THE PALGRAVE CONCISE
HISTORICAL ATLAS
OF
THE FIRST WORLD WAR

THE PALGRAVE CONCISE
HISTORICAL ATLAS
OF
THE FIRST WORLD WAR

MATTHEW HUGHES & WILLIAM J. PHILPOTT

First published 2005 by
PALGRAVE MACMILLAN
Houndmills, Basingstoke, Hampshire RG21 6XS and
175 Fifth Avenue, New York, N.Y. 10010
Companies and representatives throughout the world

PALGRAVE MACMILLAN is the global academic imprint of the Palgrave Macmillan division of St. Martin's Press, LLC and of Palgrave Macmillan Ltd. Macmillan® is a registered trademark in the United States, United Kingdom and other countries. Palgrave is a registered trademark in the European Union and other countries.

ISBN-13: 978–1–4039–0433–1 hardback
ISBN-10: 1–4039–0433–2 hardback
ISBN-13: 978–1–4039–0434–8 paperback
ISBN-10: 1–4039–0434–0 paperback

This book is printed on paper suitable for recycling and made from fully managed and sustained forest sources.

A catalogue record for this book is available from the British Library.

Library of Congress Cataloging-in-Publication Data
The Palgrave concise historical atlas of the First World War / [edited by]
  Matthew Hughes & William J. Philpott.
     p. cm.
  Includes bibliographical references and index.
  ISBN 1–4039–0433–2 (cloth) — ISBN 1–4039–0434–0 (pbk.)
  1. World War, 1914–1918—Campaigns—Maps. 2. Historical geography—Maps.
  I. Title: Concise historical atlas of the First World War. II. Hughes, Matthew, 1965–
  III. Philpott, William James.

  G1037.P3 2004
  940.3 '022'3—dc22

                                                        2004632200

  10   9   8   7   6   5   4   3   2   1
  14 13 12 11 10 09 08 07 06 05
Printed and bound in Great Britain by
The Cromwell Press, Trowbridge

Contents

Preface   vi

1. The Belligerents
2. Pre-war Offensive Military Plans
3. The Battle of the Frontiers and the Retreat
4. The Battles of the Marne and the Aisne
5. The Russian Advance into Prussia, 1914
6. German War Aims – The 'September Programme'
7. Stabilisation of the Western Front
8. The War between Austria-Hungary and Russia
9. Clearing the Seas, 1914–16
10. The Western Front – An Overview
11. War on the Periphery – An Overview
12. The Great War in Africa and Asia
13. The Allied Blockade of Germany
14. Italy Enters the War
15. The Attempts to Break the Western Front, 1915
16. Mesopotamia and the Caucasus
17. The Dardanelles Campaign (Gallipoli)
18. The Second Battle of Ypres – The Use of Gas in War
19. The Conquest of Poland – Gorlice–Tarnów
20. The Italians on the Isonzo, 1915–17
21. The Defeat of Serbia and Rumania
22. The Salonika Campaign
23. Plans for the Partition of the Ottoman Empire
24. Allied War Aims in Europe
25. The Battle of Verdun
26. The Battle of Jutland
27. The Somme Offensive I – The Plan and the First Day
28. The Somme Offensive II – The Battle of Attrition
29. The German Submarine Offensive
30. The Strategic Bombing of Britain
31. The Collapse of Russia, 1917
32. The Nivelle Offensive
33. France Under Strain, 1917
34. The Arab Revolt, 1916–18
35. Allenby's Offensive in Palestine
36. The Third Battle of Ypres (Passchendaele)
37. Malmaison – The 'Bite and Hold' Battle
38. The Battle of Caporetto – The Collapse of the Italian Army
39. The Battle of Cambrai – The Use of the Tank
40. Empires at War
41. The Treaty of Brest-Litovsk, March 1918
42. The German Spring 1918 Offensive
43. Foch's Advance to Victory – The 'Hundred Days'
44. American Operations on the Western Front
45. Breaking the Hindenburg Line, September 1918
46. The Collapse of Germany
47. Peace in the West – The Versailles Settlement
48. The Eastern Peace Settlements
49. Allied Intervention in the Russian Civil War
50. The Costs of the War, 1914–19

Bibliography   102
Index   104

Preface

When the editors of this volume were at school, the history syllabus on the First World War leapt from the assassination of Archduke Franz Ferdinand in 1914 to the Treaty of Versailles in 1919. Events in between, with the exception of the Russian revolution, were considered too pointless or too murderous – possibly too incomprehensible – for detailed examination. If the First World War is studied at all, it is generally through its literature rather than its history, which only tends to reinforce the received wisdom of confusion and casual slaughter. This accessible introductory history, which engages with the events of 1914–18 themselves, is intended to fill this gap.

In this atlas, the editors provide a clear, brief introduction to key features of the war – military, political, social and economic – which will give students of the period, whether of its history or literature, a basic understanding of its nature, and impact on the societies which fought it. This is not the first atlas of the war. Arthur Banks's *A Military Atlas of the First World War* and Martin Gilbert's *First World War Atlas* are both standard reference works, the former focussing on military operations and the latter on the political and social effects of the war. Both have been in print since the 1970s, and in the intervening years scholarship on the war has moved on. Moreover, neither Banks's nor Gilbert's atlas is accompanied by interpretive text. In this atlas, the editors for the first time combine bold sketch maps with up-to-date historical scholarship. Fifty explanatory texts on the key campaigns and political developments of the war together provide a clear introductory narrative of events on and off the battlefield. William Philpott, an expert on the western front, has provided the texts and maps covering that theatre. Matthew Hughes, a specialist on the Middle Eastern war, is responsible for the maps and texts covering the eastern and southern fronts and the global dimensions of the war.

The First World War changed both the nature of warfare, and the political structures and social fabric of the nations and empires that fought it. While the forces and methods of 1914 – infantry, artillery and cavalry armies manoeuvring against open flanks – would have been familiar to Napoleon, he would have struggled to master the armies and tactics of 1918, as did the generals who fought the war. Over four years

the full weight of science and industry had been devoted to solving the problems thrown up by stalemate on the fire-power-dominated battlefield. New weapons – tanks, aeroplanes, flamethrowers, gas – and new technologies – the internal-combustion engine, wireless telegraphy – were now key components of the military machine. Above all, the machine gun and heavy artillery came to epitomise the First World War: one the supreme weapon of defence, the other of offence. The combination of traditional forces with new weapons produced a new style of warfare – the 'three-dimensional deep battle' – a veritable Revolution in Military Affairs that created the modern-day battlefield.

To fight this war required unprecedented changes on the home front. Mobilisation of the civilian population for total war involved increased state control of the economy and society, presaging the totalitarian regimes – states organised in peacetime for fighting modern industrial war – which appeared in the inter-war years. The strains of prolonged war eventually produced tension on the home front, which spilled over into strikes, riots, peace movements and ultimately revolution. The societies of the post-war era, impoverished and split, shocked and disillusioned, were profoundly different from those of the confident age of economic growth and social progress which had preceded it. The events of 1914–18 profoundly shaped the ensuing century; a second world war, a Cold War, even contemporary troubles in the Middle East, can all be identified as a direct consequence of the experience of the First World War and the inadequate peace settlements which ended it.

The First World War was a global war. Fighting spilled over from Europe into Africa and Asia, and soldiers from North America and Australasia crossed the oceans to do their bit. In this atlas, the global dimension of the war is set alongside the main crucible of war in Europe. It must not be forgotten that it was the human, financial and psychological costs of the First World War that marked the beginning of the end for the Eurocentric, imperialist vision of the world that had dominated the preceding centuries. In this respect, the First World War was a global, world-changing conflict.

The editors would like to thank Luciana O'Flaherty at Palgrave Macmillan for her advice and patience during the preparation of this atlas.

Map 1: The Belligerents

Since the defeat of Napoleon in 1815 European peace had been maintained by means of a 'balance of power' between the five so-called 'Great Powers', Great Britain, France, Russia, Austria and Prussia. Tensions were resolved through international conferences, creating a 'Concert of Europe'. The so-called 'congress system' functioned effectively until the middle of the nineteenth century, when a series of Great Power wars redrew the map of central and southern Europe, and upset the delicate balance of power.

Prussia's wars with Austria in 1866 and France in 1870–71 established a new and powerful empire, Germany, in central Europe. Its architect, Chancellor Otto von Bismarck, sought to ensure the new Germany's security by recreating a balance of power. From this evolved the 'alliance system', an artificial balance maintained by careful diplomacy. The 1879 Dual Alliance with Austria-Hungary was to become the cornerstone of Germany's international policy until 1914. Yet after her 1866 defeat and the resulting compromise which split the monarchies of Austria and Hungary in 1867, the Habsburg empire was no longer a first-line power. Bismarck went on to buttress this alliance with the 1881 Three Emperors' League (*Dreikaiserbund*) incorporating Russia, and the 1882 Triple Alliance including Italy, another new state with Great Power ambitions, successfully keeping Germany's main rival France isolated.

Bismarck's attentions were focussed inwards. At the end of the nineteenth century rapid industrialisation was changing European society. Mass electorates, literate and politically aware, were pressing for recognition of their rights. In Germany Bismarck hoped to suppress political socialism with anti-socialist laws, and to buy off worker militancy with welfare payments. However, after 1890 the response of the new Kaiser, William II, a nationalist pursuit of world power (*Weltpolitik*) for the German empire, shattered Bismarck's carefully nurtured balance of power and set Europe on the path to general war.

After her 1871 defeat France sought an outlet for her international ambitions in imperial adventures, inevitably bringing her into conflict with Great Britain, the only world power before 1900. Bismarck's fall in 1890 gave France the opportunity to break out from her diplomatic isolation, seriously compromising Germany's dominant international position. She made a military alliance with Russia in 1892, threatening Germany with a future war on two fronts. Increasingly insecure in her imperial power, and concerned about German naval expansion and economic growth, Britain opted to settle outstanding disputes with her traditional colonial rivals, France and Russia, with Ententes in 1904 and 1907. Italy's commitment to the German alliance also weakened, as France offered, in a 1902 rapprochement, to recognise Italian colonial ambitions in the Mediterranean. Germany's leaders were feeling diplomatically isolated; *Weltpolitik* was a failure.

Two issues dominated international affairs at the turn of the century. Firstly, imperial rivalries – especially over territorial control in newly-partitioned Africa, and commercial opportunities in East Asia and the Pacific – brought tensions between Germany and the other powers. In particular two crises over Morocco, in 1905–06 and 1911, strengthened the Triple Entente's anti-German orientation. Nevertheless Great Power conferences, which resolved both Moroccan crises, remained an effective means of resolving colonial disputes without resort to armed force.

It was the second source of international tension, the perennial 'Eastern Question' – how to manage the decline of the Ottoman empire (Turkey) – which contained the seeds of Great Power conflict. Britain, France and Germany were competing to develop commercial opportunities in the Turkish empire. Germany's plan for a railway from Berlin to Baghdad was seen as a direct challenge to British commercial and imperial interests in central Asia. For their respective allies, Russia and Austria-Hungary, nationality questions were paramount. Russia's diplomatic humiliation following Austria-Hungary's annexation of Bosnia in 1908 refocussed Great Power attention on the Slavic national minorities of the region. The Balkan Wars in 1912 and 1913 between the Turks and ambitious Slavic states – Serbia and Bulgaria, supported by Greece – further destabilised the region. Austria-Hungary in particular feared the growth of Serbian power, which threatened her hold over Slav minorities within her imperial borders. Tensions came to a head following the assassination of the heir to the Habsburg throne, the pacific Archduke Franz Ferdinand, and his wife, by a Serbian nationalist, Gavrilo Princip, in the Bosnian capital Sarajevo on 28 June 1914. Germany, now with only one reliable ally, took a calculated risk to break her diplomatic isolation, backing Austria-Hungary's ultimatum to Serbia. Such high-stakes diplomacy failed, however, as Russia, the traditional protector of fellow Slavs, rallied behind Serbia. Eleventh-hour attempts by the British foreign secretary, Sir Edward Grey, and Europe's monarchs to resolve the deepening international crisis diplomatically came to nothing as pre-planned mobilisation schedules rolled into action. A third Balkan war could not be contained as Great Power interests were now involved and alliance obligations had to be honoured.

It is difficult to separate the factors which led to war in 1914: Balkan tensions, Habsburg anxieties, French and Russian ambitions, British imperial worries, rapid domestic social and political change – all catalysed by a volatile combination of German nationalism and insecurity – came together in the second decade of the twentieth century and fed into the crisis which brought about a general war in July 1914.

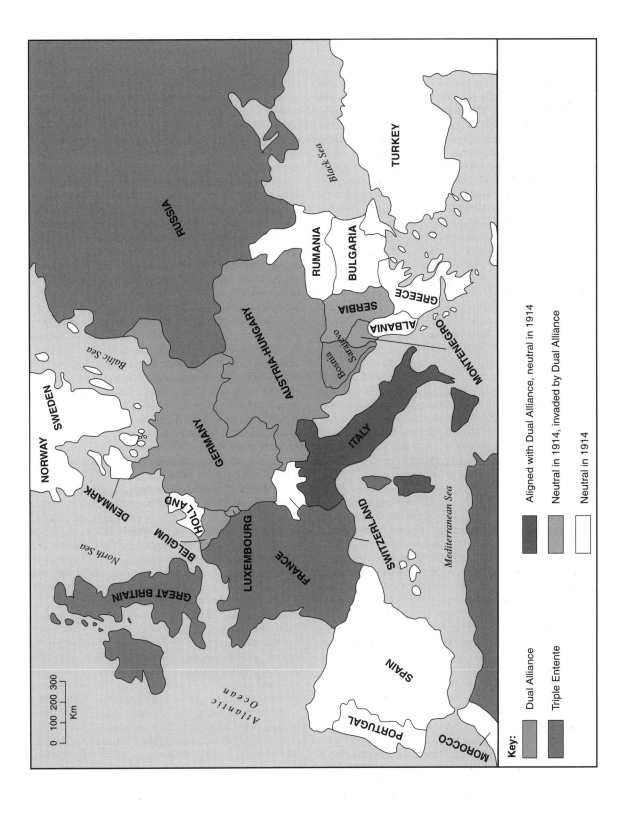

Key:

Dual Alliance

Triple Entente

Aligned with Dual Alliance, neutral in 1914

Neutral in 1914, invaded by Dual Alliance

Neutral in 1914

Map 2: Pre-war Offensive Military Plans

Militarism is considered to be one of the principal causes of the First World War. The Great Power rivalries of the early twentieth century took place against a background of expanding armies and navies, increasing armaments expenditure, offensive military planning and strident nationalistic propaganda.

There were two arms races, one at sea and one on land. Germany's 1898 decision to build an ocean-going fleet to project her world power inevitably alarmed the leading naval power, Great Britain. Britain was forced to revise her diplomatic strategy, aligning with lesser regional naval rivals – Japan, France and Russia – to meet the main challenge from Germany. Britain's introduction of the 'Dreadnought' type all-big-gun battleship in 1906 initiated a new naval race, in which Britain's wealth and efficient ship-building industry allowed her to maintain the desired 40% margin of superiority over Germany. Lesser states followed the Anglo-German lead. Italian and Austro-Hungarian 'Dreadnought' building in the Adriatic, and Russian and Turkish competition for naval mastery of the Black Sea, contributed to growing regional tensions.

In the land arms race Germany was again a principal player, competing against Russia and France. Her growing fear of war on two fronts led her to expand her military forces, putting the political, economic and social system under increasing strain. Her final pre-war army service law, in 1913, was only passed with socialist votes, after Germany's land-owners and industrialists refused to support the land tax which was to pay for military expansion. In 1914 Germany could put 2,147,000 men in the field on mobilisation. France strained to keep up. Her 1913 three-year national service law would allow her to put 1,800,000 men into the field, but in proportion to Germany this was a much heavier drain on her manpower resources – 4.5% of her population to Germany's 3.2%. Russia's manpower was almost limitless. Her pre-war military reforms would eventually allow her to put 3,400,000 men into the field; although her mobilisation was slow, railway expansion was speeding things up. Arms races spilled over into smaller states. Large, costly conscript armies and expensive foreign arms imports fuelled Balkan tensions which broke out into war in 1912.

In a time when armies were growing and finances were stretched, speed was of the essence. All states planned for rapid mobilisation and a short victorious war based on a decisive offensive campaign. The modern capitalist economic system, it was thought, would not stand the strains of a long war. Germany's strategic answer to the threat of a two-front war was the rapid defeat of France, an idea initiated in 1905 by the chief of the German Great General Staff, Alfred von Schlieffen and developed by his successor, Helmuth von Moltke. Seven German armies would envelop the French army, passing through the Low Countries, going round Paris and trapping the French forces against their frontier defences, destroying them in a final enormous battle of annihilation. All would be over in six weeks, allowing the victorious German armies to return eastwards to challenge the slowly mobilising Russian hordes. France's response, 'Plan XVII', was to mass her armies in eastern France for a disruptive counter-offensive against the invading German armies. France's allies were to furnish aid as quickly as possible, Russia by launching its partly-mobilised armies into East Prussia, and the British by rushing their small professional Expeditionary Force across the Channel to reinforce the French left wing. Meanwhile in the east the Russians and Austro-Hungarians were to launch their armies against each other in the rugged Carpathian mountains along their border. Serbia was to be immediately knocked out by a rapid three-pronged attack.

The 'cult of the offensive' which preoccupied military planners before 1914 was understandable in the light of their past military experience, but failed to take proper account of the nature of modern industrial war. Rapid railway mobilisation allowed armies to be rushed to the front, but once detrained they were limited to the speed of man and horse. The tactical power of defensive firepower would make offensive action on the battlefield itself costly and liable to failure. Strategically reserves could be rapidly re-deployed by rail to check the slow advance of foot soldiers. As well as these general weaknesses, the individual plans had political and logistical faults. The Schlieffen plan involved the violation of Belgian neutrality, guaranteed by international treaty. The Belgians themselves might resist a German invasion, and their frontier forts presented a formidable obstacle to rapid advance. The wide sweep through France would over-extend the front of attack and overstretch the German army's supply and communication lines. The French for their part underestimated the number of divisions which Germany could deploy in the west. Britain refused to commit her Expeditionary Force to France before war broke out. In such military uncertainty and over-ambition lay the seeds of disaster.

The people of Europe, thoroughly militarised by national service and nationalistic propaganda, responded positively to this belligerence. Socialist organisations preached an alternative anti-war message, calling for a general workers' strike to cripple national mobilisation in the event of war: in July and August 1914 their message went unheeded. In ironic counter-point to the assassination of Archduke Franz Ferdinand, on 31 July 1914, French socialist leader Jean Jaurès met his death at the hands of a right-wing assassin, having called on patriotic French workers to do their duty and defend *la patrie*.

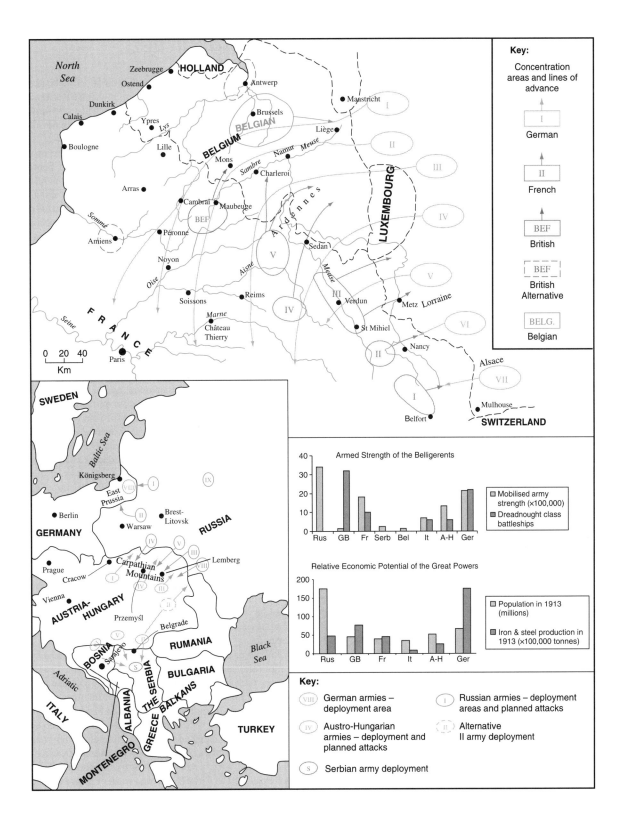

Key:

Concentration areas and lines of advance

I	German
II	French
BEF	British
BEF (dashed)	British Alternative
BELG.	Belgian

North Sea

Zeebrugge • Ostend • Dunkirk • Calais • Boulogne • Ypres • Lille • Arras • Amiens • Péronne • Noyon • Soissons • Reims • Château Thierry • Paris

HOLLAND

Antwerp • Brussels • Maastricht • Liège • Namur • Mons • Charleroi • Cambrai • Maubeuge • Sedan • Verdun • Metz • Lorraine • St Mihiel • Nancy • Mulhouse • Belfort

BELGIAN · BELGIUM · LUXEMBOURG · FRANCE · Alsace · SWITZERLAND

Lys · Sambre · Meuse · Ardennes · Aisne · Oise · Somme · Marne · Seine

0 20 40
Km

Armies: I, II, III, IV, V, VI, VII, NI, BEF

SWEDEN · Baltic Sea · North Sea

Königsberg · East Prussia · Berlin · Warsaw · Brest-Litovsk · Prague · Cracow · Vienna · Lemberg · Przemyśl · Belgrade · Sarajevo

GERMANY · RUSSIA · AUSTRIA-HUNGARY · BOSNIA · SERBIA · RUMANIA · BULGARIA · THE BALKANS · MONTENEGRO · ALBANIA · GREECE · ITALY · TURKEY

Carpathian Mountains · Adriatic · Black Sea

Armies: VIII, I, II, IV, V, III, VIII

Armed Strength of the Belligerents

(bar chart, values 0–40)

Rus, GB, Fr, Serb, Bel, It, A-H, Ger

□ Mobilised army strength (×100,000)
■ Dreadnought class battleships

Relative Economic Potential of the Great Powers

(bar chart, values 0–200)

Rus, GB, Fr, It, A-H, Ger

□ Population in 1913 (millions)
■ Iron & steel production in 1913 (×100,000 tonnes)

Key:

VIII German armies – deployment area

IV Austro-Hungarian armies – deployment and planned attacks

S Serbian army deployment

I Russian armies – deployment areas and planned attacks

II Alternative II army deployment

Map 3: The Battle of the Frontiers and the Retreat

The largest and costliest battle of the First World War occurred in its first month, when the French and British armies marched north to meet the German armies advancing through Belgium. Collectively known as the Battle of the Frontiers, this 400-kilometre (250-mile) encounter battle, stretching from Belfort on the Swiss border to Mons, quickly exposed the flaws in France's pre-war planning.

On 1 August 1914 France and Germany mobilised. On 3 August German troops violated Belgian neutrality. On 4 August the British empire declared war on Germany. Both German and allied mobilisations and concentrations went smoothly. On the western front 88 German divisions faced 82 French, 7 Belgian and 5 (later 7) British divisions. Although the allies had a slight numerical superiority in the west, poor coordination between their separate national armies, deficient intelligence and flawed tactical doctrine placed them at a disadvantage.

On 7 August, before mobilisation was complete, Joseph Joffre, France's commander-in-chief, launched his first attack against the German left flank, symbolically into the disputed territory of Alsace and Lorraine, capturing the city of Mulhouse. In the third week of August the First and Second French Armies advanced rapidly to Morhange and Sarrebourg, only to be halted by von Moltke's strengthened left wing and driven back to Nancy by the German Sixth and Seventh Armies. Joffre, believing that this show of strength in Alsace-Lorraine meant that the German centre was weak, sent his Third and reserve Fourth Armies north through the Ardennes between 21 and 23 August. After vicious close-quarter fighting, they in their turn were checked and driven back by the German Fourth and Fifth Armies. Joffre had seriously underestimated the strength of the German flanking advance through Belgium, which through the use of powerful super-heavy artillery had quickly overcome the resistance of the Belgian fortresses of Liège and Namur and driven the Belgian army back into Antwerp. Belgian warnings of the scale of the German advance through their country went unheeded, Joffre persisting in an all-out offensive when a defensive posture might have been better. On 21 August the Fifth Army and the recently arrived British Expeditionary Force (BEF) were ordered north over the river Sambre to turn the apparently exposed German right flank. In fact it was the allied left flank, held between 21 and 23 August at Charleroi and Mons by the German Second and First Armies, that was in danger of envelopment by the German forces advancing north of the river Meuse. Belatedly realising the threat to his over-extended and badly mauled forces, on 25 August Joffre ordered a general retreat southwards. The French left wing pivoted backwards on the fortress of Verdun. The French Fifth Army was obliged to conform to the retreat of its beaten neighbours, dragging the small but unbowed BEF with it. For ten days the allied armies force-marched backwards in intense heat, while Joffre strove to reorganise his armies for a counter-strike.

The German plan seemed to be going well, German cavalry ranging far west across Belgium and France, penetrating as far as Amiens. Yet such a rapid advance in turn imposed heavy strains on the stamina of the German troops and the functioning of their lines of supply. Moreover, even after such heavy defeats, the French armies were not crushed. Two successful rearguard actions on the left flank, by the II Corps of the BEF at Le Cateau on 26 August, and the French Fifth Army at Guise on 29 August, blunted the German advance and allowed the Anglo-French armies to disengage and fall back behind the natural barrier of the river Marne, east of Paris.

It is a military aphorism that no plan survives the first clash of arms, and Joffre's experience in August 1914 bears that out. Pre-war miscalculation of German intentions, and a wilful refusal to act on intelligence that contradicted pre-war perceptions, exposed the French army to strategic annihilation. An offensive operational and tactical doctrine exposed the rank and file to decimation on the battlefield. German formations on the left wing relied on the tactical defensive to dislocate French attacks. Machine guns, rifles and above all quick-firing field artillery made the battlefield uncrossable for the French infantry. French casualties in the first encounter battles were some 211,000, at a rate that was not to be exceeded for the rest of the war. The Germans too had a rude awakening to the reality of modern war when they went on the tactical offensive. At Mons the well-dug-in BEF checked over twice their number and inflicted heavy casualties with rapid and well-aimed rifle fire. In the Battle of the Frontiers as a whole German casualties, estimated at 220,000, were roughly equivalent to those of the allies. Even before the ascendancy of the machine gun, it was apparent that the First World War battlefield was no safe place for the massed infantry formations advocated by late-nineteenth-century tactical doctrine.

Joffre's response to the disaster was swift and emphatic. Blaming old, inept leaders for the defeats of the French armies he purged the high command; two army commanders, Lanrezac of the Fifth and Ruffey of the Third Army, were sacked, along with nine army corps commanders and 38 divisional commanders. Dynamic younger generals such as Maurice Sarrail, Ferdinand Foch and Philippe Pétain were promoted in their place. To regain control over the disorganised allied left wing a new French army, Manoury's Sixth, was created west of Paris. By the first week of September the French were ready to counter-attack (see Map 4).

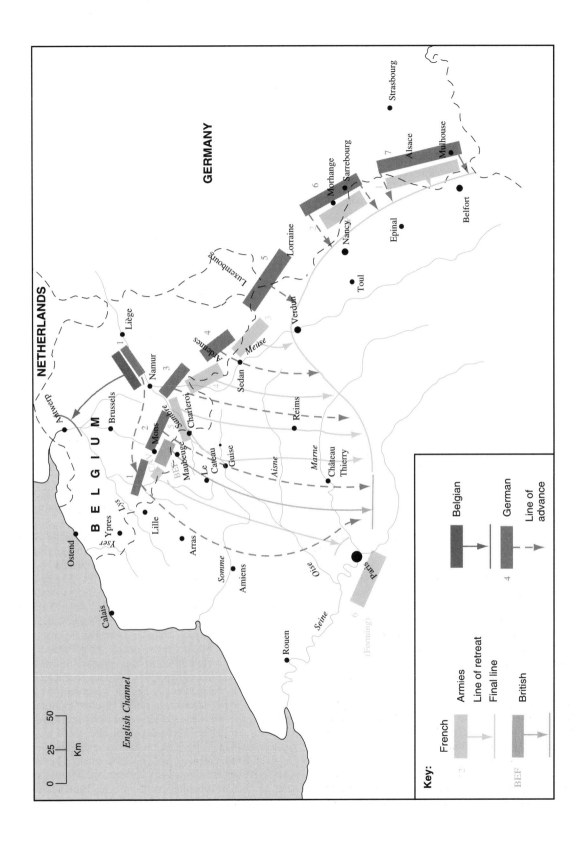

Map 4: The Battles of the Marne and the Aisne

The Battle of the Marne was not the 'miracle' of popular legend. It was a carefully prepared and hard-fought counter-attack in which the French army was able to take advantage of the dislocation of the German army's over-ambitious sweep through France. By early September the over-extension inherent in the German offensive plan started to tell. As they retreated the Belgians had destroyed their railways, leaving the invaders reliant on horsepower. Food and ammunition, expended in unprecedented amounts in the early battles, had to be brought to the attacking troops along increasingly extended and vulnerable lines of communication. The detachment of troops to besiege Antwerp and Maubeuge, and to reinforce the exposed eastern front, had weakened the right wing. Moltke now concentrated his five eastern armies on defeating the apparently beaten French. His two western armies were to close up and envelop the French left wing. Anxious about the over-extension of his front, Alexander von Kluck, commanding the First Army on the extreme right, chose to advance to the east rather than west of Paris, to keep in touch with Karl von Bülow's Second Army and reduce the distance his weary troops had to march. In this change of plan lay the seeds of disaster.

On the French side of the line the phlegmatic Joffre showed his true worth, keeping his head in a time of crisis, and looking always for the opportunity to counter-attack. His weaknesses lay in the centre and on the extreme left of the allied line. As the French line withdrew to the protection of France's strong line of frontier fortifications, Joffre was able to liberate divisions for use elsewhere on the front. He rapidly created two new armies: Foch's Ninth to shore up the centre; and Manoury's Sixth to cover Paris, and to give him effective control over operations on the left wing, where cooperation with the BEF had broken down. When aerial reconnaissance revealed von Kluck's turn east of Paris he judged that the time had come to stand and fight. Joffre decided to strike at the exposed right flank of von Kluck's army, at the same time exploiting a gap opening up between the German First and Second Armies, to destroy the German right wing. For this he needed the cooperation of the BEF, opposite the widening gap. Lord Kitchener, British Secretary of State for War, intervened personally on 1 September to restore cooperation between the British and French field armies. With his authority re-established, on 5 September Joffre ordered the retreating French armies to turn about and to engage with the enemy all along the line. French field artillery swept the ground in front of their hastily improvised defensive positions, defeating every enemy attempt to dislodge the exhausted infantry. While this desperate battle held the main body of the Germans between Paris and Verdun, the Sixth Army advanced eastwards against the flank and rear of the German First Army. The Germans came close to breaking the French centre in the St Gond marshlands, but Foch's iron resolve held: 'my centre is collapsing, my right wing falling back. Situation excellent. I attack!' he is reported to have declared in the heat of battle. Meanwhile the crisis was reached on the open flank. Von Kluck was forced to rush forces northwards to meet the threat to his exposed flank and rear. Elements of the Fifth Army and the BEF advanced northwards across the river Marne towards Château-Thierry, into the growing gap between the German First and Second Armies.

Anxious to know what was going on on his right flank, von Moltke sent a staff officer, Colonel Hentsch, with authority to issue orders on his behalf. On his arrival Hentsch saw the dangerous position the two German flanking armies were in, and to close the gap ordered their retreat northwards to prepared defensive positions on the heights above the river Aisne. The other German armies, held on the line from St Gond to Verdun, were ordered to conform to this retreat. A succession of localised British and French attacks in the last fortnight of September tried unsuccessfully to dislodge the Germans from their Aisne defences. The allied divisions lacked the heavy artillery and high explosive ammunition necessary for this new trench warfare and were easily checked. The Germans were to remain on the Aisne heights until 1917.

The Battle of the Marne was a triumph of military improvisation, for which credit should go to Joffre; and of patriotic determination, for which credit should go to the ordinary French soldier, exhausted but undefeated. Its greatest casualty was von Moltke, replaced by the younger Erich von Falkenhayn on 14 September. Germany's strategic retreat marked the ultimate failure of the over-ambitious pre-war offensive plans. Yet the 'miracle of the Marne', while it saved France, did not end the war. Quick, decisive strategic victory had proved impossible on the western front, where the presence of massive force in limited space discounted manoeuvre and encouraged head-on slogging matches, in which the firepower of modern weapons gave the advantage to the defender. In such a situation the fighting spirit of the ordinary soldier counted as much as the skill of the general. Yet the flesh and blood of the infantryman, however high his morale, could not prevail against fixed defences and machine guns. The early Anglo-French defeats on the Aisne were the first indication that a new type of battle would come to characterise the First World War.

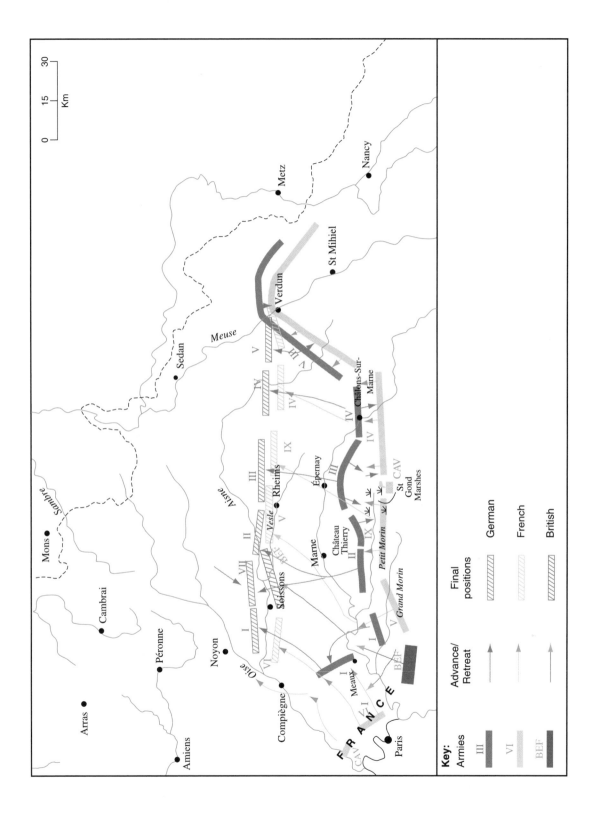

Key:

Armies		Advance/ Retreat	Final positions	
III		↑		German
VI		↑		French
BEF		↑		British

Map 5: The Russian Advance into Prussia, 1914

Lacking the military resources for an offensive on two fronts, in August 1914 Germany concentrated the great majority of her forces in the west to defeat France quickly (see Maps 3 & 4), leaving von Prittwitz's Eighth Army to hold the Russians until forces could be railed east. The focus of battle was Prussia and, in particular, East Prussia that stretched out into Russian territory.

In light of the Russian forces massing on the frontier, Russia decided to attack Germany and Austria-Hungary simultaneously. For the attack on East Prussia, the Russians used two armies, Rennenkampf's First and Samsonov's Second. Thirty Russian infantry and eight cavalry divisions faced eleven German infantry and one cavalry divisions. There were two main corridors of attack: one towards the fortress city of Königsberg (Kaliningrad) in the north; the second from the south (Russian Poland) into the German rear east of the fortress city of Thorn (Toruń) by the town of Tannenberg (Stębark). Dividing these two lines of attack were the Masurian (Mazury) lakes, 100 kilometres (60 miles) of almost impenetrable waterlands.

The presence of these lakes forced the Russians to divide their forces. Rennenkampf's First Army advanced west against Königsberg; Samsonov's Second Army moved into East Prussia from Russian-held Poland to the south. The aim was to pinch off the East Prussia salient and destroy the German Eighth Army in the field. But Rennenkampf and Samsonov failed to coordinate their attacks. This gave the Germans the opportunity to deal with each invading army in turn. It has been said that the lack of coordination was a consequence of a violent disagreement between Rennenkampf and Samsonov on a railway platform during the Russo-Japanese War (1904–05). This story is undoubtedly apocryphal but the differences between the two men were real enough.

Rennenkampf's First Army of three corps (11½ divisions) crossed the frontier on 17 August. Prittwitz's Eighth Army moved forward from its defensive line along the Angerapp (Wegorapa) river, attacking Rennenkampf's forces at Gumbinnen, 40 kilometres (25 miles) inside the frontier, on 20 August 1914. Entrenched Russian firepower checked and threw back the Germans, a situation not helped by German artillery firing on its own troops. Following the defeat at Gumbinnen, Prittwitz lost his nerve. In fact, because Rennenkampf's logistics were badly organised, he was slow in his advance to Gumbinnen and, after the battle, his troops halted. Although Prittwitz had time to reorganise his forces, in a fit of worry, with Samsonov threatening from the south, he ordered a general retreat to the Vistula (Wista) river, over 160 kilometres (100 miles) to the west, thus surrendering East Prussia.

Prittwitz never got the chance to implement his retreat. In response to complaints from Eighth Army's corps' commanders that a retreat to the Vistula was pre-mature, von Moltke dismissed Prittwitz and sent out a new commander, Paul von Hindenburg, whose steadfast mind was ably complemented by his Chief of Staff, Erich Ludendorff, and by Eighth Army's perceptive operations officer, Maximilian Hoffmann. Ludendorff and Hindenburg, who met for the first time on the platform of Hannover railway station on 22 August, arrived at Eighth Army HQ on 23 August where Hoffmann presented them with a new plan. It was Hoffmann's plan that Hindenburg and Ludendorff executed to great effect.

Hoffmann wanted to make the most of the Russians' decision to divide their forces either side of the Masurian lakes. Realising that transport problems had greatly slowed Samsonov's advance, Hoffmann's plan called for one cavalry division to screen Rennenkampf's force while the rest of Eighth Army, utilising the Germans' superior rail network, redeployed against Samsonov. This plan dovetailed with Russian strategy as Rennenkampf, believing that he was going to have to invest the fortress of Königsberg, paused his advance. As the Russians sent many military messages *en clair* (uncoded), the Germans knew about this halt.

Aerial reconnaissance and a reinforcement of one cavalry division and two infantry corps from France helped the Eighth Army when it delivered its blow against Samsonov on 26 August. The plan was for a huge battle of encirclement that would strike the flanks and envelop Samsonov's force, spread out over 100 kilometres (60 miles), without reconnaissance, without information and pushing blindly towards the Allenstein–Osterode line. Hoffmann's plan worked. By 29 August, German forces were across Samsonov's rear, cutting his line of retreat. Trapped Russian forces (2½ corps) dissolved into leaderless mobs. The battle was over by 30 August. Part of a Russian division hemmed in by Bössau lake drowned, hence the legend of Russian soldiers driven into lakes and swamps to die. Declaring 'The Emperor trusted me. How can I face him again?' Samsonov shot himself. The victory at Tannenberg saved East Prussia from invasion. It shattered the Russian Second Army, which suffered over 50,000 casualties, the loss of 92,000 prisoners and 400 guns. Hindenburg then shifted his troops back to face Rennenkampf, who had done nothing during Tannenberg. Some historians have even questioned Rennenkampf's loyalty, using this as an explanation for his gross inaction in late August.

It was now the turn of Rennenkampf's First Army. Eighteen German divisions faced nine Russian. The first battle of the Masurian lakes (5–13 September) failed to replicate the encirclement of Tannenberg. Although defeated, Rennenkampf conducted a fighting retreat in which he fell back to the frontier, suffering over 100,000 casualties. In both battles, the Russians suffered 300,000 casualties and lost 650 guns to 100,000 German casualties.

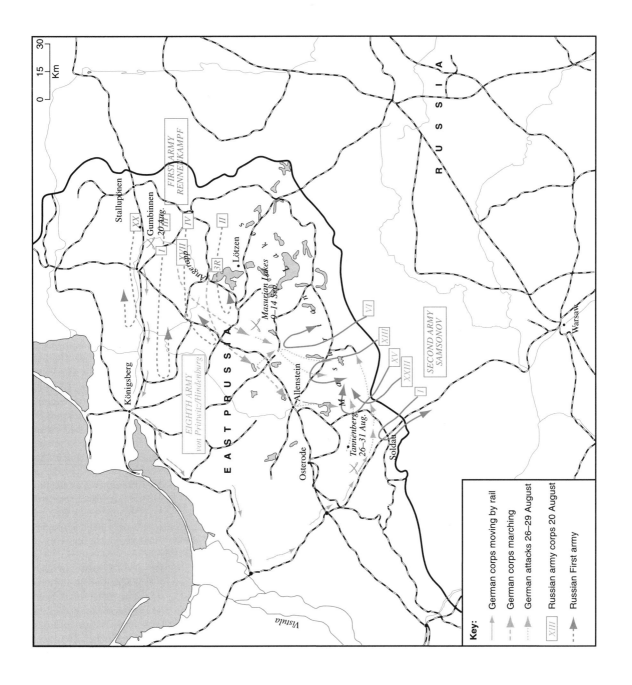

Map 6: German War Aims – The 'September Programme'

On 9 September 1914 Chancellor Bethmann Hollweg announced Germany's 'September Programme' of war aims. Whether this statement of territorial demands and military and economic ambitions was a triumphant response to early victories, or a pragmatic recognition that the war would not be short, and that the German people had to be made aware of what they were fighting for in a lengthy life-or-death struggle, the pre-emptive formulation of war aims was and remains controversial.

Although couched in defensive terminology, Germany's war aims were expansionistic. Territorial annexations, economic domination and military control would provide, Bethmann Hollweg promised, 'security for the German Reich in west and east for all imaginable time'. As such, Germany's war aims were an expression of the social-Darwinist philosophy of imperialistic competition which had underpinned pre-war arms races and colonial rivalries. *Weltpolitik* may have failed in peacetime, but war presented an opportunity to achieve Germany's global ambitions.

In Europe Germany wished to impose her hegemony, through a combination of territorial expansion and economic control. In the east Russian territory in Poland and the Baltic would be annexed. Subsequently, in a concession to national self-determination, it was proposed that dependent satellite states should be set up in Poland and the Ukraine at Russia's expense. In the west Luxembourg and important economic regions of France and Belgium – the Longwy-Briey iron-ore field and the Belgian Channel ports, Antwerp, Zeebrugge and Ostend – would be incorporated within the German empire to boost Germany's economic capacity and secure her against future British and French hostility. France, Belgium and the Netherlands would be incorporated in a German-dominated economic union – *Mitteleuropa* – which would stretch from the Atlantic coast in the west to Poland in the east, and from Scandinavia in the north to Turkey in the south. Africa would become a German-dominated continent. French, Belgian and Portuguese colonies in central and southern Africa would be incorporated into a central Africa economic region – *Mittelafrika* – which would supply German industry with raw materials. Control of the Atlantic and Red Sea coasts would secure German command of key international routes, a check on British power. With Germany's economic interests assured, Britain's economic and commercial hegemony could be effectively challenged.

War aims were not fixed, but evolved in response to changes in the diplomatic and military situation. Consequently the detail of German ambitions changed as the war went on, although her stated war aims remained true to the principles of 1914: ensuring German economic and strategic security and weakening Britain's commercial superiority. By 1916 she was prepared to compromise her more extreme demands in an attempt to split the Entente and secure a separate peace with France, Russia or Belgium, which would enable her to focus on her main enemy, Great Britain. Yet Germany's success on the battlefield – everywhere her armies fought on foreign territory – precluded the sort of concessions that would have been needed for a compromise peace. As war went on German domestic politics polarised around the issue of war aims. The political peace (*burgfrieden*) which the left and right had agreed on the outbreak of war finally collapsed in 1917. In July the Social Democratic and Centre parties supported a 'peace resolution' in the German parliament (*Reichstag*) which called for a negotiated peace 'without annexations and indemnities', as advocated by the Socialist International. The response of the right, the foundation of the nationalist German Fatherland Party (*Deutsche Vaterlandspartei*) committed to opposing 'the all-devouring tyranny of Anglo-Americanism', staked the future of the Imperial regime on a victorious peace.

The punitive peace imposed on Russia at Brest-Litovsk in March 1918 showed the world what German victory would mean in practice (see Map 41). The simultaneous 'Peace Offensive' on the western front (see Map 42), was to be the last gasp of Germany's ruling military elite, who hoped that victory would stave off the growing social unrest on the home front. The allies, aware of what a German victory would mean for their sovereignty and power, fought back ferociously and turned the tables on the German army. Germany's request for an armistice, on 4 October 1918, marked the end of an era. Beforehand the military had handed political power to liberal and socialist politicians who favoured President Wilson's 'Fourteen Points' as a basis for peace (see Map 24). By the terms of the 1919 Treaty of Versailles it was to be Germany which suffered territorial annexations, economic subordination and military emasculation. In the terms of that treaty lay the roots of another conflict (see Map 47).

In the 1960s the historian Fritz Fischer famously argued that Germany's September Programme of war aims represented the climax of a conscious policy of German expansionism which had its roots in the *Weltpolitik* of the pre-war years; that Germany had sought war as a means to assert her world power. This controversial thesis has been much debated by historians, and consensus has yet to be reached. It has subsequently been argued, for example by Volker Berghahn, that German *Weltpolitik* had proved a costly failure by 1914. It was not planned aggression, but fear and insecurity, which motivated Germany. Only through a formal consolidation of her power in Europe, and recognition of her global influence, could she hope to secure her future as a Great Power. Paradoxically, in pursuing such an imperialist agenda uncompromisingly she turned the rest of the world against her and brought about her own defeat and humiliation.

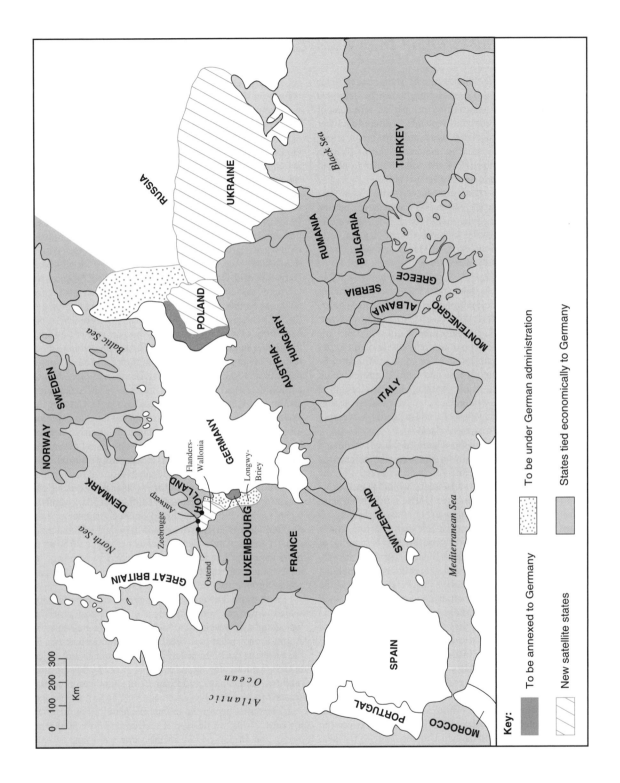

Key:

■ To be annexed to Germany

▦ To be under German administration

▨ New satellite states

░ States tied economically to Germany

Map 7: Stabilisation of the Western Front

Following the establishment of static trench lines from the river Aisne eastwards, both sides attempted to secure victory by turning the open western flank of the battlefront. Between mid-September and mid-October 1914 divisions were hurried westwards, but neither side could secure decisive strategic advantage in this 'race to the sea'. By November 1914 the solid trench front had consolidated all the way to the Channel coast.

In September German strategy was unfocussed. The new German commander, Erich von Falkenhayn, pushed at the left and centre of the main French front, at Verdun and Soissons, while at the same time deploying forces to the north to envelop the exposed French left wing. None of these operations proved decisive.

The allies hoped to use their advantage in cavalry to make a wide outflanking movement across Belgium. To this end the BEF was relocated from the river Aisne to Flanders in early October. Falkenhayn too wished to sweep westwards to the Channel coast, but before he could do so the key fortress of Antwerp, refuge of the Belgian field army after it had been separated from its allies in August, had to be reduced. Whether the British and French armies could re-deploy northwards before Antwerp fell, and rest their flank on that secure bastion, was crucial. Allied disagreements on the strategy to be followed proved acute, preventing decisive action on the northern flank.

Nothing epitomised the chaos in allied command more than the improvised and unsuccessful defence of Antwerp. The British wanted to march directly to the city's relief, fearing that the Belgians would abandon this vital port if not rapidly assisted. Joffre's priority was to defeat the German forces advancing into France by an offensive towards Lille, and he felt that first line troops could not be spared for Antwerp. At the beginning of October British Royal Marines and naval reservists, the only available troops, were despatched to reinforce the Belgian defences. Winston Churchill, the First Lord of the Admiralty, hurried to Antwerp to encourage the exhausted Belgians to hang on until more substantial reinforcements arrived. Britain's last regular division, the 7th Division, was to follow, he promised, along with a corps of French marines and territorials. In the first week of October the super-heavy German artillery which had subdued Belgium's frontier fortresses in August was brought to bear on Antwerp's defences, and the outlying defence works were systematically reduced. Without consulting his allies Joffre diverted the promised French corps to cover the redeployment of the BEF around Béthune. The 7th Division could not relieve Antwerp alone; its task was now to cover the escape of the exhausted Belgian field army along the coast. Antwerp surrendered on 10 October, before Joffre's offensive commenced.

As British and French divisions arrived in the north they were thrown into allied operations to advance eastward and capture Lille. Initial progress against a weak German cavalry screen was not sustained as new German divisions, released by the fall of Antwerp, came into line. General Foch, assigned the task of coordinating the actions of the French, British and Belgian armies, hastily established a defensive line from Nieuport on the coast to Arras, to hold off repeated German pushes to break through to the Channel ports. The fighting centred around the Belgian town of Ypres. To the north the Belgians took up position on the extreme left of the allied line behind the river Yser. Hard pressed by the enemy they protected their thinly-held line by inundating the river's flood plain. Between mid-October and mid-November successive German assaults were launched against Anglo-French positions further south. Fighting was particularly heavy in the BEF's sectors at Ypres and Armentières, where the battalions of Britain's pre-war regular army sacrificed themselves in the allied cause. British and French formations became inextricably mixed in a confused and costly mêlée that became known as the First Battle of Ypres. In this confused tactical engagement the actions of individuals and small units could prove decisive. On 31 October the recapture of the Gheluvelt crossroads by the 2nd battalion of the Worcestershire regiment prevented a decisive German breakthrough. Both sides were by now desperate for reserves, Britain throwing newly arrived Indian Army divisions into the battle, and ultimately sending battalions of her second-line Territorial Army across the Channel to bolster the defence. The fighting reached its climax on 10 November, when young, enthusiastic but ill-trained volunteers from the German universities attempted to rush British machine guns at Langemarck. German casualties, some 70%, were horrendous: the Langemarck blood-sacrifice was to become the most potent patriotic myth which sustained the German nation through four further years of war.

With this failure and the onset of cold weather the battle settled down into watchful defence. The opposing armies had fought themselves to a standstill. A half-hearted Anglo-French attempt to break through the German line in the north in mid-December came to nothing, and allied leaders paused for thought. How would they restore mobility to a static battlefield in the new campaigning season?

The casualties of the mobile battles of 1914 were the heaviest of the whole war. The Germans lost 80,000 at Ypres, the British 54,000 in the same battle and 90,000 since the outbreak of war. The French lost 265,000 killed in 1914. Armies took to trenches in the interest of self-preservation in the face of murderous firepower. A new type of static siege warfare had begun.

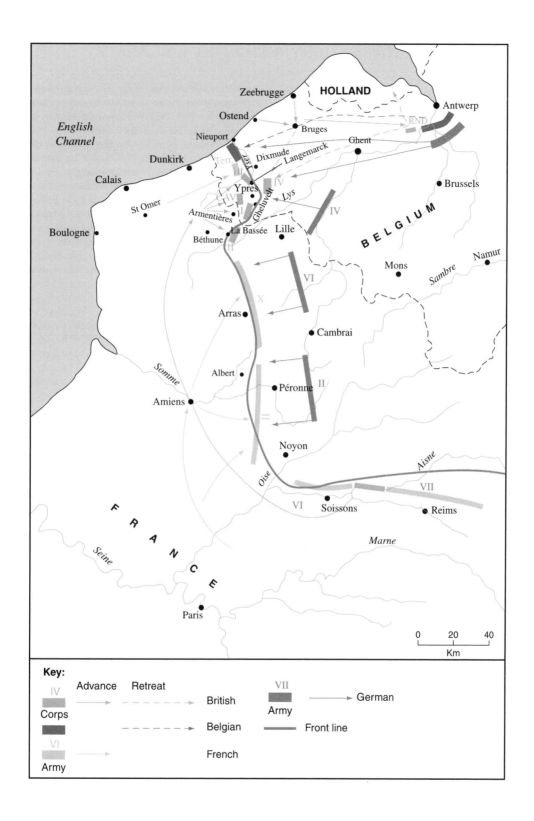

Map 8: The War between Austria-Hungary and Russia

In Vienna, there was a large gap between ideals and reality when it came to war. The poorly equipped Austro-Hungarian army was recruited from a great variety of ethnic groups, often with doubtful loyalty to the emperor. Mobilisation posters in 1914 came in 15 languages for an army that was 44% Slav, 28% German, 18% Hungarian, 8% Rumanian and 2% Italian, which created command problems between the German-dominated officer corps and the men. But the main difficulty in 1914 was the over-ambitious plans of the Austro-Hungarian commander, Conrad von Hötzendorf, whose lament that he deserved a better army was echoed by his men's complaint that they deserved a better commander. Life in the Austro-Hungarian army is well described in Jaroslav Hašek's book *The Good Soldier Švejk*.

In 1914, Conrad divided his army into three: *A Staffel* (A Echelon), 38 divisions in Galicia facing the Russians; 8 divisions in the *Minimalgruppe Balkan* (Balkan Task Force) by Serbia; and *B Staffel* – the Second Army of 13 divisions – in reserve. If Conrad wanted to get *B Staffel* to Galicia on Austria-Hungary's slow troop trains, he would need to do so no later than five days after mobilisation began (the fifth day being 1 August). Believing that Serbia could be defeated before Russia mobilised, Conrad committed *B Staffel* to the Serbian front before a more rapid than expected Russian mobilisation forced him to re-deploy it to Galicia. Thus, *B Staffel* left the Serbian front before it could win a victory but got to Galicia in time to participate in a defeat.

The main Austro-Hungarian fortresses at Lemberg (L'vov or Lwów), Kraków and Przemyśl protected Galicia. Thereafter the main line of resistance for the 480-kilometre (300-mile) front lay along the Carpathian passes. Russian plans called for the deployment in Galicia of four armies and, by the end of August 1914, the Russians had deployed 71 divisions. Conrad deployed three armies of 47 divisions (plus *B Staffel* that arrived by 8 September) that advanced on 23 August with catastrophic results. Deployed on a front of 280 kilometres (175 miles) and dangerously split, Conrad's men fanned out, heading north into Poland and east into the Ukraine, increasing attack frontage and diluting their strength. The result was battles in late August and early September 1914 at Gnila Lipa, Komarów and Zlóta Lipa. Believing that he was winning, in the face of overwhelming contrary evidence, Conrad tried to outflank and encircle the Russians. He was, however, trying to outflank a stronger force with a weaker force and, looking at total defeat, he ordered a general retreat of some 240 kilometres (150 miles) to the Carpathians, leaving behind 150,000 men besieged in Przemyśl (which fell in March 1915). In three weeks, Austria-Hungary had lost 400,000 men, including 300,000 prisoners-of-war. The army also lost

experienced officers and men; their replacements, riddled with nationalism, were less reliable and liable to desert. The Russians lost 250,000 men and 100 guns and made little effort to pursue their disorganised opponent. After the Lemberg disaster, there was a series of confused indecisive battles (October–December 1914) as the Russians attacked in an extended line from Poland to Galicia. By Christmas, Austria-Hungary had established a defensive line from the Vistula to Tarnów and the line of the Carpathians. Total Austro-Hungarian casualties for 1914 numbered 750,000.

The main operation in 1915 was Russia's defeat at Gorlice–Tarnów (see Map 19) that led to the 'great retreat' of Russian forces from Poland, pushing back the front line hundreds of kilometres. In 1916, the key operation was Russia's impressive 'Brusilov offensive'. On 14 April 1916, Russian commanders assembled at Stavka, Russia's high command. The feeling was that an offensive was futile and resources best conserved to meet the Central Powers' attack expected in the summer. Alexei Brusilov, facing Austro-Hungarian troops, felt differently. Knowing that much of the Austro-Hungarian army was ready to desert, he argued for simultaneous attacks against Austria-Hungary in his sector and German forces in the north – to stop Germany sending troops south to assist Austria-Hungary. Stavka decided that after Brusilov attacked Alexei Evert would assault the Germans.

Brusilov emphasised the need for meticulous planning and preparation, good intelligence and shell conservation. Ultimate success, however, depended on Evert helping Brusilov. As Evert prevaricated, Brusilov postponed his attack until 4 June, with Evert promising to attack five days later. The attack succeeded brilliantly: along a 320-kilometre (200-mile) stretch of front, Austro-Hungarian lines collapsed and Russian infantry streamed into unscarred country. Mass desertions by Austro-Hungarian Slav units followed. The Russians took hundreds of thousands of Austro-Hungarians prisoner. Untroubled by Evert, the Germans rushed reserves south to stiffen the line. Evert finally launched a limited attack on 23 June: too little, too late. Had he supported Brusilov Austria-Hungary might have collapsed. The Brusilov offensive resulted in Germany taking overall charge of military strategy on the eastern front. Austro-Hungarian forces were no longer capable of independent action.

Russia's last major offensive came with the 'Kerensky offensive' in June/July 1917. Within two weeks, this poorly conceived and executed attack east of Lemberg had failed, entire units deserting or refusing to fight. To improve morale, Russia raised a women's 'battalion of death', the idea being that when men saw their womenfolk fighting they would be shamed into carrying on the war. By 3 August, everything gained in the offensive had been lost, along with 30,000 prisoners and 200 guns.

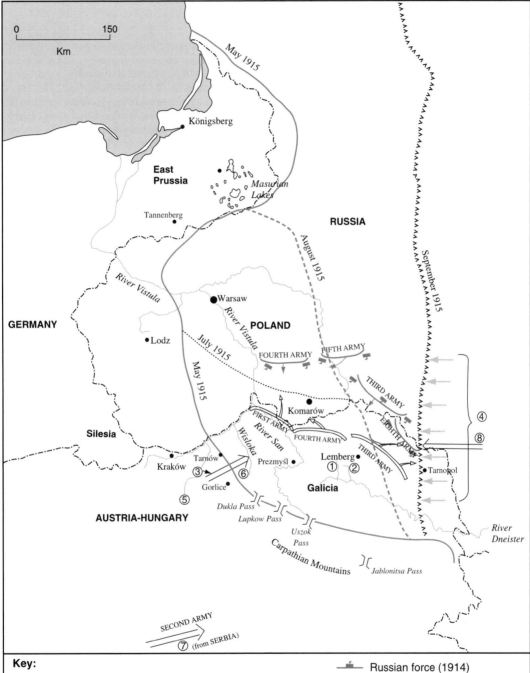

Km

0   150

East Prussia

Königsberg

Masurian Lakes

RUSSIA

May 1915

August 1915

Tannenberg

GERMANY

River Vistula

River Vistula

Warsaw

POLAND

July 1915

Lodz

May 1915

Silesia

FOURTH ARMY

FIFTH ARMY

THIRD ARMY

September 1915

EIGHTH ARMY

④

⑧

Wisloka

FIRST ARMY

River San

Komarów

FOURTH ARMY

THIRD ARMY

Tarnów

Kraków

③

⑥

Prezmyśl

Gorlice

⑤

Dukla Pass

Lupkow Pass

Lemberg

① ②

Galicia

Tarnopol

AUSTRIA-HUNGARY

Uszok Pass

Carpathian Mountains

Jablonitsa Pass

River Dneister

SECOND ARMY

⑦ (from SERBIA)

Key:

① = Gnila Lipa (river)

② = Zlóta Lipa (river)

③ = Gorlice–Tarnów offensive 1915

④ = Brusilov offensive 1916

⑤ = Dunajec river

⑥ = Wisloka river

⑦ = *B Staffel* (from Serbia) 1914

⑧ = Kerensky offensive 1917

   Russian force (1914)

   Austrian-Hungarian force (1914)

——— May 1915

·········· July 1915

– – – August 1915

∧∧∧ September 1915

Map 9: Clearing the Seas, 1914–16

Excepting for the battlecruiser *Goeben* and light cruiser *Breslau*, both of which evaded the Royal Navy in the Mediterranean and escaped to Turkey, the only significant German naval force at large in August 1914 was Maximilian Graf von Spee's East Asiatic Squadron, based in China at the German-controlled port of Tsingtao (Qingdao), but at sea in the mid-Pacific in August 1914: two armoured cruisers, the *Scharnhorst* and *Gneisenau* (eight 8.2-inch guns), and, when all assembled, four light cruisers: *Emden*, *Dresden*, *Nürnberg* and *Leipzig*. Spee detached from his squadron *Emden* (ten 4.1-inch guns), captained by Karl von Müller, for commerce raiding in the Indian Ocean. It attacked merchant shipping and sank in Penang harbour a French destroyer, *Mousquet*, and the Russian light cruiser, *Zhemchug*, which had no lookouts posted, whose crew was below deck consorting with Chinese prostitutes (60 of whom went down with the ship) and whose captain was away in town. Eventually, the Australian cruiser *Sydney* (eight 6-inch guns) chased down the *Emden*, crippling it off the Cocos (Keeling) Islands (9 November). Müller's exploits tied up a considerable number of Entente warships, disrupted the passage of trade in the Indian Ocean and threatened the passage of troop convoys from Australia to Europe. Meanwhile, the light cruiser *Königsberg* (ten 4.1-inch guns) – operating off east Africa when the war started – was blockaded in the Rufiji river delta in German East Africa where she evaded capture until two British shallow-draft monitors wrecked her in July 1915.

On 1 November 1914, Spee's main force ambushed Christopher Cradock's British Western Atlantic Squadron off the Chilean port of Coronel sinking with all hands two old cruisers, *Good Hope* and *Monmouth*. In response to the Royal Navy's first major defeat in 100 years, Britain's First Sea Lord, Jackie Fisher, sent Frederick Sturdee with the battlecruisers *Inflexible* and *Invincible* (eight 12-inch guns) to the South Atlantic. They were coaling at the Falkland Islands when Spee arrived to raid Port Stanley and with four armoured cruisers and two light cruisers they pursued the fleeing Germans. In the ensuing battle later that day (8 December 1914), Sturdee sank almost the entire German squadron. Only *Dresden* escaped, hiding out in the South Pacific until found and scuttled in the Juan Fernández Islands in March 1915. Although an important victory, British gunnery and range finding at the Falklands battle were poor: only 7% of shells found their target, or one hit per gun every 75 minutes. Neither had Spee's weaker force tested British battlecruiser armour. Spee's cruises captured the public imagination and caused difficulties for the Entente, but the losses inflicted were slight, and cannot be compared to the German submarine threat later in the war (see Map 29).

Closer to home in the North Sea, the British and Germans fought two naval battles in 1914 and 1915. On 28 August 1914, the Royal Navy raided enemy shipping off the German naval base of Heligoland. The arrival of Sir David Beatty's strong British battlecruiser force turned the battle. In the ensuing Battle of Heligoland Bight, the British sank the German light cruisers *Köln*, *Mainz* and *Ariadne*, plus a destroyer. In 1914 and early 1915, Franz von Hipper's German battlecruisers bombarded Britain's east coast (see Map 30). The Royal Navy awaited its reckoning with 'Hipper's babykillers'. It came on 23–24 January 1915 when Hipper set sail for the Dogger Bank area of the North Sea to lay mines and destroy fishing boats (believed to be gathering intelligence). Informed of this move by naval intelligence, five of Beatty's battlecruisers sailed out to confront Hipper's force of three battlecruisers (plus the old semi-battlecruiser *Blücher*). At 08.50 on 24 January, Beatty sighted Hipper's ships, which promptly fled south. A running battle ensued at extreme ranges up to 20,000 yards (18,300 metres). *Blücher*, terminally damaged, capsized. A steel door that kept a huge fire from reaching the magazine saved *Seydlitz* from destruction. German fire badly damaged Beatty's flagship *Lion*, after which poor British signalling allowed the Germans to escape. While the Germans learnt lessons about handling volatile gun cordite from the *Seydlitz* incident, the British erroneously concluded that Dogger Bank vindicated the superiority of their battlecruisers. While British victories, Heligoland Bight and Dogger Bank were marred by serious shortcomings in gunnery (and also signalling) that, un-remedied, would be disastrous at Jutland in 1916.

There was also the menace of mines and German submarines (U-boats, *Unterseeboote*). On 22 September 1914, off the Dutch coast, the submarine U-9 torpedoed and sank in a row three old British cruisers, *Aboukir*, *Hogue* and *Cressy*, a portent of the power of the submarine. Germany concentrated its limited submarine force on *Handelskrieg* – counter-blockade trade warfare against Entente (and neutral) merchant shipping. Unrestricted submarine warfare – in which the U-boat gave no warning, instead torpedoing without coming to the surface to see if the target ship was Entente or neutral – raised the possibility of antagonising neutral states, notably America. In February 1915, Germany declared the waters around Britain a 'war zone'. On 7 May 1915, U-20 sank the passenger liner *Lusitania* off the west coat of Ireland, killing 128 US citizens (of 1198 drowned). Unrestricted attacks threatened to bring the US into the war and in August–September 1915 the Germans moderated their submarine attacks. Germany's decision to reintroduce unrestricted submarine warfare in February 1917 would help bring America into the war.

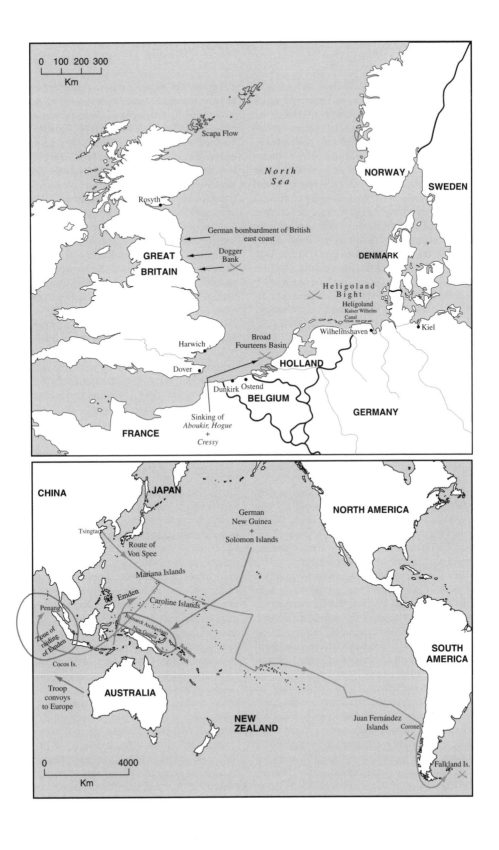

Map 10: The Western Front – An Overview

By the end of 1914 the western front had assumed the basic shape which it was to keep until 1918. For more than 700 kilometres (440 miles) the opposing armies faced each other in a series of improvised entrenched positions. The small Belgian army, supported by a detachment of the French army, held the short northern sector from Nieuport to Dixmude. With most of Belgium occupied by the Germans, King Albert, sovereign and commander-in-chief, chose to adopt a defensive posture for the duration of the war, hoping that by keeping his army in the field he would be able to secure Belgian independence at any future peace conference. South of the Belgians the British army held the line from the Ypres salient into Picardy. As the British army increased in size it took over more of the line from the French, whose manpower resources continually declined as the war went on. By March 1918 the British held 123 kilometres (76 miles), from Poelcapelle to Barisis. The rest of the line was held by the French army. Their divisions were concentrated on the active front from Soissons to the St Mihiel salient, the 250 kilometres (156 miles) to the Swiss frontier being considered by both sides a strategically unimportant sector which could be lightly held with resting formations.

As the front consolidated in late 1914 the Germans chose their defensive positions carefully, wherever possible siting their trench lines on high ground, overlooking the allied positions. These ridges presented the allies with a tactical and strategic objective; securing them would in turn allow the allies to dominate the German rear areas, destabilise the German defensive system, and restore mobility to field operations. These commanding heights, whose names have come to symbolise the western front – Passchendaele, Messines-Wytschaete, Aubers, Vimy, Thiepval, the Chemin des Dames, Mort Homme – were to be the focus of three years of attritional warfare.

Initially the allies thought that concentrating sufficient force on one point of the German front would allow them to 'break through' the trench line into the German army's communications net and rupture the whole front (see Map 15). This proved impossible with the limited matériel at their disposal. The inertia of crossing the firepower-dominated battlefield, with limited mobility and poor communications, blunted infantry assaults. Any breaches forced could be plugged by the enemy, who could bring up reserves more rapidly than the attacking troops could advance. Successful counter-attacks could then be delivered against exhausted and depleted attackers – ground taken would often be lost. With 'break through' impossible a new kind of linear siege warfare, drawing on the methods and weapons of bygone eras – saps, tunnels, mines, mortars, grenades – developed. As the battle in France and Flanders went on, the opposing defensive systems became more elaborate. Behind the front line both sides dug successive defensive positions, each with swathes of protective barbed wire, complicated webs of fighting and communication trenches, and mutually supporting fortified strong-points. This gave depth to the defence and insured against an enemy breakthrough. Below the ground elaborate systems of tunnels and mines were dug, to penetrate the enemy's trench system by stealth. The art and science of defensive organisation reached its peak in the Hindenburg line, specially prepared for a German retreat in 1917.

Day-to-day existence in the trenches was difficult but not impossible. On quiet sectors of the front, or between offensives, a 'live-and-let-live' system might operate, both sides allowing the other to get on with day-to-day trench routine with limited interference. Actual fraternisation between the opposing armies, such as the famous Christmas truce of 1914, was rare, and frowned on by the high command. It did not survive the intensification of warfare after 1915. Time spent in the front line was limited, a regular system of reliefs ensuring that no man spent long periods under fire. However, front line service inevitably took its toll; as well as casualties from enemy action, disease – trench foot, pneumonia, rheumatism and above all the psychological strain of 'shell shock' – slowly sapped the strength and morale of front line units.

The static and apparently stalemated western front has come to epitomise all that was wrong with the First World War – unimaginative generals sacrificing the lives of brave men in futile offensives. This misrepresentation needs correction. To contemporary military professionals the western front represented a measurable military problem: how to break the static front and restore mobility to warfare, in the absence of strategic surprise and open space. Potential solutions were to be found in technology, matériel, tactics or operational methods – or in practice a combination of all four. Armies experienced a 'learning curve' as they struggled to identify, experiment with and solve the practical challenges of extended siege warfare. The constant dynamic between more-sophisticated attack and improved defence made the problem all the more intractable. Individual technical developments – artillery, gas, tanks, aircraft, wireless communications – had to be integrated with new tactical methods – artillery–infantry cooperation and 'storm-troop' tactics for example. From this interplay evolved new 'deep battle' doctrines – 'break in', 'bite-and-hold' and ultimately 'break out'. Over four years a veritable 'Revolution in Military Affairs' occurred on the western front. The infantry–cavalry–artillery tactics of 1914, which would have been reasonably familiar to Napoleon, were replaced by all-arms combined operations, allowing the front to be broken in 1918 and the German army to be defeated in modern mobile warfare (see Map 44).

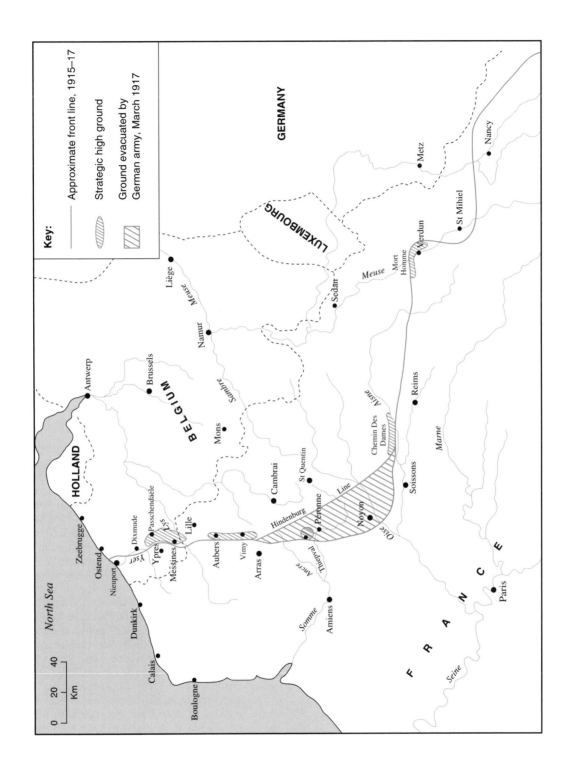

Map 11: War on the Periphery – An Overview

While the main theatres of the First World War were the western and eastern fronts, the war involved a great deal of fighting in peripheral theatres. These included Italy (see Maps 20 and 38), Salonika (see Map 22), Gallipoli (see Map 17), the Caucasus (see Map 16), Africa, the Far East (see Map 12), Palestine (see Map 35) and Mesopotamia (see Map 16). On the high seas, the German threat was largely eradicated by early 1915, but German commerce raiders continued to attack shipping throughout the war (see Map 9). There were also low-level conflicts in the Western Desert of Egypt (the Senussi), in South Africa (the Maritz revolt), in Nyasaland (Malawi) (John Chilembwe's revolt), in the Hedjaz with the Hashemite Arab revolt against the Turks (see Map 34), in the Yemen with Turkish forces facing British-controlled Aden, and in Russia when Allied forces intervened towards the end of the war (see Map 49). These all suggest that the First World War was a 'world' war and not just another European civil war.

The Entente powers, with their control of the high seas, dominated war on the periphery, launching a series of offensives designed to punch their way into enemy territory to which the Central alliance had to respond. Warfare on the periphery raised debates on strategy and often resulted in quite severe civil–military disputes over strategy. In Britain, there was a long tradition of maritime warfare, identified by the British military thinker Basil Liddell Hart as the 'indirect approach' – a British 'way of warfare' that emphasised a strategy of attacking an enemy through support for continental alliances and attacks though sideshow military theatres that would drain enemy resources. By 1916, with France and Russia waning, this was no longer possible and Britain for the first time committed a large conscript army to the western front, the main theatre of operations.

However, this did not preclude ongoing peripheral operations in Italy, the Balkans and the Middle East. In Britain this provoked a debate between 'easterners' and 'westerners'; between those keen to pursue alternative military campaigns that would break the deadlock, and those arguing for the commitment of all resources to the main, western European, theatre. Famously, the British Prime Minister David Lloyd George was a firm supporter of an 'easterner' strategy, while his Chief of Imperial General Staff, William Robertson, was the 'westerner' who argued the case for directing all men and matériel to support Douglas Haig's operations in France. For Lloyd George, peripheral operations were more than just a means of defeating Germany by 'knocking away the props', as he characterised it. They represented a means whereby Britain could gain enemy territory that could be of value as a bargaining tool in any peace talks. If the war ended without a clear-cut victor such spoils of war would help Britain dominate the peace settlement.

Lloyd George's long-running dispute with Robertson dominated British strategic planning in 1916 and 1917. In February 1918, Lloyd George finally got rid of Robertson, and he forced through the allied Supreme War Council a strategy document, Joint Note 12, that called for holding operations in France while the main weight of British offensive operations in 1918 be directed against the Ottoman empire. However, the threat of the Ludendorff offensives from March 1918 (see Map 42) meant that Joint Note 12 was forgotten as the western front again dominated strategic thinking. Before Lloyd George could once again argue for peripheral operations the war ended.

There were similar 'westerner' versus 'easterner' debates in France and Germany during the war. In France, Aristide Briand, Justice Minister and later Prime Minister, clashed with Joffre, the army commander, over participation in the Dardanelles/Gallipoli campaign and on sending a French expeditionary force to Salonika, an operation that was intimately tied up with France's complicated civil–military relations during the war. In Germany, Hindenburg and Ludendorff, in command on the eastern front, pushed for victory in that theatre before a victory on the western front. In 1916, this dispute culminated in Hindenburg and Ludendorff replacing Erich von Falkenhayn as Chief of Staff, after which they triumphed over Russia before attacking in France in 1918.

The debates over peripheral strategy show that in the key Entente states such as Britain and France the politicians remained in charge throughout the war. Military advisers in these countries had immense influence but at the end of the day elected politicians ultimately decided strategy. Haphazard and imperfect as this system may have been, it did mean that both politicians and generals brought the best of their skills to the war with the former using the latter's advice to decide strategy. This resulted in some wasteful peripheral operations (such as Gallipoli) but was a far better way of managing the war than the system in Germany where, by 1916, Hindenburg and Ludendorff and the Third Supreme Command had effectively taken charge of the war, sidelining both politicians and the Kaiser. As in the Second World War, German strategy was skewed by the lack of civilian input into strategic decision-making and this was a key reason why Germany lost both world wars.

Peripheral operations also allowed the Entente powers to make good use of imperial resources that, close to hand, were readily available to fight in African and Asian theatres, thus freeing up troops for the war in France. It also meant that the Entente powers ended the war in control of large swathes of enemy territory that could be used at the peace talks to ensure that key war desiderata (such as the destruction of the German empire) were met.

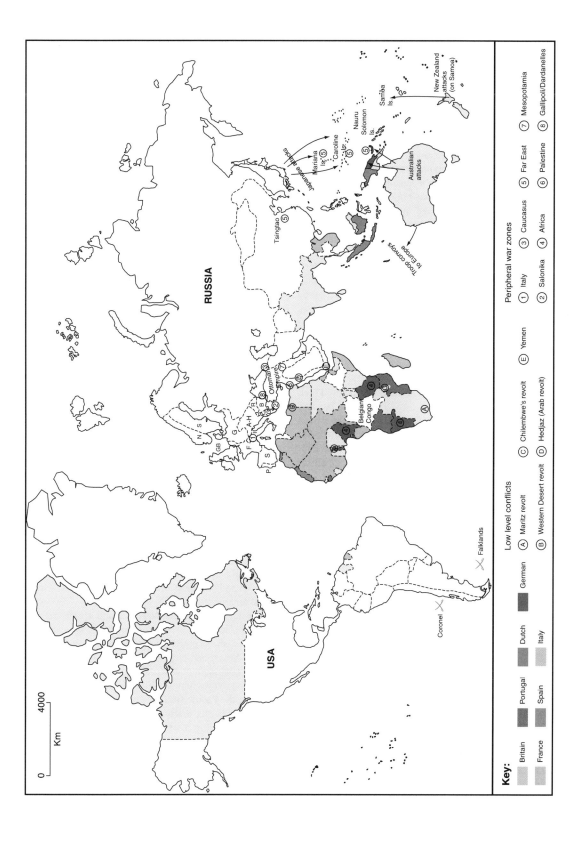

Key:

Britain	Portugal	Dutch	German
France	Spain	Italy	

Low level conflicts

Ⓐ Maritz revolt Ⓒ Chilembwe's revolt Ⓔ Yemen
Ⓑ Western Desert revolt Ⓓ Hedjaz (Arab revolt)

Peripheral war zones

① Italy   ③ Caucasus   ⑤ Far East   ⑦ Mesopotamia
② Salonika ④ Africa   ⑥ Palestine   ⑧ Gallipoli/Dardanelles

RUSSIA

USA

Tsingtao

Belgian Congo

Ottoman Empire

Troop convoys to Europe

German squadron

Mariana Is. ⑤

Caroline Is. ⑤

Nauru

Solomon Is. ⑤

Samoa Is.

New Zealand attacks (on Samoa)

Australian attacks

Coronel ✕

Falklands ✕

0 ⎯ 4000

Km

Map 12: The Great War in Africa and Asia

Africa was dragged into the First World War because it was almost completely controlled by European powers. While militarily Africa was a sideshow, there was fighting there as Entente armies conquered Germany's African colonies. Moreover, both sides mobilised Africa's resources and manpower, touching the lives of vast numbers of Africans, and proving the value of empire as a strategic resource. Because of appalling communications, the major military difficulty was not defeating the enemy but reaching him. The war here involved small columns operating with little artillery support, the machine gun being the heaviest weapon used in most engagements. Troops from Britain, France, Belgium and Portugal (from 1916) assaulted Germany's African colonies in Togoland (Togo), Cameroons (Kamerun), South-West Africa (Namibia) and East Africa (Tanganyika/Tanzania). Locally recruited soldiers and porters played a vital part in these campaigns. In Togoland on 12 August 1914, a sergeant-major of the West African Frontier Force fired the first shot of the African war; on 25 November 1918, two weeks after the war had ended in Europe, the last German-led forces in East Africa surrendered at Abercorn.

Togoland fell quickly. As the Germans had based their most powerful wireless station in Togoland, its loss restricted communications with Berlin. Bounded by British and French colonies, German forces in the Cameroons, short of munitions, held out in the northern highlands until 1916, after the bulk of the force had escaped to Spanish-controlled Muni. Britain and France then divided Togoland and the Cameroons between them. Meanwhile, in an example of local empire building, South African forces attacked German South-West Africa. A revolt of pro-German white Afrikaners in South Africa (September–October 1914), led by a South African officer, S.G. Maritz, delayed the invasion. Eventually, loyal South African forces quelled the revolt, after which they invaded South-West Africa by land across the Orange river and from the sea, by Lüderitz and Walvis Bay. The last German forces surrendered at Tsumeb in July 1915. Casualties were low: more South Africans died in Maritz's revolt than in fighting the Germans.

The major campaign of the war in Africa was in German East Africa against German-led *askaris* (locally-raised African levies) reinforced by a small police force plus the guns and crew of the wrecked German ship *Königsberg*. Under the overall command of Paul von Lettow-Vorbeck, 218 Europeans and 2542 *askaris* were divided into some 21 companies, each with 150–200 *askaris* led by German officers and NCOs. The Germans repulsed a bungled Indian Expeditionary Force landing at Tanga. Thereafter, Lettow-Vorbeck kept his force in being until 1918, tying down large numbers of Entente troops desperately needed elsewhere.

He avoided major battles, instead invading at different times Mozambique, Northern Rhodesia and Nyasaland. While Lettow-Vorbeck kept fighting until after the war was over, his command in East Africa is not as impressive as is often thought. His sustained defence of the colony only lasted from March 1916 to November 1917, comparable in length to the German defence of the Cameroons, and he had no theory of guerrilla war, preferring classic German theories of envelopment and the decisive battle.

Two million Africans served in the war as a whole, as either soldiers or labourers, and some 200,000 were killed in action or died. Africa was used as a vast pool of manpower, with hundreds of thousands of men from Belgian, British, French, German and Portuguese Africa employed as porters and soldiers, many dying from disease, especially malaria (as did many white troops). While the war certainly dented European racial superiority in Africa, too little is known about black Africans' experience of the war.

While Germany was no danger to Japan, the latter – allied to Britain in 1902 – wanted the German port of Tsingtao (Qingdao) on the Chinese coast. Germany also had extensive island colonies in the Pacific in Micronesia (Mariana and Caroline Islands), Papua New Guinea and Samoa. Britain was keen for Japan to join the war, assuming that Japan's armed forces, especially the navy, would help in the fight against Germany in the Pacific. As long as Japan remained neutral and Britain concentrated on the war in Europe, Germany stood a reasonable chance of defending Tsingtao. Once Japan entered the war on 23 August 1914, it was only a matter of time. Without naval support, the German governor of Tsingtao drew in men and matériel for a siege against 60,000 Japanese troops plus a small Anglo-Indian contingent. First contact was on 18 September 1914, the main advance beginning on 25 September against a German garrison of 184 officers and 4390 men. The Japanese employed a gradual siege warfare approach – using air-power – and, running out of ammunition, the Germans sought an armistice on 7 November.

Japan, Australia and New Zealand also attacked and occupied Germany's colonies in Micronesia and New Guinea. Japan occupied the Micronesian islands in October 1914; in November, New Zealand took German possessions to the east of longitude 170 (Samoa) while Australia got those to the west (New Guinea). While the collapse of Germany's empire in the Pacific freed up British and Entente forces for the war in Europe, it also represented the rise of Japan as a major regional power whose aim was to expand her empire across the Pacific and into China. Japan soon started to express her desire for expansion by fortifying the recently conquered German possessions and by presenting China with a series of demands in 1915 (the twenty-one demands) that tried to extend further Japanese influence over China.

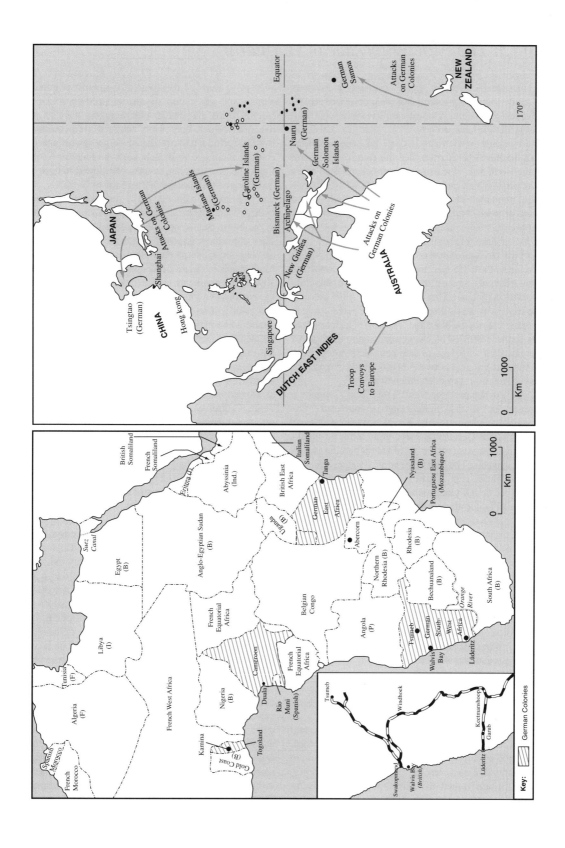

Map 13: The Allied Blockade of Germany

Blockade by land or sea of an enemy's overseas trade was a long-established weapon of war. It targeted the enemy's home front, knowing that in a long war imports and exports were vital. In 1914, an Entente blockade of Germany's overland trade was difficult, but the Royal Navy controlled the two routes in and out of the North Sea – the English Channel and the Faroes gap – through which passed the vast bulk of Germany's merchant shipping. Thus, a naval blockade could starve Germany of world trade. Moreover, Germany's strategy of keeping its surface fleet in port during the war abandoned its seaborne foreign trade to the Royal Navy.

As naval blockade threatened the right of neutral powers to trade freely, the 1856 Declaration of Paris had concluded that only a line of ships off the enemy's coast blockading its ports was acceptable. This was 'effective' blockade and, close to the enemy coast, it need not trouble neutral shipping unless it tried to run the blockade. The 1909 Declaration of London further restricted blockade, challenging the right of belligerents such as Britain to stop neutral shipping cargo on 'continuous voyage' between neutral ports, even if the ultimate destination was an enemy power.

When war began, the risk of losses from Germany's submarines, destroyers, mines, and shore-based guns made it too dangerous for the Royal Navy to enforce a close blockade of Germany's ports. Only a distant blockade of Germany across the Straits of Dover and the Faroes gap was practicable. The North Sea ports of neutral Holland and the Scandinavian states (Norway, Sweden and Denmark), inside the blockade zone, were potential transshipment points for trade with Germany. Thus, Britain would have to stop and check all shipping going into the North Sea, turning back cargoes bound for Germany. This threatened to upset not just the European neutrals, but also America's worldwide shipping fleet.

Hoping not to antagonise neutrals, Britain avoided the word 'blockade' until 1916, preferring the phrases 'economic warfare' or 'control and examination based on force'. Initially, as only certain goods were marked out as contraband and so liable for seizure, cargoes bound for Germany passed through the blockade. Britain's definition of contraband expanded massively as the war unfolded, to include basic commodities such as foodstuffs. Britain eventually drew up an extensive list of goods marked as contraband, against the wishes of neutral states (and Germany) wishing to trade freely.

Weaknesses in the system allowed Scandinavia and Holland to supply Germany with imported goods. Indeed, in 1916, food exports to Germany from the Scandinavian countries and Holland were 25% higher than in 1913. Gradually Britain turned the screw on the neutrals. In 1915, she brokered deals with European neutrals in an attempt to stop the re-export to Germany of goods from abroad and the export of neutral produce to Germany. Neutral firms that traded with Germany went on a black list, after which they were debarred from trading with Britain, forbidden to use British cargo vessels and refused coaling facilities at British ports around the globe. By 1918, the Scandinavian powers had agreed to trade quotas that stopped the passage of all goods to Germany.

If persuasion failed, there was always the physical reality of the blockade. Naval patrols across the entrances to the North Sea stopped all merchantmen for inspection. They rigorously imposed the idea of continuous voyage, making neutral ships prove that cargoes were not 'contraband' goods intended for Germany. In 1915, Britain stopped 3098 ships across the Faroes gap, very few ships evaded the patrols. No ship, it seems, got past the Dover patrol that year. Britain pressed every kind of vessel into service: armed passenger liners, trawlers, drifters and motorboats. Extensive minefields encouraged neutral ships to report for inspection before being escorted through the minefields. By the end of 1915, the blockade fleet numbered some 3000 ships. The blockade across the narrow Straits of Dover was easier than in the Faroes gap, where the Tenth Cruiser Squadron kept perpetual watch in rough seas for shipping that it examined and brought back to the Orkneys if there was any question of suspicious cargoes. Eventually, the threat of German mines and submarines pressed back the blockade line from the shorter Shetlands–Norway gap towards the Faroe islands.

Facilitating the acceptance of blockade was the fact that Germany's counter-blockade strategy of submarine warfare was far more dangerous to neutral shipping (see Map 29). Unrestricted submarine warfare indiscriminately killed neutral (including American) sailors. Britain's blockade, while intrusive and irritating, was only dangerous to those neutral ships that declined to submit to a search. America generally accepted the blockade, helped by the fact that in two years only four Americans lost their lives because of British action against neutral shipping.

While historians disagree on the impact of the blockade, once the war stabilised into a long conflict it was an important weapon against Germany. By 1916, the blockade was starving Germany of much-needed supplies, such as nitrates and copper for munitions production. Germany bypassed the blockade by exploiting the resources of occupied Europe, but this compared poorly to access to global trade. It also developed *ersatz* (substitute) products to replace previously imported goods. The blockade reduced Germany's war effectiveness, lowering morale and provoking discontent among German civilians living on a reduced calorific intake as imports of foreign foodstuffs declined to almost nothing. The blockade against Germany continued until July 1919.

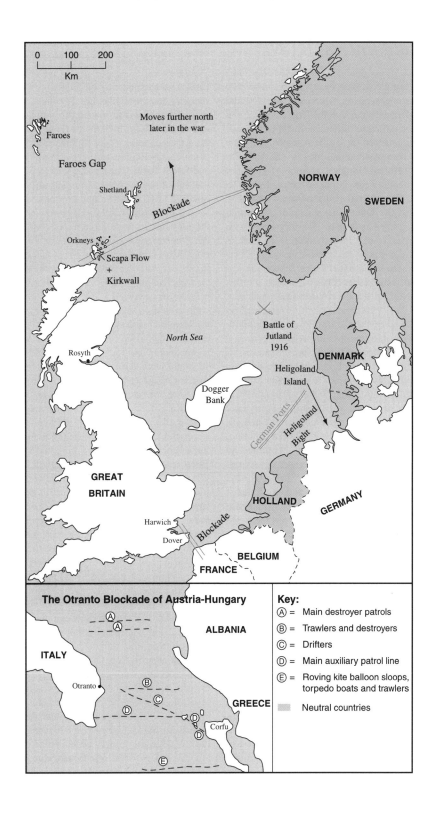

0   100   200
Km

Moves further north
later in the war

Faroes

Faroes Gap

Shetland

NORWAY

SWEDEN

Orkneys

Blockade

Scapa Flow
+
Kirkwall

North Sea

Battle of
Jutland
1916

DENMARK

Rosyth

Dogger
Bank

Heligoland
Island

German Ports

Heligoland
Bight

GREAT
BRITAIN

HOLLAND

GERMANY

Harwich

Blockade

Dover

BELGIUM

FRANCE

The Otranto Blockade of Austria-Hungary

Ⓐ
Ⓐ

ALBANIA

ITALY

Otranto

Ⓑ

Ⓒ

Ⓓ

Ⓓ

GREECE

Corfu

Ⓓ

Ⓔ

Key:

Ⓐ = Main destroyer patrols

Ⓑ = Trawlers and destroyers

Ⓒ = Drifters

Ⓓ = Main auxiliary patrol line

Ⓔ = Roving kite balloon sloops,
torpedo boats and trawlers

Neutral countries

Map 14: Italy Enters the War

When the First World War began, Italy was a second-order European power, allied to Germany and Austria-Hungary through the Triple Alliance of 1882. While Italy had no serious differences with Germany – indeed, she formally renewed the Triple Alliance in 1912 – she had irredentist claims stretching back to the 1860s to the Italian-speaking Austro-Hungarian region of Trentino/South Tyrol which soured the Triple Alliance. Italy also claimed Istria and Trieste (citing the presence of Italian speakers) and wanted the Dodecanese islands, occupied in 1912, to be recognised as Italian. The differences with Austria-Hungary meant that Italy remained neutral in 1914. Italian socialists and pacifists opposed the war, and she was militarily weak; she had a largely agrarian economy, a shortage of raw materials (especially coal), deep internal social divisions, a weak army and a disinterested population. So, on 2 August 1914, the Italian government seized on the lack of consultation by the Central Powers formally to declare its neutrality, a decision that surprised no one.

When the early campaigns of the war proved indecisive, the Italian government, led by Prime Minister Antonio Salandra, slowly shifted its allegiance towards the Entente. This was evident in the movement of Italian troops from the border with France to the one with Austria-Hungary over the winter of 1914–15. Italy's king, Victor Emmanuel III, Salandra and Foreign Minister, Baron Sidney Sonnino, were the driving forces in the move to war, supported by an eclectic grouping of political and cultural revolutionaries including the radical journalist Benito Mussolini, the nationalist writer Gabriele D'Annunzio and the Futurist artist Filippo Marinetti (who thought that war would help to modernise Italy). The Italian population divided into those who supported neutrality, those keen on intervention and those uninterested in war. The government, meanwhile, accelerated its military build-up and, fearful of Austro-Hungarian expansion into Albania, occupied the Albanian port of Valona (Vlöre).

Salandra's talk of Italy's national interests – or *sacro egoismo* – along with the actions of his interventionist foreign minister Sonnino, made an accommodation with Austria-Hungary difficult. The conservative Sonnino, committed to Italian colonial expansion, was sure that prolonged neutrality would wreck Italy's chances of post-war territorial gains. While at first Sonnino was keen on siding with Germany, its check on the western front (see Map 4) made him re-assess the situation and seek to support whichever side looked like winning. Thus, Sonnino had discussions with both sides in late 1914 and early 1915, but Italy's territorial *irridenta* made any settlement with the Central Powers highly unlikely.

By December 1914, Salandra stated publicly Italy's opposition to the Central Powers' war aims and to Austro-Hungarian expansion in the Balkans. In response, Germany sent her former chancellor Bernhard von Bülow with a powerful diplomatic mission to build contacts with non-interventionist politicians. In early 1915, von Bülow and the Austrian ambassador to Italy tried to satisfy Sonnino's demands for Italian territorial expansion in the Balkans and South Tyrol. They made some progress, but Germany was unable to get Vienna to offer the Italians territory in South Tyrol, Trieste and Albania. Austria-Hungary's formal rejection of Italian demands in April 1915 opened the door for Entente diplomacy, with the advantage that the Entente powers could offer Austro-Hungarian land to Italy. Moreover, with the Central powers heavily engaged in the war, the reversal of the Triple Alliance seemed like an attractive and risk-free operation for Italy.

On 26 April 1915, Italy signed the Treaty of London with Britain, France and Russia. In return for Italy joining the war, the London pact accepted Italian territorial claims in Europe and Asia Minor, and promised extensive military and economic aid for Italy. Italy would get reparations, the Trentino/South Tyrol region, Trieste, Istria, the Dalmatian/Adriatic coast (excepting the port city of Rijeka/Fiume) and parts of southern Turkey around Adalia. With the exception of South Tyrol, Trieste and Istria, these areas contained very few if any Italians. Italy's far-ranging territorial claims would cause problems after the war with some Entente politicians arguing that they had offered too much territory in the rush to sign Italy up for the war. When the Bolsheviks published the secret territorial provisions of the Treaty of London, it caused an outcry in Greece and Serbia, whose territory had been promised to Italy, and from those inside Italy opposed to what they saw as an expansionist, unnecessary war.

In May 1915, as war approached there were orchestrated pro-war demonstrations. On 13 May 1915, parliamentary opposition to the war led to the resignation of Salandra's cabinet. Three days later the King re-instated Salandra when it was found impossible to appoint a neutralist administration. Salandra's re-appointment gave him the mandate for war and, although 74 left-wing deputies opposed war, the Italian army was mobilised and war declared against Austria-Hungary on 23 May 1915 (Italy did not declare war against Germany until 1916). Once in the war, military policy passed almost entirely to the Chief of Staff, Luigi Cadorna, who led the Italian army from 1915 to 1917 on eleven costly and disastrous offensives against Austria-Hungary along the river Isonzo (see Map 20). Italy's lacklustre military performance in the war adversely affected her post-war efforts to secure all of the territorial demands of the Treaty of London and she finished the war feeling that she had been short-changed territorially (see Map 48).

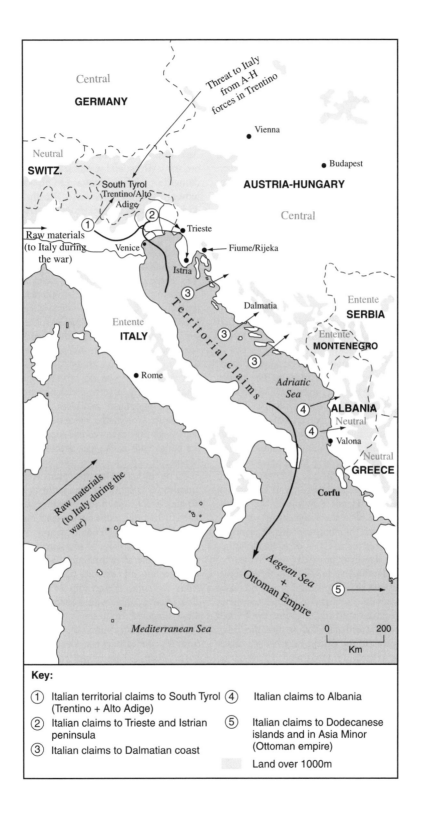

Key:

① Italian territorial claims to South Tyrol (Trentino + Alto Adige)

② Italian claims to Trieste and Istrian peninsula

③ Italian claims to Dalmatian coast

④ Italian claims to Albania

⑤ Italian claims to Dodecanese islands and in Asia Minor (Ottoman empire)

Land over 1000m

Map 15: The Attempts to Break the Western Front, 1915

In 1915, Joffre chose an offensive strategy to liberate France's occupied northern *departments*. Given the allies' superiority on the western front – there were 113 allied divisions opposing 98 German in January – he believed that force could be concentrated against a point or points on the German front to achieve a breakthrough. Others, notably Britain's war minister, Lord Kitchener, doubted that the western front could be broken until greater resources were available, and sought easier strategic gains in other theatres. Nevertheless the western front remained the principal Anglo-French theatre, in which growing British military resources were concentrated.

Since the German line in France constituted a deep salient, Joffre chose to concentrate his attacks against its flanks, in Artois and Champagne, in the expectation that a breakthrough to Lille, Douai and Mézières would disrupt the German army's lateral railway communications behind their front and force a general retirement. The first allied attacks were launched in the spring. On 16 February the French Fourth Army attacked in Champagne. On 10 March the British First Army launched a diversionary attack in Artois against the village of Neuve Chapelle. The French made limited progress. After one month a 3-kilometre (2-mile) advance had cost 43,000 casualties. The British operation, on a much smaller scale, was initially successful. After a surprise 35-minute hurricane bombardment the two attacking divisions stormed the enemy's front trenches. They penetrated to a depth of over 1 kilometre (⅔ mile), seizing Neuve Chapelle village, at the cost of 2300 casualties. Yet it was only a tactical success – a breakthrough remained elusive. Before Henry Rawlinson, the British commander, could commit his reserves the enemy's reserves came up to counter-attack, blunting the British advance. Follow-up operations over the next few days cost a further 10,000 casualties, for little extra ground.

Joffre renewed the offensive in May on a larger scale. In Artois on 9 May the French Tenth Army attacked Vimy ridge, breaking into the German defensive system. Six weeks of back-and-forward fighting cost the French 102,000 casualties, the Germans 73,000, but the ridge remained in German hands. The British First Army's attack against Aubers ridge to the north made no progress on the first day, owing to insufficient ammunition for the supporting artillery bombardment. The resulting 'shells scandal' destabilised British politics, forcing the Liberal Prime Minster, Herbert Asquith, to set up an all-party coalition government. A Ministry of Munitions, headed by David Lloyd George, was established to manage the production of war matériel. Despite its initial failure the First Army continued to attack for a fortnight in an unsuccessful attempt to secure Aubers ridge. While offering some support to the French attacks further south, the battle cost the British

army a further 30,000 casualties. This failure convinced the First Army's commander, Douglas Haig, of the need for methodical preparation and lengthy bombardment to overcome the German fixed defences.

The final series of attacks took place in September. Again the scale of operations was increased, and attacks on the Artois and Champagne fronts were timed to coincide. The French attacked on both fronts on 25 September. Twenty divisions of Tenth Army attacked on a 35-kilometre (22-mile) front in Artois; 27 divisions of Second and Fourth Armies advanced on a 40-kilometre (25-mile) front in Champagne. Weight of numbers alone was not enough to do better than before. Again a 4-kilometre (2½ mile) penetration beyond the German first position was contained and counter-attacked from the second defensive system. Another 192,000 casualties failed to secure the elusive breakthrough. The German army suffered 150,000 casualties in preventing it. The British First Army's supporting attack, across the difficult ground of the Loos coalfields, repeated the familiar pattern. Assisted by gas for the first time, five British divisions crossed the German first position. However, in expectation of more limited results the three reserve divisions had been held well back under GHQ control, and were unable to advance quickly enough to exploit this success. When thrown against the undamaged German second position on the second day of the battle with inadequate artillery support they were cut to pieces.

The allied offensive plans for 1915 were over-ambitious. Despite their superiority in manpower on the western front, which increased as more British divisions arrived, they lacked the matériel and munitions – particularly heavy artillery which could support a deeper advance – to force their way beyond the enemy's forward defensive system. Time after time allied infantry would capture the enemy's forward defences, but fail to make further progress. After the early momentum of an attack stalled, bloody close-quarter fights would continue for days or weeks over these disputed front line positions, such as the Notre-Dame-de-Lorette spur, on Vimy ridge, fought over countless times between December 1914 and September 1915, when it was finally captured by the French. The opposing armies left 42,000 dead on that hill alone. Attrition, rather than manoeuvre warfare, became the fallback strategy in 1915. It was costly for defenders as well as attackers – in 1915 the German army suffered 615,000 casualties, predominantly on the western front. Such mêlées would not win the war, but they would teach both attackers and defenders alike the tactics and operational methods of close-order trench fighting. In 1916 this strategy and method would intensify in the attritional battles of Verdun and the Somme (see Maps 25, 27 and 28).

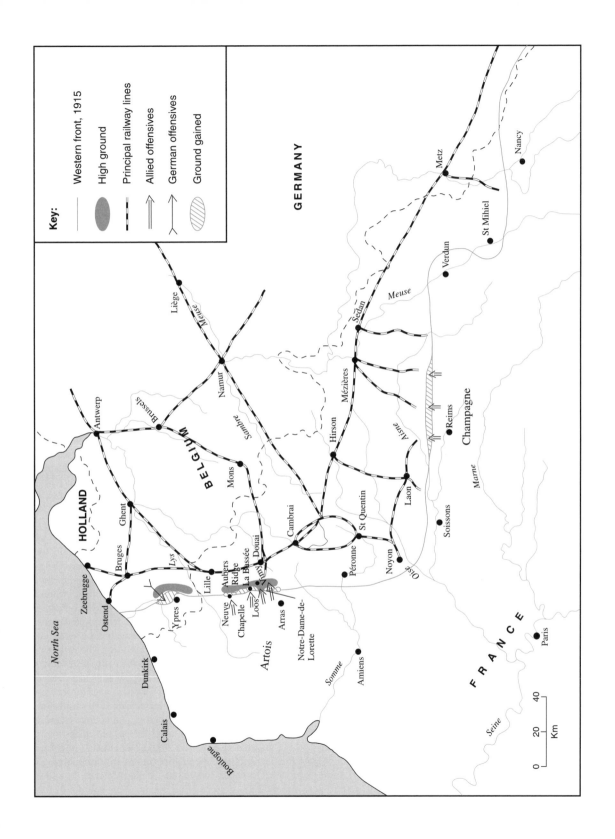

Key:

Western front, 1915	
High ground	
Principal railway lines	
Allied offensives	
German offensives	
Ground gained	

North Sea

HOLLAND

GERMANY

BELGIUM

FRANCE

Calais
Boulogne
Dunkirk
Zeebrugge
Ostend
Bruges
Ghent
Antwerp
Brussels
Liège
Namur
Mons
Ypres
Lille
Aubers Ridge
Neuve Chapelle
La Bassée
Loos
Vimy
Douai
Arras
Notre-Dame-de-Lorette
Artois
Cambrai
Péronne
Amiens
St Quentin
Noyon
Soissons
Laon
Reims
Champagne
Hirson
Mézières
Sedan
Metz
St Mihiel
Verdun
Nancy
Paris

Meuse
Sambre
Lys
Somme
Seine
Oise
Aisne
Marne
Meuse

0 20 40
Km

Map 16: Mesopotamia and the Caucasus

Turkey entered the war on the side of the Central Powers in November 1914. In response, the war in Mesopotamia (Iraq) began when in November 1914 India sent a naval expedition to Basra to protect British interests – notably oil in southern Persia. Under the control of the Indian government, British and Indian land forces at Basra pushed into southern Mesopotamia, using the Tigris and Euphrates rivers for their advance. Initial success spurred the force into thinking that it could capture Baghdad, 400 kilometres (250 miles) upriver (in a straight line) from Basra. Although London had reservations about an advance to Baghdad, it failed to stop the Mesopotamia force, under the overall command of John Nixon, from advancing inland. Nixon's force was ill-equipped for the task ahead. He failed to build up the logistics needed to take an army deep into enemy territory. Port facilities at Basra were poor; thereafter, supply to the front relied on limited numbers of small boats that negotiated the Tigris and Euphrates rivers in the face of intense heat and a hostile local population. Nixon's failure to realise that the campaign depended on proper logistics ruined it (Nixon retired on the grounds of ill-health in early 1916).

Having captured An Nāṣirīyah and Al 'Amārah (May–July 1915), thus clearing southern Mesopotamia, in September 1915 the 6th Indian division (nine Indian and three British battalions), spearheading Charles Townshend's Expeditionary Force D, raced up the Tigris. It defeated the Turks at Es Sinn just south of Al Kūt (Kūt al Imāra) before advancing on Baghdad. The Turks checked Townshend's over-extended force at Ctesiphon, 30 kilometres (19 miles) south of Baghdad in November 1915 after which Townshend's exhausted men fell back on Kūt al Imāra, where a bend in the river offered a suitable defensive line. In early December, the Turks invested Kūt. The fear of losing the besieged 6th Division galvanised the British and Indian governments into deploying three new divisions to relieve Kūt. But the chaotic supply arrangements in Mesopotamia delayed the deployment of this force, giving the Turks time to tighten their grip, building defensive works south of the town to block any relief force.

Townshend issued erroneous statements that he could only hold out for two months, forcing the hand of the relief force. In a series of bloody battles ending in April 1916, the Turks held the hastily assembled relief force. After suffering 23,000 casualties, the relief force got to within 11 kilometres (7 miles) of Kūt but no further. Townshend failed to introduce rationing until it was too late, and on 29 April 1916 his starving garrison of some 10,000 men surrendered, 4000 of whom would die in captivity. Townshend spent his time as a prisoner in comfort, more worried about his post-war reputation than the suffering of his men.

Kūt was a tremendous blow to British prestige. Once the garrison surrendered the recriminations began. The lack of proper medical services was one area of concern, many soldiers having suffered terribly because of this. The British government assumed direct control over the Mesopotamia campaign in the summer of 1916, appointing (Frederick) Stanley Maude as commander-in-chief. By the autumn of 1916, Maude had at his disposal some 150,000 troops. Maude's first task was to expand the port facilities at Basra and reorganise the supply lines to the front line. Having done this, Maude set out to avenge the defeat at Kūt, advancing against an outnumbered and outgunned enemy. He attacked in December 1916, defeating Turkish forces at Kūt, before advancing on Baghdad, which he took on 11 March 1917. Maude died in November 1917 from cholera. His replacement was the commander of III Indian Corps in Mesopotamia, William Marshall, who launched a final offensive in October 1918 that cleared the Turks from all of northern Mesopotamia, capturing Mosul (and its potential oil reserves) on 2 November 1918.

The Caucasian front is one of the least-studied campaigns of the First World War. Russia and the Ottomans had traditionally clashed in the Caucasus, and so once the latter entered the war the two sides deployed troops for a confrontation in the mountainous mass of eastern Asia Minor. Keen to expand east into the Caucasus, the Ottoman minister of war, Enver Pasha, gathered two armies at Erzurum, which he personally led in an offensive towards Ardahan and Sarikamish (Sarikamiş). The result was a disastrous defeat in terrible weather. At high altitude and in mid-winter, thousands of Turks died of cold in Enver's ill-fated expedition. The Russians repulsed another Turkish attack in the summer of 1915. In 1916, the Russians counter-attacked and were spectacularly successful. Fighting in harsh terrain and with limited logistical support, the Russians nevertheless took the fortress of Erzurum in February 1917. Using naval forces to support the advance, the Russians then switched to the coast, taking Trabzon in April 1917. The Russian revolution in March 1917 put a halt to large-scale Russian operations. By then the Russians had pushed deep into eastern Turkey, past Lake Van (Van Gölü). The Bolshevik revolution in November 1917 led to the collapse of Russian forces in the Caucasus as Russian soldiers deserted en masse. With Russia's collapse, Turkish forces re-occupied territory lost in 1916 and 1917 before launching an offensive into the Trans-Caucasus region, capturing Baku in September 1918. In 1915 and 1916, as part of the war in the Caucasus region, the Ottomans targeted the local Christian Armenian population and the resulting genocide by the Ottomans led to the deaths of some 1 million Armenians, a portent of the Nazis' 'final solution' of the Second World War.

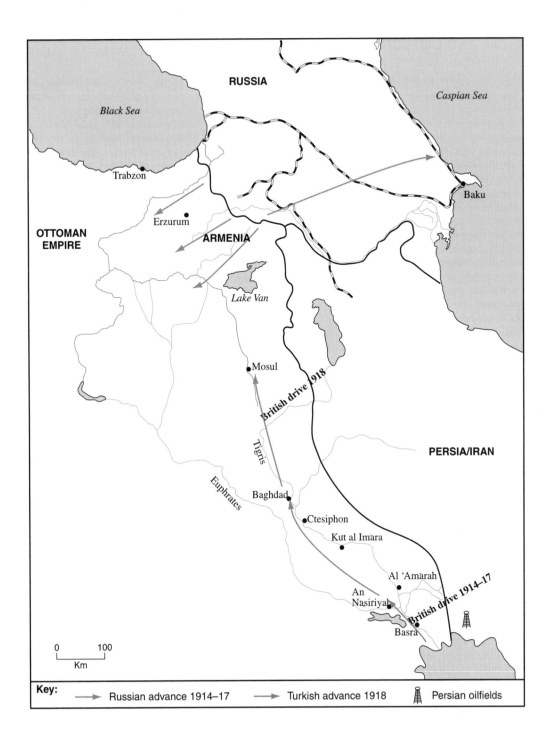

RUSSIA

Black Sea

Caspian Sea

Trabzon

Baku

OTTOMAN
EMPIRE

Erzurum

ARMENIA

Lake Van

Mosul

British drive 1918

Tigris

PERSIA/IRAN

Euphrates

Baghdad

Ctesiphon

Kut al Imara

Al 'Amarah

An
Nasiriya

British drive 1914–17

Basra

0   100
Km

Key: → Russian advance 1914–17   → Turkish advance 1918   ⛩ Persian oilfields

Map 17: The Dardanelles Campaign (Gallipoli)

In 1915, the Entente launched naval and land operations to knock the Ottoman empire (Turkey) out of the war with a single decisive blow. The brainchild of the mercurial British First Lord of the Admiralty, Winston Churchill, the initial plan took advantage of the Entente's naval superiority. Obsolescent Entente warships were to force the narrow Dardanelles Straits, after which warships could threaten the Turkish capital, Constantinople (Istanbul). An Anglo-French fleet assembled off the Gallipoli peninsula and in February–March 1915 it fought its way up the Dardanelles, in the face of fixed and mobile Turkish and German shore batteries, three shore-mounted torpedo-tubes and minefields. While the larger ships engaged the shore batteries, trawlers swept for mines. This was a slow process, with the capital ships retiring at dusk to return the following day. The naval force made steady progress, passing the outer forts, and was approaching the final set of defences at the Chanak (Canakkale) narrows on 18 March 1915 when it hit a recently laid undetected minefield. The French battleships *Bouvet* and *Gaulois* and the British *Ocean*, and the British battlecruisers *Irresistible* and *Inflexible*, were sunk, beached or badly damaged. The British admiral, John De Robeck, withdrew his fleet and on 22 March he met Ian Hamilton, in charge of land forces, to tell him that a naval assault was impossible. While bolder spirits pointed out how close they were to breaking through the Straits, with the Turks demoralised and low on ammunition, De Robeck's cautious counsel prevailed and the British and French planned an amphibious assault on the Gallipoli peninsula.

For the difficult task of launching an amphibious assault, Hamilton had at his disposal six divisions: the British 29th Division and Royal Naval Division, two divisions of the Australian and New Zealand Army Corps (ANZAC), and two divisions of the French *Corps expéditionnaire d'Orient*. From 22 March to 25 April, these units gathered on the island of Lemnos, while Hamilton devised a hasty plan to assault Gallipoli. With poor intelligence on the Turks, and eschewing a landing at Bulair, Hamilton decided to make his main assault on the relatively flat tip of Cape Helles, with French forces making a diversionary landing at Kum Kale. The ANZACs would land at the one practicable landing site on the seaward side of the peninsula (famous as Anzac Cove) while the 29th Division landed at five sites from west to east around Cape Helles: Y, X, W, V and S beaches. Hamilton's plan made little sense. His force was inadequate to clear the peninsula, but without doing this, the Turkish shore forts remained to bar the naval route to Istanbul. A landing at Bulair might have cut off the peninsula but Hamilton's force was too weak to advance across the rough terrain separating Bulair from Istanbul. Only if the Turks chose to do nothing could Hamilton succeed. But forewarned of the preparations for an amphibious assault the Turks busied themselves building defensive works on Gallipoli, under the command of a German general, Otto Liman von Sanders.

On 25 April, an invasion armada gathered off Gallipoli. After a naval bombardment, steam-powered pinnaces towed boats full of troops ashore, casting them adrift close to the shore to be rowed to the beach. There was only one specialised landing ship with holes cut in her bows for landing troops, the old collier *River Clyde*, to be landed at V beach. The ANZAC troops got off to a bad start, landing 1.6 kilometres (1 mile) north of the planned landing site (for reasons which have never been properly explained) below steep, tangled bluffs. Unless the ANZACs could reach the crest of the high ground they ran the risk of being hemmed in, dominated by an enemy holding the high ground. In the dense gullies above their landing site, the ANZACs proved unable to dominate the high ground and were forced to establish a shallow defensive perimeter overlooked by the enemy.

While the landings at Kum Kale and Y, X and S beaches at Cape Helles were largely unopposed, at W and V beaches the few Turks present put up fierce resistance, raking the landing beaches with concentrated machine-gun fire with devastating results. But by the evening of the 25 April men were ashore at all the beaches. The Turks rushed the 19th Division to the area, under the command of Mustafa Kemal, to take up positions on the high ground. Helped by Hamilton's lack of offensive momentum, Kemal's men held the ANZACs, but were unable to push them off their beachhead. At Cape Helles, the 29th Division, reinforced by the French and the Royal Naval Division, attacked the village of Krithia, 6 kilometres (4 miles) inland. Soon western-front style trench deadlock set in as the British struggled unsuccessfully to take Krithia.

To break the deadlock, Hamilton devised a new amphibious assault at Suvla Bay for 6/7 August that would link up with an attack from Anzac Cove. But the new landing at Suvla Bay achieved little, a hastily assembled force led by Kemal blocking the dilatory British advance. After the Suvla Bay fiasco, Charles Monro replaced Hamilton and he recommended withdrawing from a lost battle. The British evacuated Suvla/Anzac Cove and Cape Helles (10 December 1915 to 8 January 1916), without a man being lost, the one successful part of the ill-fated campaign. Turkish casualties numbered some 300,000 to Entente losses of 265,000. Although their casualties were relatively slight, for the ANZACs Gallipoli became a symbol of their coming of age as nations; for the Turks, Gallipoli was a material triumph that saved their country; for the British, it was one of the most poorly mounted and ineptly controlled operations in modern British military history.

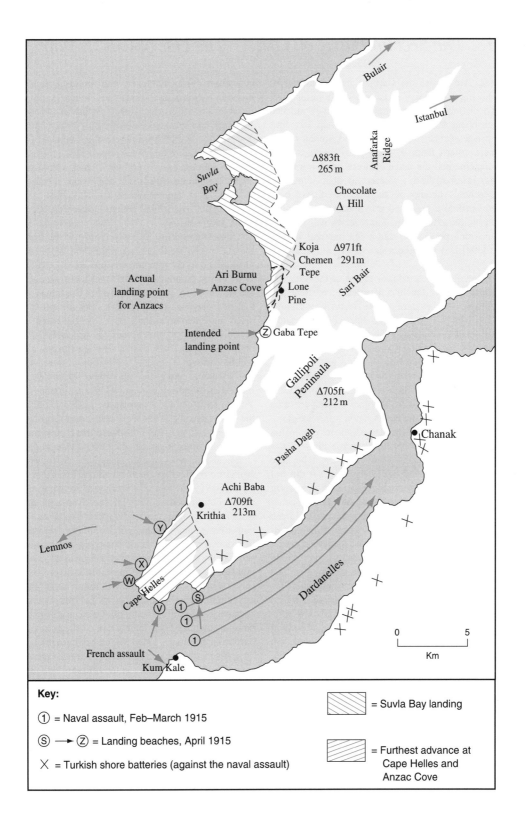

Bulair

Istanbul

Suvla
Bay

Δ883ft
265 m

Anafarka
Ridge

Chocolate
Δ Hill

Koja   Δ971ft
Chemen   291m
Tepe

Actual
landing point
for Anzacs

Ari Burnu
Anzac Cove

Lone
Pine

Sari Bair

Intended
landing point

Ⓩ Gaba Tepe

Gallipoli
Peninsula

Δ705ft
212 m

Pasha Dagh

Chanak

Achi Baba
Δ709ft
213m

Krithia

Lemnos

Ⓨ

Ⓧ

Ⓦ

Cape Helles

Ⓥ Ⓢ
   ①
   ①

   ①

Dardanelles

French assault

Kum Kale

0   5

Km

Key:

① = Naval assault, Feb–March 1915

Ⓢ ⟶ Ⓩ = Landing beaches, April 1915

✕ = Turkish shore batteries (against the naval assault)

= Suvla Bay landing

= Furthest advance at
  Cape Helles and
  Anzac Cove

Map 18: The Second Battle of Ypres – The Use of Gas in War

On 22 April 1915 the German army launched its only major offensive on the western front for 1915. To distract from the major offensive launched simultaneously on the eastern front (see Map 19), four divisions struck against the Canadian and French troops holding the northern flank of the Ypres salient. A new weapon supplemented the usual artillery bombardment – chlorine gas released from cylinders to float across the enemy's trenches. Although not the first use of gas – both French and German armies had previously used tear-gas shells, with limited effect – the Ypres attack was the first occasion in which poison gas had a real tactical impact on the battlefield. It initiated a new era of industrialised warfare.

French colonial and territorial troops of the 45th and 87th Divisions holding the line between Steenstraat and Poelcapelle bore the brunt of the first attack. Although they had received warnings of an impending chemical attack, the French generals had been dismissive and were taken completely by surprise. Corporal Jim Keddie of the 1st Canadian Division, holding the line to their right, witnessed 'a horde of Turcos [French colonial soldiers] making for our trenches, some were armed, some were unarmed. The poor devils were absolutely paralysed with fear.' Yet while terrifying, the new weapon was not particularly lethal. Estimates of gas casualties in the initial attack range from 200 to 625 men. Keddie himself was gassed: 'it makes your eyes smart and run, I became violently sick, but it passed off fairly soon'. It did not prevent the Canadians improvising a defence to prevent the Germans breaking through the gap made by the fleeing French and pushing on to Ypres. In fact the gas had been too successful. The Germans had not expected such a collapse of the enemy's defence, and had no fresh reserves on hand to exploit the breach. Moreover, the advancing troops hung back through fear of their own gas. The French were able to rally and consolidate a new defensive line along the Yser canal, some 3–5 kilometres (2–3 miles) behind their original line. The Germans had made a large dent in the allied line north of Ypres, securing a foothold across the Yser canal at Steenstraat and shrinking the British salient, which was now a long finger of ground vulnerable to artillery fire from the left-rear. If the lost ground could not be recaptured the salient was untenable.

Field Marshal French expected the French to recapture the ground which they had lost, restoring the integrity of the salient. Over the following week a succession of confused attacks and counter-attacks took place on the northern flank of the salient. The allied line held, although the French lacked the fresh reserves needed to recapture the lost ground. Horace Smith-Dorrien, commander of the British Second Army in the salient, recommended its evacuation. French refused, and Smith-Dorrien was dismissed. Nevertheless, since the French could make no progress the order was given to withdraw the British line 5 kilometres (3 miles) to a less exposed position in front of Ypres at the end of April. The battle continued for several weeks, although the Germans made little progress in their push to capture Ypres itself. On 15 May a French counter-attack recaptured Steenstraat and forced the enemy back over the Yser canal. Overall the battle cost the German army 35,000 casualties, and the allies 70,000, of whom 60,000 were British.

The German use of gas was seen to mark the end of the era of 'civilised' warfare in the First World War. 'War has nothing to do with chivalry any more,' wrote German Third Army commander Karl von Einem the day after the gas attack. There were to be no more Christmas truces like that of December 1914, as both sides increased their war effort and intensified their hatred for the enemy. The use of poison gas on the battlefield had been specifically banned by the 1899 Hague Convention governing the conduct of war. Germany's violation of international law was another to add to the catalogue of 'atrocities' on which the allies founded their anti-German propaganda effort. Yet in order to avoid a permanent tactical disadvantage on the battlefield the allies were obliged to respond in kind. By the end of 1915 both French and British armies had made their own chlorine gas attacks. As the war progressed the chemical industries of both sides were tasked with developing more effective chemical agents for use at the front. By late-1915 the German army was employing the more deadly chlorine compound, Phosgene, an acute respiratory irritant effective up to 48 hours after inhalation. The most notorious poison, dichlorethylsulphide ('mustard gas'), introduced in 1917, caused blistering and burning of the skin, acute blindness, and severe bronchial pneumonia if inhaled. A more effective means of delivery by artillery shells was also developed, which removed the reliance on a favourable wind when releasing gas from cylinders. Gas became an integral component of the complicated artillery bombardments of the later years of the war. While not particularly lethal – only 3% of gas casualties died – it neutralised defenders (demoralised by its presence and encumbered by anti-gas respirators) more effectively than high-explosive shells in the initial stages of an attack.

Poison gas, above all, epitomises the horror of the First World War battlefield. A silent, terrifying and crippling weapon, its wide-scale employment illustrates the immorality and lethality possible in modern industrial war. Fear of its use against Germany prevented one gas victim, Corporal Adolf Hitler, from using it on the battlefield in the Second World War. However, he found an even more horrific use for it, in the gas chambers of the Nazis' extermination camps.

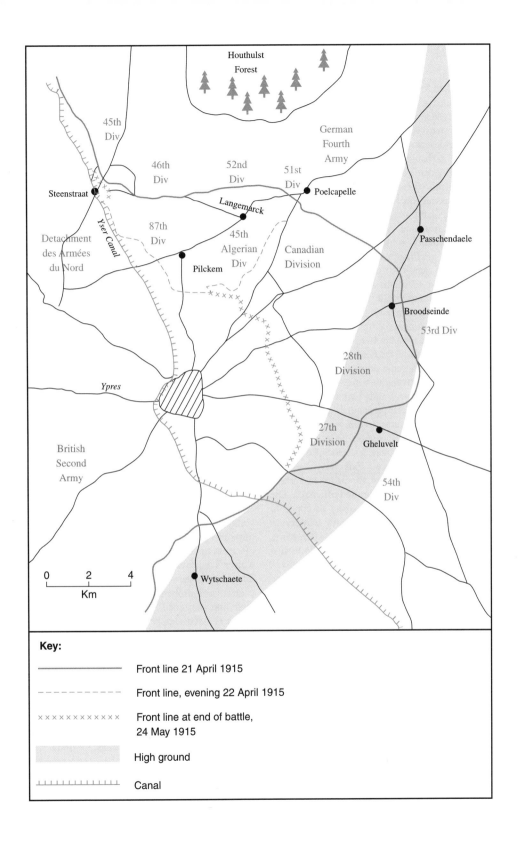

Houthulst
Forest

45th
Div

46th
Div

52nd
Div

51st
Div

German
Fourth
Army

Steenstraat

Poelcapelle

Langemarck

Yser Canal

87th
Div

45th
Algerian
Div

Pilckem

Canadian
Division

Passchendaele

Detachment
des Armées
du Nord

Broodseinde

53rd Div

28th
Division

Ypres

27th
Division

Gheluvelt

British
Second
Army

54th
Div

0   2   4
Km

Wytschaete

Key:

———————	Front line 21 April 1915
– – – – –	Front line, evening 22 April 1915
x x x x x x x x x x x x	Front line at end of battle, 24 May 1915
▓▓▓	High ground
⊥⊥⊥⊥⊥⊥⊥⊥	Canal

Map 19: The Conquest of Poland – Gorlice–Tarnów

Having checked Russia's offensive in 1914 into East Prussia at the battles of Tannenberg (Stębark) and Masurian (Mazury) lakes, Germany went on the offensive on the eastern front in 1915, occupying Russian-controlled Poland and pushing deep into Russia. In February 1915, in the second battle of the Masurian lakes, the Germans pushed the badly deployed Russian Tenth Army back 100 kilometres (60 miles) to Kovno (Kaunas), clearing East Prussia of Russian forces. But Russian forces to the south still occupied Poland and stood at the mouth of the Carpathian passes, threatening Austria-Hungary. In March 1915, the Russians finally took the besieged Austro-Hungarian fortress of Przemyśl, along with 120,000 Austro-Hungarian prisoners. The Russian menace to Austria-Hungary compelled the Germans to act to ensure the survival of their ally, more especially as Italy joined the war on 23 May against Austria-Hungary.

Alongside Austro-Hungarian forces, the Germans planned a major offensive for May 1915 that would lead to a tremendous victory known as the Gorlice–Tarnów offensive. While the German supreme commander, Erich von Falkenhayn, preferred to concentrate forces on the western front, Paul von Hindenburg and Erich Ludendorff, commanding forces in the east, persuaded him to release eight divisions for an attack against Russia, arguing that this was necessary to relieve pressure upon the hard-pressed Austro-Hungarians holding the southern sector of the front. While agreeing to an offensive, Falkenhayn vetoed Hindenburg and Ludendorff's plan for an encirclement battle in Poland in favour of a more limited offensive. The plan was for a new German Eleventh Army equipped to western-front standards, especially with heavy artillery, to be deployed to the Austrian front. Its job was to break into the Russian lines in the narrow gap between the river Vistula (Wisła) and the Carpathian mountains by the Polish towns of Gorlice and Tarnów. A breakthrough here would force back the Russians in the Carpathians to the south, relieving pressure on Austria-Hungary. 120,000 German and Austro-Hungarian troops were massed against 56,000 men of the Russian Third Army. The Russians were short of guns, rifles and ammunition; forward trenches were shallow and insufficiently strong; they lacked training and had no effective reserves. Moreover, von Mackensen, the Eleventh Army's commander, worked well with his Austro-Hungarian counterparts, blending the two national forces into one fighting unit.

In April 1915, troop trains moved east through Germany, taking men to assembly areas near Cracow (Kraków) where they took over the line from Austro-Hungarian troops. Unlike the cramped western front, they found a vast no-man's land separating the two forces, in places 4 kilometres (2½ miles) wide, in which peasants were still living and tending their fields. With a substantial superiority in men and guns, the Austro-German Gorlice–Tarnów offensive opened on 2 May with a four-hour preliminary bombardment. The tactics employed were a portent of the breakthrough tactics used by the Germans later in the war: a hurricane artillery bombardment followed by rapid infantry infiltration to maintain offensive momentum. It was not a question of breaking in, but of breaking through enemy defences. In 1915, these tactics worked against weak Russian defences. Although not massive by western-front standards, the bombardment at Gorlice–Tarnów of one gun every 70 metres (75 yards) was extraordinary for the eastern front. Unprepared mentally and physically for such a barrage, shell-shocked Russian troops surrendered en masse or fled. As the break-in widened, it deepened. The Russian Third Army retreated 80 kilometres (50 miles) to the river Wisloka (Wisłok), before falling back to the river San, where, short of rifles and artillery, it was strung out on an extended front and outflanked by Austro-German forces to the north and south. The Russian high command (Stavka), hampered by a poor railway system and distracted by operations to the north in Courland (Latvia), failed to send any reinforcements. The Russians found temporary refuge behind the San and Dniester (Dnestr) rivers before German and Austro-Hungarian forces renewed the offensive. Przemyśl was recaptured by the Germans on 4 June. The Russians retreated east toward Lemberg (L'vov or Lwów), which they lost on 22 June, pulling back the entire Russian line as they withdrew.

At meetings with the Kaiser in June 1915, Ludendorff argued, once again, for an immense encirclement battle – similar in style to the failed Schlieffen plan – with attacks through Kovno and Vilnius (Vilna) towards Minsk to cut off Russian forces in Poland. But Falkenhayn, with the Kaiser's approval, convinced him to adopt a more modest scheme when the offensive was renewed in July. Falkenhayn's caution was probably justified: as the Russians retreated their line shortened, just as the Germans were outpacing their extended supply lines. Reinforced in mid-June, the Germans launched three simultaneous offensives in July 1915 to clear Galicia, Poland and the Baltic region. While they escaped encirclement, the Russians lost Warsaw (4 August), Kovno (17 August), Brest-Litovsk (25 August), Grodno (2 September) and Vilnius (18 September). Concerned by threats elsewhere, Falkenhayn halted the offensive in September 1915. Gorlice–Tarnów pushed the Russians back hundreds of kilometres, out of the rich provinces of Galicia and Poland. Russia recovered in 1916, but Gorlice–Tarnów was a strategic shift on the eastern front, ending the threat of a Russian invasion of Austria-Hungary. The eastern front now ran from Riga in the north to Czernovitz in the south.

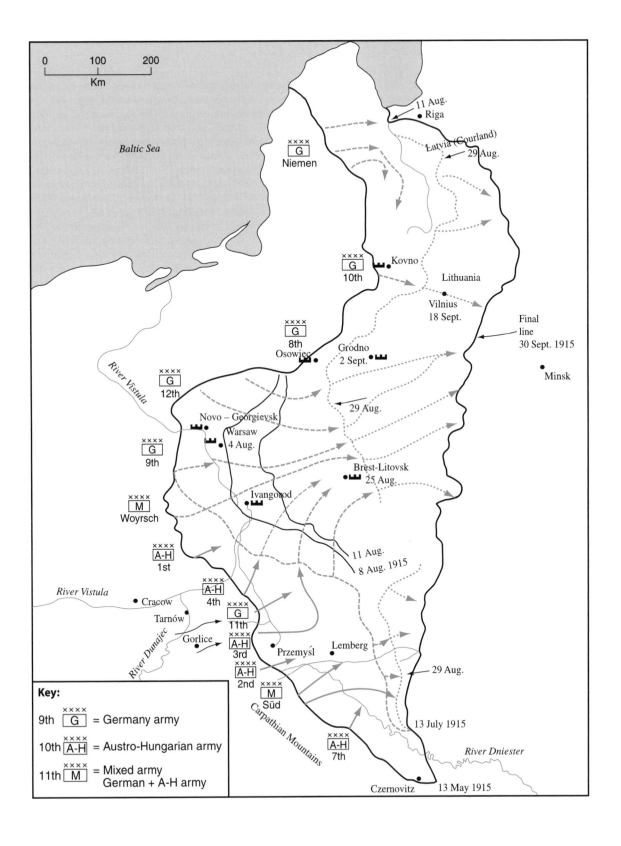

Baltic Sea

11 Aug.
• Riga

××××
G Niemen

Latvia (Courland)
29 Aug.

××××
G 10th ═ Kovno

Lithuania

• Vilnius
18 Sept.

Final
line
30 Sept. 1915

××××
G 8th Grodno
Osowiec 2 Sept.

• Minsk

River Vistula

××××
G 12th

29 Aug.

Novo – Georgievsk

××××
G 9th Warsaw
4 Aug.

Brest-Litovsk
25 Aug.

××××
M Woyrsch Ivangorod

11 Aug.
8 Aug. 1915

××××
A-H 1st

River Vistula

××××
A-H 4th • Cracow

Tarnów
××××
G 11th

Gorlice
××××
A-H 3rd • Przemyśl • Lemberg

29 Aug.

River Dunajec
××××
A-H 2nd
××××
M Süd

13 July 1915

Carpathian Mountains

××××
A-H 7th River Dniester

Czernovitz 13 May 1915

Key:

9th ×××× G = Germany army

10th ×××× A-H = Austro-Hungarian army

11th ×××× M = Mixed army
German + A-H army

Map 20: The Italians on the Isonzo, 1915–17

The mountainous nature of the Austro-Italian frontier determined the course of the war on the Italian front. Except for a short 32-kilometre (20-mile) section of front by the Adriatic coast, the 600-kilometre (380-mile) front line stretched across mountainous or very mountainous terrain. Looking down on the north Italian plain, the Austro-Hungarian army dominated the Italian front, but with the exception of a May–June 1916 *Strafexpedition* ('punishment expedition') offensive from the Trentino (South Tyrol/Alto Adige) salient towards Padua (Padova), Austro-Hungarian forces remained on the defensive from May 1915 to September 1917, taking advantage of their fixed positions on the higher ground. Thus, when Italy took the offensive she would have to fight her way forwards through Austro-Hungarian defences and, for most of the front, extensive mountain ranges. Moreover, Austro-Hungarian troops in the Trentino salient were a permanent threat to the Italian rear.

Although Italy had too few *alpini* mountain troops to launch a major attack along the high alpine peaks that stretched from the Stelvio and Tonale passes in the west to the Dolomites, Carnic (Carnia) and Julian Alps in the east, small bands of specialist mountain infantry fought among these mountain peaks at altitudes reaching up to almost 4000 metres (13,000 feet). There were also bursts of intense fighting along the southern section of the Trentino salient near Rovereto and Asiago as Italian forces pushed towards Trento (Trient). But the main theatre of war for Italy was the short stretch of relatively flat land by the coast along the Isonzo river and the hilly land just to the north where it was possible to mass large armies. So, from June 1915 to September 1917, Italy's supreme commander, Luigi Cadorna, fought eleven Isonzo battles, to capture the Austro-Hungarian port of Trieste before pushing on to Vienna. He poured the bulk of Italy's men and matériel into the attritional Isonzo battles, all fought in roughly the same area, which exceeded the western front in terms of high casualties for minimal ground gained.

Along the Isonzo, Austro-Hungarian forces dug themselves in from 2245-metre (7365-feet) Monte Nero (Krn) in the north – where flying shell fragments wounded a Sergeant Benito Mussolini – to the rocky limestone Carso (c.300 metres high/1000 feet) and Bainsizza (c.600 metres high/1950 feet) plateaux to the south. The Austro-Hungarian army facing Italy was initially weak – seven divisions in May 1915 – but reinforced and on the defensive, it held the Italians. Cadorna massed a superior force in the Second and Third Armies to break this line but his tactics and operational method were imperfect. He had just seven divisions and insufficient artillery support for the first Isonzo battle (23 June–8 July). Thereafter, as trench deadlock set in, strong enemy defences in rough terrain confounded his poorly planned and executed attacks. While not a bad general, Cadorna's style of command was rigid and very authoritarian: during the war, he dismissed 217 generals and 255 colonels, and instituted a ferocious system for disciplining his mainly peasant conscript army. Moreover, the Italian army was poorly prepared for war, having just 120 heavy guns in May 1915. Discontent on the home front adversely affected the men, further lowering morale. By Christmas 1915, Italy had launched four Isonzo battles that had achieved very little. Italian losses of some 160,000 casualties in 1915 exceeded those of Austria-Hungary but the latter's high command, now fighting on three fronts (Serbian/Balkan, Russian and Italian), was sufficiently worried to request German help against Italy, which was not forthcoming. By 1916, Austria-Hungary had been forced to deploy 35 of its 65 mobilised divisions to the Italian front.

In 1916, as part of the Chantilly plan to coordinate offensives on all Entente fronts, the Italians prepared more offensives. The objective of the fifth Isonzo battle, which opened on 11–12 March, was the town of Gorizia (Görz/Gorica). Bad weather set in, and then the May 1916 *Strafexpedition* distracted the Italians. Once the Trentino front had stabilised, Cadorna resumed the attacks on the Isonzo, with 22 Italian divisions deployed for the sixth Isonzo offensive in August 1916 against 9 Austro-Hungarian. Gorizia fell (9 August) but when the offensive ended on 17 August the total gain was only 5 kilometres (3 miles). The capture of Gorizia prompted Cadorna to launch three more offensives east of the town in late 1916 (seventh, eighth and ninth Isonzo battles), none of which breached the Austro-Hungarian defences. For the tenth battle in 1917, Cadorna outnumbered the Austro-Hungarians three-to-one and, with a long preliminary bombardment, he managed to push to within 15 kilometres (9 miles) of Trieste by June 1917. Austro-Hungarian counter-attacks clawed back some of the ground lost before Cadorna launched his last offensive in August 1917. Fifty-two Italian divisions massed along a long stretch of the front, including *arditi* ('men of daring') shock troops, attacked on 19 August in the eleventh and greatest Isonzo offensive. On the brink of collapse on the Isonzo, Austria-Hungary appealed to Germany for help. This time she agreed to help and diverted forces for a huge counter-offensive at Caporetto on the upper Isonzo – also known as the twelfth battle of the Isonzo – which broke the Italian line (see Map 38). Casualties in the eleven Isonzo battles totalled 582,000 for Italy versus 344,000 for Austria-Hungary, often the result of rock splinters from artillery exploding in the stony terrain (many men were blinded). In the eleven Isonzo battles, the Italians lost over 115,000 men killed to 90,000 Austro-Hungarians.

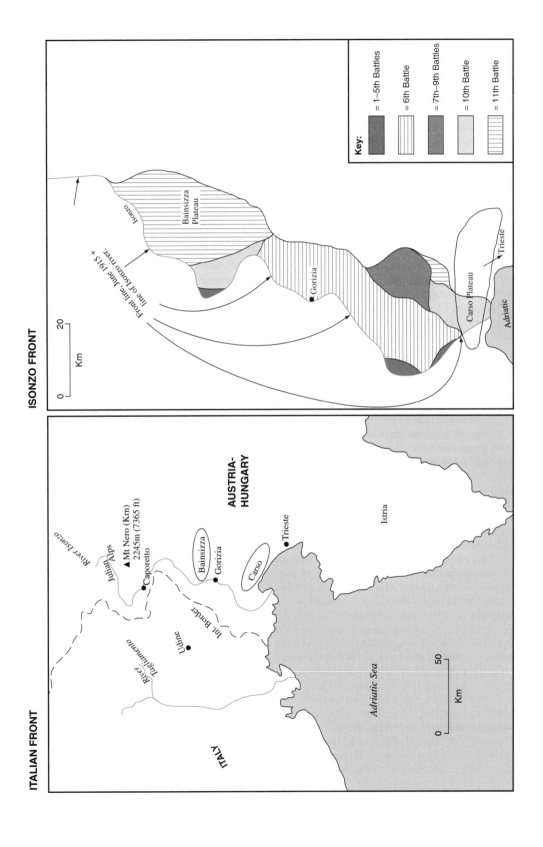

ITALIAN FRONT

ISONZO FRONT

Key:
= 1–5th Battles
= 6th Battle
= 7th–9th Battles
= 10th Battle
= 11th Battle

Map 21: The Defeat of Serbia and Rumania

Austria-Hungary declared war on Serbia on 28 July 1914, the first time that war was declared by telegraph. On 12 August, Austro-Hungarian forces commanded by Oskar Potiorek invaded north-west Serbia. Serbian forces led by *voivod* (commander-in-chief) Radomir Putnik responded with spirited counter-attacks, between August and early December 1914, along the rivers Jadar, Drina and Kolubara, forcing the Austro-Hungarians out of Serbia. Belgrade was back in Serbian hands by 15 December 1914. While the victories of 1914 over Austria-Hungary were a huge success for Serbia, she lost 100,000 men in battle, with many more soldiers and civilians dying in a typhus epidemic behind Serbian lines.

In 1915, the pattern of war in the Balkans had changed. The Ottoman empire had joined the Central Powers in October–November 1914. If the Central alliance were able to win over the neutral state of Bulgaria, it would open up the possibility of a contiguous land route along the 'Orient railway' from Berlin to Istanbul. Bulgaria could also threaten Serbia's eastern flank should Austria-Hungary decide to attack Serbia for a second time. Diplomatically, the Central Powers had the upper hand, as they were able to offer Bulgaria large tracts of Serbian land in Macedonia in return for entering the war.

For the second invasion, the Central alliance fielded 600,000 troops, against which Serbia and its ally, Monte-negro, had barely 300,000 men. On 6 October 1915, one Austro-Hungarian (the Third) and one German army (the Eleventh) attacked Serbia. On 11–12 October, Bulgarian forces attacked Serbia, declaring war the next day. Britain, France and Russia responded by declaring war on Bulgaria. A hastily organised Anglo-French landing at the neutral Greek port of Salonika came too late to assist the Serbs (see Map 22). Two Bulgarian armies deployed from the east against Serbia. Even before Bulgaria was formally in the war, Belgrade had fallen (9 October). The Bulgarian First Army took Pirot (24 October) and Nish (Niš) (5 November), where it joined up with Austro-German forces advancing from the north. With their country cut in two and all major towns in enemy hands, the Serbs in late November to December 1915 embarked on a desperate retreat west to Durazzo (Durrës), where allied warships evacuated the remnants of the typhus-ridden Serbian army to Corfu. Austro-Hungarian and Bulgarian forces subsequently pushed into northern and central Albania, establishing a line from the Vijosë river to Lake Ohrid (Ohridsko). The Entente retained a base at Valona in southern Albania. The Entente had been unable to help Serbia and Montenegro, and so had lost its hold on the central Balkan region. The defeat of Serbia in 1915 gave the Central alliance temporary mastery over the Balkans, opening up a land route to Istanbul, thus allowing the Germans to

re-supply the Ottoman empire for the rest of the war. By early 1916, only Greece and Rumania remained neutral.

The key event in 1916 was Rumania's decision to enter the war on the side of the Entente. Offered the Austro-Hungarian regions of Transylvania and Bukovina, and spurred on by the success of the summer 1916 Brusilov offensive (see Map 8), Rumania entered the war on 27 August 1916. This would prove to be her undoing as her 800,000-strong army had little modern weaponry, a poor domestic arms industry, a badly trained officer corps and supply lines dependent on imports from Russia. When Rumania's army went into action on 27–28 August 1916, the Brusilov offensive had lost momentum. Exposed to possible attacks from Bulgaria in the south and Austria-Hungary in the west, the Rumanians deployed their First, Second and Fourth Armies along the Carpathian mountain passes and invaded Transylvania, while their Third Army took up positions along the river Danube and in the Dobrudja facing Bulgaria. A rapid response by the Austro-Hungarians, stiffened by German, Bulgarian and Ottoman reinforcements, checked the Ruma-nians in Transylvania, before they launched a counter-attack.

In early September 1916, Central alliance forces led by the German general August von Mackensen advanced from the south into the Dobrudja, taking the towns of Cernavoda and Constanţa, threatening the Rumanian capital, Bucharest. Another German-led force, commanded by Erich von Falkenhayn, penetrated the Vulcan pass in the Carpathians and engaged Rumanian forces along the river Argeşel in late November and early December 1916. Meanwhile, on 23 November, Mackensen switched his focus of operations to Wallachia, crossing the Danube at Sistove (Svishtov) and turning the Rumanian positions facing Falkenhayn along the river Alt (Olt). On 6 December 1916, Mackensen and Falkenhayn's forces entered Bucharest. As with the Serbs in 1915, the Rumanians were forced into a hasty retreat, this time to the safety of Russian-held Moldavia. The front then stabilised along the river Sereth (Siret). The lack of a coordin-ated Entente strategy contributed to Rumania's rapid defeat. An Anglo-French attack from Salonika to help Rumania faltered and, once again, an ally in the Balkans was defeated. The remnants of the Rumanian army, with French help, rebuilt itself into a fighting force of some 500,000 men and counter-attacked in the summer of 1917, culminating in the battle of Mărăşeşti in August 1917. Rumanian forces simply could not sustain such battles and, with the news of the Russian revolution, Rumania entered peace talks with the Central alliance culminating in the Treaty of Bucharest (7 May 1918), a harsh settlement that turned Rumania into a vassal state. On 10 November 1918, with Austria-Hungary and Bulgaria effectively defeated, Rumanian forces again took the field, thus staking Rumania's claim at the peace talks.

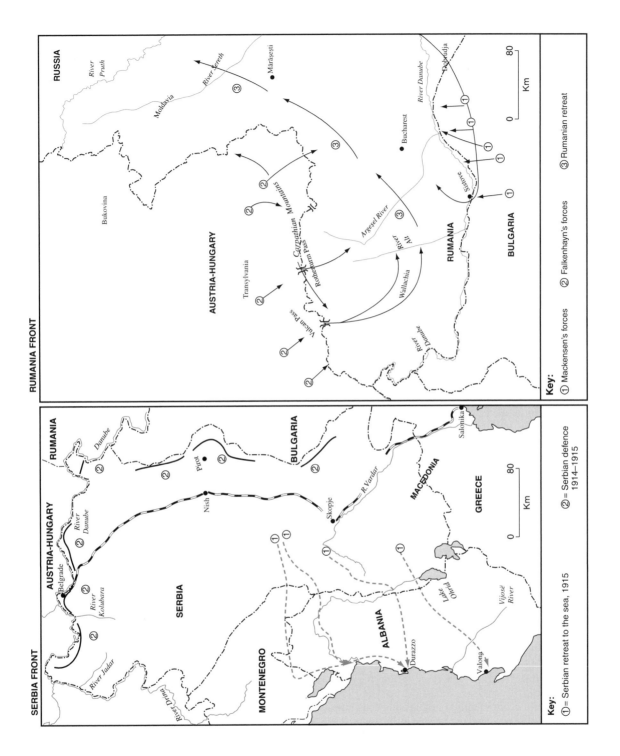

SERBIA FRONT

AUSTRIA-HUNGARY

RUMANIA

Belgrade

River Drina

River Jadar

River Kolubara

② River Danube

② Danube

SERBIA

Nish

Pirot ②

② ②

BULGARIA

MONTENEGRO

① ①

ALBANIA

Durazzo

Valona

Vijosë River

Lake Ohrid

①

Skopje

R. Vardar

MACEDONIA

GREECE

Salonika

0   80

Km

Key:

① = Serbian retreat to the sea, 1915

② = Serbian defence 1914–1915

RUMANIA FRONT

RUSSIA

River Prut

Moldavia

River Sereth

Bukovina

Mărăşesti •

③

③

AUSTRIA-HUNGARY

Transylvania

②

②

② Carpathian Mountains

Vulkan Pass

Rothenturm Pass

② ②

Wallachia

River Alt

Argesel River

③

RUMANIA

• Bucharest

River Danube

Dobrudja

① ①

① ①

Sistove

①

①

BULGARIA

River Danube

0   80

Km

Key:

① Mackensen's forces   ② Falkenhayn's forces   ③ Rumanian retreat

Map 22: The Salonika Campaign

The railway from the strategically important port city of Salonika (Thessaloniki) in northern Greece to Belgrade via Skopje (Uskub) offered a direct route to embattled Serbia. In September 1915, with Bulgaria mobilising for an attack on Serbia, Britain and France accepted an offer from the pro-Entente Greek prime minister Eleutherios (Elephferios) Venizelos to land troops at Salonika. The force at Salonika was initially composed of Anglo-French units, many of which had come from Gallipoli. It was reinforced by the Serbian army in exile on Corfu, Italians and a small Russian contingent. It remained until the war's end.

The force landed on 5 October 1915, the same day that the pro-German Greek king, Constantine I – who was married to the Kaiser's sister – forced Venizelos to resign. On 6 October 1915, the Central Powers invaded Serbia. Anglo-French units at Salonika pushed north up the Vardar (Axios) river valley to help the Serbs. It was too little, too late (see Map 21). The Serbs retreated through Albania to the Adriatic coast while the Salonika force retired back to the city. Bulgarian and German forces (with some Turkish units) then gathered along the Greek–Serbian and Greek–Bulgarian borders, while the Greek army, supposedly neutral, handed Greece's Fort Ruppel, which commanded the Struma (Strimón) valley, to the Bulgarians (26 May 1916). In response to these threats, the supreme commander at Salonika, the French general Maurice Sarrail, transformed the city into a fortress surrounded by fieldwork defences. He took full control of the city from the Greeks in mid-1916, establishing the city as an alternative centre for pro-Entente Greek forces and politicians, a policy that embroiled the garrison in internal Greek politics.

While France was keen on the Salonika operation, senior British military advisers to the British government, such as William Robertson, Chief of the Imperial General Staff, were never convinced of the usefulness of peripheral operations such as Salonika, which took troops away from the main western front. By early 1916 the number of British troops at Salonika exceeded 150,000. Robertson vigorously urged a withdrawal from Salonika but political factors made this difficult. The defeat at Gallipoli had lowered Anglo-French prestige in the Balkans and the Entente could ill-afford for Greece to join the Central Powers.

Sarrail's record of military achievement against the Central Powers was not impressive. On 10 August 1916, Entente troops began preliminary attacks at Lake Dorian (Dojran) before a general autumn 1916 offensive. German-Bulgarian forces pre-empted this with attacks on the western and eastern extremities of Sarrail's line. In the west, the reconstituted Serbian army in the Flórina sector retreated to Lake Ostrovo (Vegorrítis). Fighting then continued along the Crno (Crna) river east of Flórina. In the eastern sector of the front, the Bulgarians took the Greek town of Serres (Sérrai) in the Struma valley on 25 August, threatening the port of Kavala (Kaválla) whose Greek garrison surrendered without a fight on 14 September 1916. Under pressure, Sarrail put a halt to the faltering offensive at Lake Dorian.

When Sarrail's troops did finally attack towards Skopje in September 1916, he hoped that this would relieve the hard-pressed Rumanians (see Map 21). Sarrail's forces took Monastir (Bitola) in the western sector of the front on 19 November 1916 but they advanced no further. As the British struggled up the Struma valley, operations descended into western front-style trench deadlock. Checked, allied troops sat out the winter doing little. By early 1917, Sarrail had some 600,000 men at his disposal – a mixture of French, British, Serbians, Italians and Russians that made command and control difficult. This force was more nominal than real as the unhealthy, swampy climate of Salonika was a breeding ground for diseases such as malaria, paratyphoid and dysentery, which left much of Sarrail's force in hospital and reduced his fighting strength to about 100,000.

Sarrail attacked again in March 1917. A Franco-Serbian force advanced on a line between Monastir and Lake Prespa, while the British spearheaded an attack at Lake Dorian. Advances were minimal: a few hundred metres were won at the cost of some 15,000 casualties. By the end of May, with Russian units in mutiny, Sarrail called off the offensive, and the front became static. Marie Guillaumat replaced the unpopular Sarrail in December 1917. In July 1918, another French commander, Louis Franchet d'Esperey, replaced Guillaumat. In June 1917, with Venizelos back in power, Greece entered the war (29 June 1917), adding 250,000 men to the Salonika force. On 15 September 1918, at the war's end, the Salonika force launched the Vardar offensive against weary and ill-equipped Bulgarian opposition. The Bulgarians broke, and by 25 September their retreat had become a rout. The Salonika force advanced deep into enemy territory, reaching the Danube by the armistice. Serbian forces re-occupied Belgrade on 1 November 1918, by which time Bulgaria had surrendered (30 September).

This final victory should not overshadow the fact that the Salonika expedition did very little, except tie up large numbers of Entente troops that could have been used more fruitfully elsewhere. Although battle casualties were low – a reflection of the general inactivity of the front for most of the war – casualties from disease, notably malaria, invalided some 400,000 men. The Germans were right to dub the front 'the greatest internment camp in the world'.

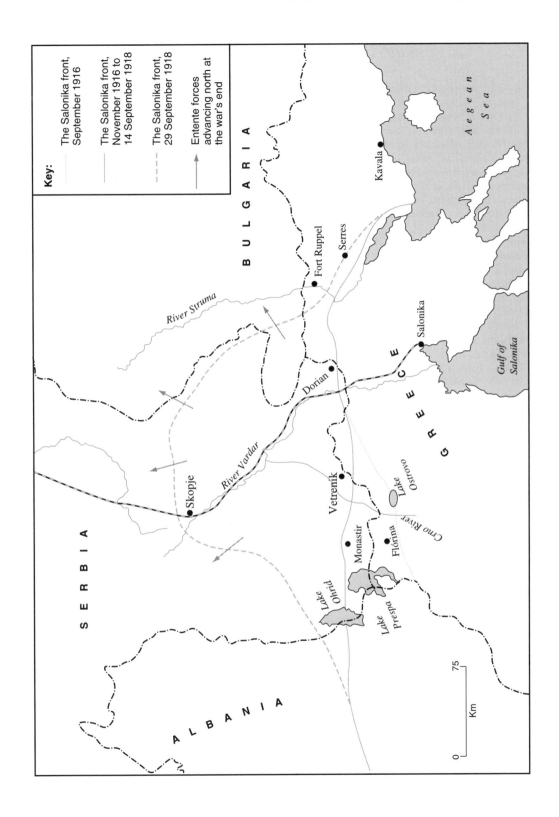

A e g e a n
S e a

B U L G A R I A

Kavala

Fort Ruppel

Serres

River Struma

Salonika

Gulf of
Salonika

Dorian

G R E E C E

Vetrenik

River Vardar

Lake
Ostrovo

Skopje

Crno River

Monastir

Florina

S E R B I A

Lake
Ohrid

Lake
Prespa

0 ————— 75
Km

A L B A N I A

Map 23: Plans for the Partition of the Ottoman Empire

As the military campaigns in the Caucasus, Mesopotamia, the Dardanelles and Palestine against the Ottoman empire developed (see Maps 16, 17 and 35), Britain realised that she would need to decide on the future of captured enemy territory. Fighting in an alliance, it was very difficult for Britain to ignore the wishes of her principal allies, France, Italy and Russia, all of whom had interests in the region, as well as local Hashemite Arabs from the Hedjaz and Zionists (Jewish nationalists), both keen on gaining territory and independence in the region.

In 1915, a committee, chaired by Maurice De Bunsen, was appointed to look into the future status of the Ottoman empire. Before 1914, Britain had been broadly supportive of the integrity of the empire, largely because Britain was more fearful of a powerful expansionist Russia to the north. De Bunsen's committee raised for the first time the possibility of partitioning the empire. However, the decisive act in 1915 came when Britain, through the Constantinople agreements, agreed to Russian control of the Straits zone around Istanbul (Constantinople). This represented a real change in policy, a reflection of Britain's need to curry favour with Russia notwithstanding Britain's previous attempts to exclude Russia from the Straits.

In 1916, Britain negotiated with the Hashemite Arabs of the Hedjaz for their entry into the war. This forced another set of negotiations for partition, between Britain (led by Mark Sykes) and France (led by François Georges Picot), usually known as the 'Sykes–Picot' agreement, which Russia subsequently signed. Suspicious of Britain's alliance with the Hashemites and worried that she was going to be excluded from Syria and Lebanon, in which she had a traditional interest, France was keen to pin Britain down to agree French territory once the war was over. Meanwhile, Russia expanded her territory in eastern Anatolia/Armenia. The Sykes–Picot agreement caused much furore later as it seemed to clash with subsequent promises made by the British and French in 1917 and 1918 to the Arabs and the Zionists. In fact, the 'Sykes–Picot' deal was a necessary precursor for Britain's invasion of Palestine, as without it France was reluctant to sanction Allenby's advance (see Map 35).

The Sykes–Picot arrangement divided the region into four zones: British, French, International and Russian. Each of the British and French national zones was further divided into territory that would be directly controlled by the colonial power (blue and red areas) and semi-autonomous territory (zones A and B) in which the colonial power would supply advisers, money, etc. The autonomous zones were a rather thin attempt to disguise the avaricious and imperial nature of the deal. The international zone (which included a British enclave at Haifa/Acre) covered Palestine, over which all the major Christian powers felt they had an interest. In 1917, by the treaty of Saint-Jean de Maurienne, Italy was brought into the deal, gaining territory in Adalia in southern Turkey.

A further problem arose in late 1917 and 1918 when Britain (and to a lesser extent France) made four sets of promises – three to the Arabs and one to Zionists – which opened up a Pandora's Box that continues to bedevil the Middle East. In November 1917, the British Foreign Secretary, A.J. Balfour, wrote an ambiguously worded letter to Lord Rothschild, a leading Zionist, in which he stated that Britain would view with favour the establishment of a national home for the Jews in Palestine. The Balfour Declaration has gained considerable notoriety as it seemed to state that Britain would encourage Jewish immigration and settlement to Palestine, a land already inhabited by Arabs. In fact, while there were pro-Zionist elements in the British War Cabinet, Britain issued the declaration for a variety of reasons, not least the wish to garner Jewish support in states such as America. Moreover, the 'Balfour Declaration' helped Britain evade its promise to internationalise Palestine, as the Zionists could help the British control Palestine, thus helping to counter annoying French demands that Palestine be ruled by an international administration.

Britain's desire to exclude France from the region also helps explain why Britain then made more ambiguous promises to the Arabs in 1918 through the Hogarth Message, the Declaration to the Seven and the Anglo-French Declaration, all of which strongly suggested that Britain was also promising the Arabs (notably the Hashemite Arabs of the Hedjaz) independence, including in Palestine, a land which now seemed to be promised to two sets of people, one of which lived there and one of which wanted to live there.

At the end of the war, Britain was in a commanding position: Russia had collapsed and British or British-led armies had conquered and occupied Palestine, Lebanon, Transjordan, Syria and Mesopotamia; France was marginalised. This meant that at the Paris peace talks in 1919, the British extended their zone of control to include all of Palestine and the oil-rich region of Mosul. After some considerable diplomatic fighting, France eventually got Britain to agree to her having Lebanon and Syria, a decision that forced Britain to end her support for the Hashemite regime led by Prince Feisal that Britain had helped install in Damascus in 1918. Eventually, in 1922–23, the League of Nations formally agreed that Britain should get Palestine, Transjordan and Iraq (Mesopotamia) as Class A Mandates, while France would get Syria and Lebanon, also as Class A Mandates. The status of Class A Mandates meant that these territories should have been granted independence fairly quickly, something that did not fully happen until after the Second World War.

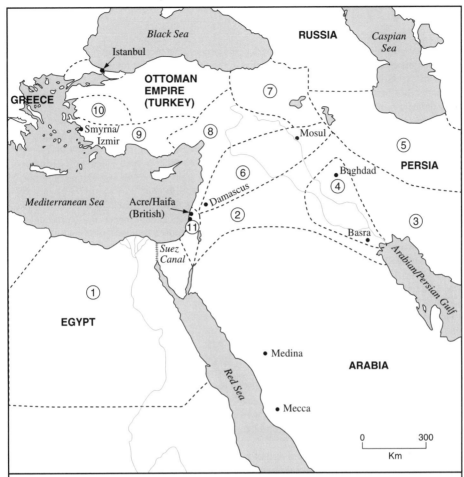

Key:

1. Egypt (British Protectorate from 1914)
2. British sphere of influence under 'Sykes-Picot' agreement (Zone B)
3. British sphere of influence in Iran/Persia
4. Direct British rule under 'Sykes-Picot' agreement (Red Area)
5. Russian sphere of influence in Iran/Persia
6. French sphere of influence under 'Sykes-Picot' agreement (Zone A)
7. Direct Russian rule under 'Sykes-Picot' agreement
8. Direct French rule under 'Sykes-Picot' agreement (Blue Area)
9. Direct Italian rule under St. Jean de Maurienne treaty
10. Italian sphere of influence under St. Jean de Maurienne treaty
11. International Zone of Palestine (Minus British enclave at Haifa/Acre)

Map 24: Allied War Aims in Europe

Unlike Germany, the allies did not immediately formulate war aims on the outbreak of war. In part this reflected disagreements between the allies themselves, and in part a desire not to give hostages to fortune, since allied diplomacy in the early years of the war was targeted at bringing in neutrals on the allied side, and breaking up the hostile alliance by offering concessions to one or more of Germany's allies. Often these diplomatic initiatives were contradictory and counterproductive. To bring Italy into the war on the allied side in 1915 she was offered territorial rewards at expense of Austria-Hungary and Turkey (see Maps 14 and 23). Such promises would stand in the way of a separate peace settlement with Austria-Hungary in 1917. Clearly, war aims were a diplomatic minefield which had to be negotiated with caution.

In the early years of the war allied war aims were necessarily vague. The allies' principal war aim, although nebulous, was to maintain the cohesion of the alliance in the face of German attempts to negotiate a separate peace with one or other of the allied nations. On 5 September 1914 France, Russia and Britain signed the Pact of London, in which they pledged themselves not to seek a separate peace with Germany. Publicly stated war aims were vague and idealistic. The defeat of 'Prussian militarism' and the restoration of Belgian independence and neutrality were causes which would appeal to domestic and international opinion. Territorially the allies' most public objective was the return of the 'lost provinces' of Alsace and Lorraine, annexed by Germany in 1871, to France.

Allied secret diplomacy involving the redistribution of territory following a decisive allied victory dominated the agenda till 1916. For Britain, whose principal objectives were essentially extra-European, victory meant colonial gains at German and Turkish expense. This in itself caused tensions with France, who had her own plans for expansion in Asia Minor (see Map 23). In the summer of 1916 for the first time the individual allied nations had begun to think about their post-war desiderata, in terms both of territory and less tangible objectives such as national security, economic advantage, compensation for war damage and fulfilling peace promises to their populace. For Britain this meant eliminating the German naval and commercial threat through the destruction of Germany's naval power and the annexation of German colonies. For France it meant draconian restrictions on Germany's war-making capacity, and a large financial indemnity. In Europe, France hoped permanently to weaken the German economy by gaining control of the industrial areas on Germany's western frontier, the Ruhr and the Saarland, either by direct annexation or by splitting them off from Germany to form a separate state. In June 1916 an inter-allied Economic Conference met in Paris to endorse French proposals to impose a financial indemnity and economic sanctions on the Central Powers following an allied victory. Belgium, which had not signed the Pact of London, was a potential weakness in the allied coalition. Fearing that Belgium would make a separate peace with Germany, on 14 February 1916 the allies issued the Declaration of Saint Adresse, promising the restoration of Belgian independence and compensation, possibly through incorporation of the formerly independent Duchy of Luxembourg. Belgium also sought the French-speaking canton of Malmédy, on her eastern border.

This new approach to war aims reflected changed international circumstances. Firstly, the allies had to respond to the proposed meditation of neutrals – by the American President Woodrow Wilson in December 1916, and Pope Benedict XV in August 1917. Secondly, as in Germany, domestic tensions had emerged as war weariness set in. The Entente's political leaders had to come up with a 'moral' agenda for continuing the war as the political left, and indeed Russia after the February 1917 revolution, moved towards supporting the international socialist agenda of a 'peace without annexations or indemnities'. Thirdly, the hope that the rival alliance might be split by separate peace offers necessitated clear agreement on terms. Indeed, by the end of 1916 it was generally believed that the war would end with a negotiated peace, and that the best the allies could hope to achieve by fighting on was a 'peace with advantage'. Moreover, the advantage had to be gained against both enemy and allies, since if there was a negotiated compromise settlement it was important to secure a strong position for the possible renewal of hostilities at a later date. For this reason, neither the British empire nor Italy would subsequently honour the economic agreements made in Paris in 1916.

The situation was further complicated by America's entry into the war in April 1917, as an 'associated power' of the Entente, with the avowed objective of fighting to secure a fair peace settlement. Furthermore, the Bolshevik seizure of power in Russia, rapidly followed by Lenin's call for a 'democratic' peace (with a European workers' insurrection to achieve it if necessary), forced the belligerents to respond. President Wilson's idealist international agenda, epitomised by his 'Fourteen Points' published in January 1918, contrasted sharply with the imperialist ambitions of America's allies. While supporting the restoration of Belgian independence and the return of Alsace and Lorraine to France, Wilson's more internationalist visions, such as the freedom of the seas and the right of national minorities to self-determination, cut across the national interests of her allies. Such allied disagreements remained unresolved while the war continued, and would be disputed later at the Paris Peace Conference (see Map 47).

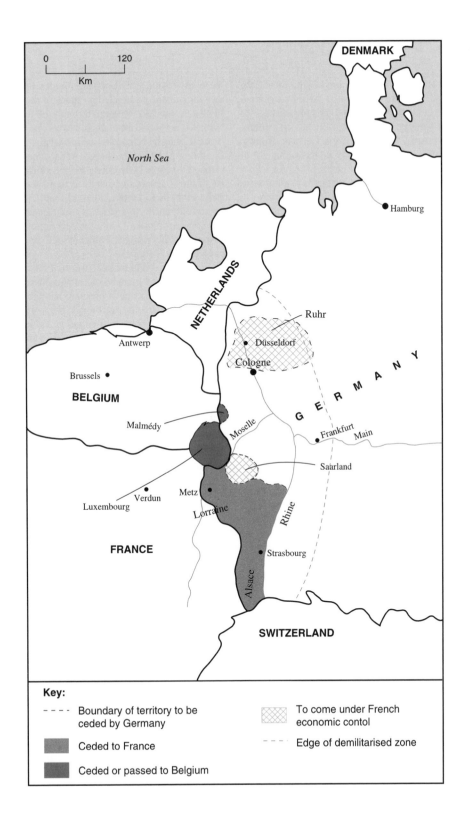

Map 25: The Battle of Verdun

The ten-month battle of Verdun is symbolic of the costly and indecisive offensives of the attritional phase of the First World War. It epitomises the style of warfare of the machine age. Above all it was an artillery battle, in which men endured what the German infantry officer and author Ernst Jünger characterised as the 'storm of steel' for little perceptible result.

At the start of 1916 Falkenhayn sought a solution to the war's strategic stalemate. Successful defence in the west, and large territorial gains in the east, had not broken the unity and resolve of the allies. Falkenhayn believed that if the French army, already weakened by their unsuccessful 1915 offensives (see Map 15), could be broken, French national morale would collapse, and France would seek a separate peace. This would leave the British empire, increasingly the mainstay of the alliance, isolated. He determined to attack the French army at a point which could not be relinquished without profound consequences for national morale. The French army would be forced to stand and fight, and would 'bleed to death' – a strategy of pure attrition.

The point chosen was the ancient fortress town of Verdun, bastion of the eastern end of the western front. Verdun sat in the valley of the river Meuse, protected by a ring of obsolescent forts on the wooded heights to the north and east of the town, the most important of which were Forts Douaumont (dubbed 'the key to Verdun') and Vaux. Although the forts had been stripped of most of their heavy guns for use elsewhere on the front, as prominent features in the otherwise desolate landscape they were hastily organised for defence and were to form the focal points of the early fighting. The whole position formed a salient against which German infantry and artillery could be concentrated.

On 21 February 1916, the Germans attacked on the right bank of the Meuse with ten infantry divisions supported by 1200 guns. The French army resisted heroically, but was pushed steadily back. Fort Douaumont, whose small garrison was taken by surprise, fell on 25 February; Fort Vaux, better defended, fell on 7 June after a week of hand-to-hand fighting in the fort's maze of underground passages. New weapons of mass destruction, such as phosgene gas and flamethrowers, were employed by the attackers in an attempt to break through the stubborn French defence. The French army's position became increasingly desperate as the 'mincing machine', as the French soldiers dubbed the battle, steadily ground down the manpower and morale of both armies. Sixty-six French and 48 German divisions passed through the inferno. Only by prodigious effort were the French front line formations kept supplied by continuous convoys along a single road, the *voie sacrée* ('Sacred Way'), under constant enemy shelling. On 25 February Joffre appointed Philippe Pétain, soon to be dubbed the

'hero of Verdun', to supervise the defence. On 6 March the German army extended its attack to the left bank of the Meuse. It managed to break through the French front line, but failed to capture the high ground at Côte 304 and Le Mort Homme, which became the scene of desperate hand-to-hand fighting in the ensuing weeks. 'What scenes of horror and carnage,' recorded one young French officer shortly before his death. 'I cannot find words to translate my impressions. Hell cannot be so terrible. Men are mad!' The battle ground on for four months in a series of costly small-scale offensives and counter-offensives, until the opening of the battle of the Somme in July obliged Falkenhayn to suspend offensive operations at Verdun.

In the final months of 1916 the French, now directed by Robert Nivelle, mounted a counter-offensive to recapture the lost forts. Using new 'creeping barrage' artillery tactics perfected by Nivelle the French regained Fort Vaux on 2 November and Fort Douaumont on 25 November. By the end of the battle in December, both armies had lost heavily for little appreciable change in the position on the ground. In the 1916 fighting German losses were around 100,000 killed or missing, while the French army lost over 160,000. Psychological wounds among the survivors were immeasurable.

Verdun can be seen as a turning point in the conduct and perception of the war. The 'blood and fire' of Verdun permanently changed the nature of warfare, and broke the spirit and cohesion of pre-war society. After 1916 the war became one of desperate survival on both sides. In France the *Union Sacrée* of 1914 broke down. After the indiscriminate execution of Verdun the ordinary *poilus* no longer accepted the senseless sacrifice of their lives. In 1917 the French army was to mutiny in protest against the incompetence of the high command (see Map 33). In 1917 Germany went through a similar domestic crisis as the political left started to call for an end to the militarist-capitalist war.

In August 1917 the French renewed the offensive at Verdun to recapture the high ground on both banks of the Meuse, which still allowed the Germans observation over their front line positions. Compared with the costly small-scale actions of 1916, the second battle of Verdun demonstrated the sophisticated development of combined-arms tactics in the French army by 1917. Pétain, by now commander-in-chief, chose to employ overwhelming firepower to economise on human lives. The attack by eight divisions on 20 August was supported by 2800 guns, and employed new small-unit infantry tactics. Following up the intensive barrage closely, the well-trained French infantry overwhelmed the shocked German defenders of Le Mort Homme and Côte 344 before they had time to react. The ground contested at the point of the bayonet for ten months in early 1916 was re-conquered in five days with fewer than 10,000 French casualties.

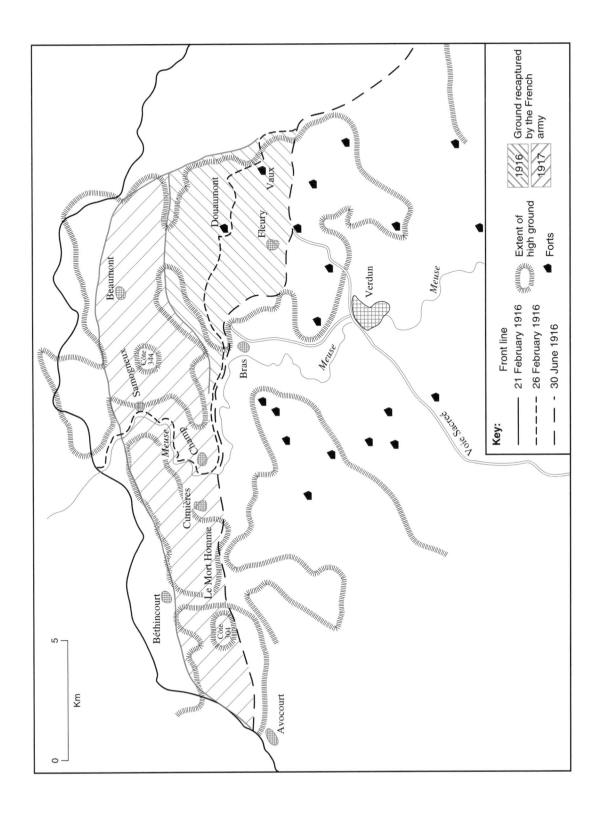

Key:

Front line
— 21 February 1916
--- 26 February 1916
– – 30 June 1916

Extent of high ground

Forts

Ground recaptured by the French army
1916
1917

Beaumont

Samogneux
Côte 344

Douaumont

Vaux

Fleury

Verdun

Meuse

Bras

Béthincourt

Cumières

Le Mort Homme
Côte 304

Champ

Meuse

Avocourt

Voie Sacrée

Meuse

Km
0   5

Map 26: The Battle of Jutland

Only once during the First World War did Britain's Grand Fleet and Germany's High Seas Fleet meet in battle: at Jutland (Skagerrak) in the North Sea between Norway and Denmark (31 May–1 June 1916) where some 250 ships and 70,000 sailors clashed in an engagement that was a German tactical victory but a strategic success for the British. The origins of the battle lay in the appointment in January 1916 of Reinhardt Scheer to command the German High Seas Fleet. Before his arrival, the main battle fleet had largely stayed in port, unwilling to take on the might of John Jellicoe's British Grand Fleet. Scheer, a more aggressive admiral, planned a raid on Britain's east coast that would entice David Beatty's British Battlecruiser Fleet based at Rosyth onto German submarines and the High Seas Fleet. Scheer dropped the plan to raid the east coast, settling on a less ambitious sweep off the western Danish coast, again with the aim of luring out the lighter British battlecruisers. Leading Scheer's fleet would be Franz von Hipper's scouting fleet, 40 fast vessels built around a core of five battlecruisers that would act as the bait, while Scheer's battleships followed at a safe distance.

The British, however, had access to German naval codes through the work of the code-breakers in the naval intelligence unit known as 'Room 40' and, knowing that Scheer had left port on the morning of 31 May, the Grand Fleet set sail from its base at Scapa Flow. By coincidence, Jellicoe, who knew the High Seas Fleet had left port but did not know its destination, sailed for the area off Denmark where Scheer was deploying his ships. Scheer would now have to deal with the whole of the Grand Fleet.

While the British had superiority in battleships and battlecruisers, the lighter, faster battlecruisers had weak armament protection. British ships also lacked the sophisticated gunnery control systems of German ships and they suffered from a gun-loading system that made them liable to magazine explosions. The Germans also had heavier, more effective shells. Thus, as the ships sailed into action, while the big gun balance sheet of British guns of 12- to 15-inch calibre against German 11- and 12-inch guns was in Britain's favour, there was a question mark over the quality of British ordnance.

The British ships sailed in two groups. First to reach Jutland was Beatty's scouting battlecruisers from Rosyth: six battlecruisers accompanied by four modern (superdreadnought) *Queen Elizabeth*-class battleships. The latter were, however, lagging behind the battlecruisers. After a chance encounter, Hipper and Beatty's battlecruisers engaged at 15.45 on 31 May at a range of some 13 kilometres (8 miles). The action went very badly for the British. The battlecruiser *Lion* (Beatty's flagship) would have blown up but for the bravery of a marine who flooded his burning turret. Worse was to follow. At 16.03, the battlecruiser *Indefatigable* blew up and sank after being hit by the 11-inch guns of the German battlecruiser *Von der Tann*. The battlecruiser *Queen Mary* was the next to be hit, sinking in 90 seconds at 16.25 after receiving a full broadside from the 12-inch guns of the German battlecruiser *Derfflinger*, leaving behind a huge pall of smoke. 'There seems to be something wrong with our bloody ships today' was Beatty's laconic comment. Finally, at around 16.30 the four *Queen Elizabeth* battleships came into range with their 15-inch guns at about 17 kilometres (11 miles), giving Beatty the advantage. Then at 16.42 Beatty spotted, behind the van of the German battlecruisers that he was engaging, the rest of the German High Seas Fleet. Outgunned, he turned to the north, his *Queen Elizabeth* battleships wreaking heavy damage on the chasing Germans. Hipper and Scheer chased Beatty, unaware that steaming south to the battle zone was Jellicoe's Grand Fleet. With darkness approaching Jellicoe arrived, sighting Beatty's flagship *Lion* at 18.00. From his flagship, the battleship *Iron Duke*, Jellicoe manoeuvred his fleet to cross the 'T' of the German High Seas Fleet, allowing maximum firepower to be concentrated on the enemy. In the ensuing mêlée, a third British battlecruiser, *Invincible*, was sunk (18.33) after a shell penetrated a turret, causing a flash-fire that reached the magazine. Split in two, her two extremities stood up in the water, a reminder of the inherent weaknesses of the British battlecruiser design.

In danger of being destroyed by the superior battleships of the Grand Fleet, at 19.35 Scheer ordered his entire High Seas Fleet to conduct a complicated but often practised 180-degree about turn manoeuvre. This was accomplished as the murk of night descended, presenting the Grand Fleet with a brief glimpse of an enemy almost destroyed. Jellicoe had missed his chance of sinking the German fleet, a fact that would provoke much debate after the battle. Exchanges of gunfire continued through the night until 02.30 on 1 June when there were final contacts between British light cruisers and destroyers and escaping German ships. Keen to avoid the mines and submarines near the German shore, Jellicoe called off the pursuit by 03.00 on 1 June. The Germans escaped by circling to the rear of the British and, shepherding his crippled ships, Scheer reached the safety of the Horns Reef light by 03.30.

Jutland was a half-fought battle broken off by the Germans before it began in earnest. The Germans claimed a victory based on sinking more ships and killing more British sailors (over 6000 dead to the Germans' 2500). Although the Royal Navy had missed an opportunity to decide the naval war, Germany's High Seas Fleet never again sailed out to do battle with Britain's Grand Fleet. The Germans had assaulted their jailer before going back to prison.

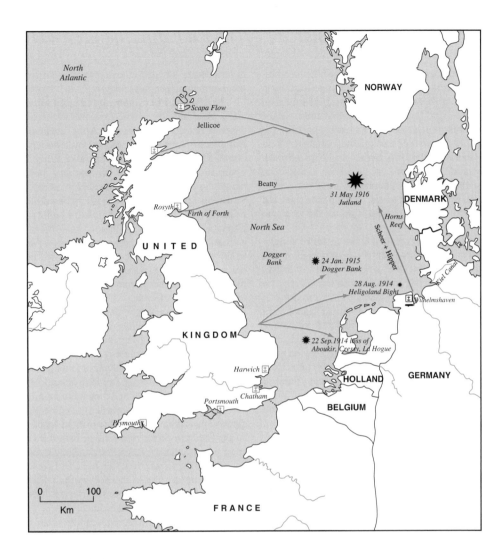

Forces at Jutland

	No. of ships (with ships lost in brackets)	
	German	British
Battleships	16 (1*)	28
Battlecruisers	5 (1)	9 (3)
Pre-dreadnought battleships	6	–
Armoured cruisers	–	8 (3)
Light cruisers	11 (4)	26
Destroyers	61 (5)	78 (8)
Seaplane carriers	–	1
Minelayers	–	1
Total	99 (11)	151 (14)
Total tonnage lost	62,230	111,980

*Pre-dreadnought

Map 27: The Somme Offensive I – The Plan and the First Day

The allied strategic plan for 1916, agreed by the allies' military leaders at Joffre's headquarters at Chantilly in December 1915, called for coordinated offensives on all allied fronts. The Anglo-French contribution on the western front was to be a combined offensive astride the river Somme. Britain would commit her volunteer New Armies for the first time, to muster an Anglo-French attacking force of 65 divisions, 40 French and 25 British. By the time the offensive commenced on 1 July 1916 events elsewhere had reduced the campaign's size and scope – attrition had replaced decision as the strategic objective for 1916.

There was early disagreement between Joffre and the new British commander-in-chief, Douglas Haig, on the nature and objectives of the Anglo-French offensive. Joffre wanted the relatively inexperienced British army to conduct a preliminary 'wearing-out' offensive to draw in German reserves before the French army launched a decisive breakthrough attack. Haig objected to such a subsidiary role. On 14 February 1916, Joffre and Haig agreed that there would be no preliminary wearing-out attack. The British would attack alongside the French on the Somme at the beginning of July, supporting them in the main French attack to the south. Such inter-allied disagreements continued to trouble the alliance before and during the offensive.

With the French committing three armies to the offensive, and the British one, overall coordination of planning was in the hands of the commander of the French northern army group, Ferdinand Foch. In the initial plan the British were to attack the high ground to the north of the river Somme (the Thiepval–Martinpuich–Combles ridge) and push on to the Bapaume–Péronne road, thus outflanking the main German position which the French were to attack later. Events between February and June altered the scope of the attack and the roles of the two armies. French reserves were diverted south to shore up the defences of Verdun, and the French role in the battle was steadily diminished. British reserves too were reduced after they took over the front held by the French Tenth Army. In these changed circumstances Foch, who judged that a decisive offensive was now impossible, wanted to postpone the attack until 1917. Fearing that French support would not be forthcoming, Haig wished to mount a purely British attack from Ypres against the Belgian coast later in the year. Yet for Joffre the need to act in concert with other allied offensives, and to relieve German pressure on Verdun, made it imperative that an Anglo-French offensive be launched as soon as possible. It was agreed in May that the Somme offensive would commence in late June, although with the roles reversed. The British army would play the main attacking role. Yet for the subsidiary French offensive to the south

to succeed it was still essential for the British to capture the dominating Thiepval ridge.

The British offensive plan relied on a heavy preliminary bombardment to destroy the successive lines of German defences. The Fourth Army commander, Henry Rawlinson, wanted to proceed systematically, taking one German defensive position at a time. Haig, more optimistic that the British army's new heavy artillery would destroy the enemy's defences, wished to push on as far and as fast as possible in the first assault, to secure the ridge in one bound and if possible follow up to the Bapaume–Péronne road. Haig's views prevailed. When zero-hour came the inexperienced British infantry, heavily laden with equipment to consolidate its hold on the conquered enemy positions, was to advance at a measured pace across no-man's land. No significant resistance was expected.

At 7.30am on 1 July 1916 13 British divisions went over-the-top. While the heaviest so far, the British preliminary bombardment was spread far too thinly to destroy all German defences. In particular, wire-cutting was incomplete and deep German dugouts remained untouched. The British army experienced its worst ever day of battle. Over 57,000 casualties were suffered including more than 19,000 dead. Partially-cut wire and untouched machine-gun positions quickly blunted the initial impetus of the attack, particularly on the northern sector of the front, between Gommecourt and Fricourt villages, where the attacking divisions hardly got beyond their own front line trenches. West of Fricourt there was partial success, the XV and XIII Corps capturing the German first position on the forward slopes of the ridge, between Mametz and Montauban.

The French Sixth Army's attack was much more successful. Five divisions attacked astride the Somme. Supported by a heavier and better-orchestrated bombardment, and using more sophisticated small-unit infantry tactics, they captured all their objectives in the German defenders' first position with relatively light casualties. Since the ridge that dominated the French front remained in German hands they could push no further.

The first day of the Somme remains a metaphor in Britain for military incompetence. Inexperience and over-ambition combined to produce disaster. Haig knew that his troops were not yet ready for such an offensive, but was constrained by allied strategy. His subordinates were inexperienced in managing such large-scale operations. His troops were brave but inadequately trained in trench warfare. In contrast the French, experienced from their 1915 combats and the defence of Verdun, demonstrated more effective tactical and operational methods. Yet this alone would not produce a decisive breakthrough. Attrition remained the only strategic option.

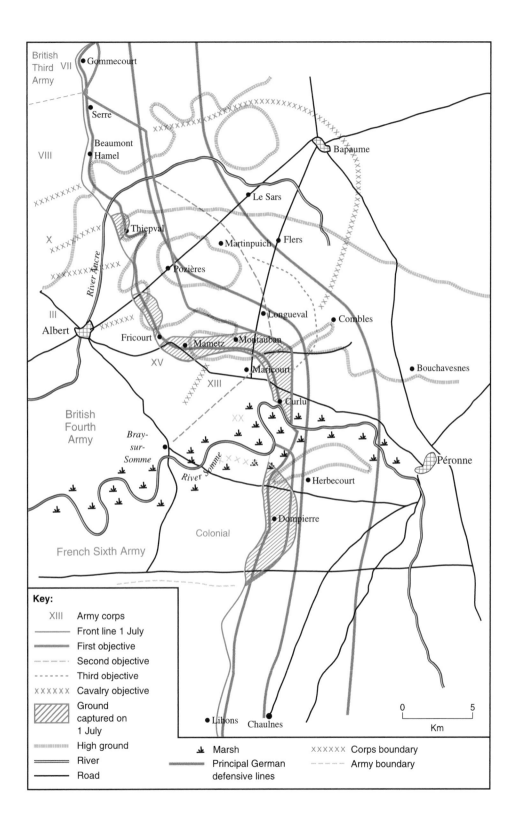

British
Third
Army

VII • Gommecourt

• Serre

VIII

Beaumont
• Hamel

Bapaume

Le Sars

X

• Thiepval

• Martinpuich • Flers

• Pozières

III

Albert

• Longueval • Combles

Fricourt •

Mametz • Montauban

XV

• Maricourt

• Bouchavesnes

XIII

• Curlu

British
Fourth
Army

XX

Bray-
sur-
Somme

River Somme

Péronne

• Herbecourt

• Dompierre

Colonial

French Sixth Army

• Lihons
Chaulnes

River Ancre

Key:

XIII   Army corps

——   Front line 1 July

——   First objective

– – –   Second objective

- - -   Third objective

xxxxxx   Cavalry objective

▨   Ground
captured on
1 July

||||||| High ground

═══   River

——   Road

⚓   Marsh

═══   Principal German
defensive lines

xxxxxx   Corps boundary

– – –   Army boundary

0   5

Km

Map 28: The Somme Offensive II – The Battle of Attrition

The limited gains of the first day of the Somme presented the allied command with a dilemma. Should they continue the battle, or halt the offensive? The lengthy logistical preparations required to mount such a battle prevented a rapid redeployment of men and resources to attack on another part of the front. The broader parameters of allied strategy obliged the Anglo-French armies to maintain pressure on the enemy, partly to relieve Verdun and partly to prevent the transfer of German reserves to the eastern front, where Brusilov's summer 1916 offensive was enjoying considerable success (see Map 8). Above all, there had been enough success on the southern sector of the front on 1 July to suggest that the German defensive position could be broken into. Continued pressure it was judged would wear down the fighting strength of the German army – in time a complete collapse might occur. For these reasons the campaign was to be prolonged for 4½ months. Little ground was won, and no decisive breakthrough ever appeared likely. Yet the muddy crawl over the Picardy hills, which severely stretched Germany's powers of resistance, imperceptibly turned the course of the war in the allies' favour.

The first phase of the battle, until the middle of September, was a slow push forwards to capture objectives which had not been won on the first day, in order to establish a line for renewing a general offensive. The shattered villages and woods on the forward slopes of the ridge – Thiepval, Pozières, Contalmaison, Combles, High Wood, Delville Wood and Trônes Wood – became the focal point of bloody small-unit actions as British and French battalions attacked and German reserves counter-attacked. In this attritional struggle the British learned quickly, acquitting themselves well in the gruelling forward advance. Their artillery support doctrines in particular made rapid progress, the creeping barrage, employed by their French allies to support the infantry's advance, being adopted as standard practice. Tactical innovation – for example the successful surprise dawn attack which captured the Bazentin villages and Longueval on 14 July – helped the British divisions improve on their initial disaster. Having secured the ridge line by the end of August, the allies were ready to renew the joint attack in strength. On 15 September 23 British and French divisions attacked on the line Thiepval–Vermandovillers, the British revealing their greatest tactical innovation, the tank. The new armoured fighting vehicles came as a surprise to the Germans, and their appearance contributed significantly to the successful advance on the British sector of the front, notably in the capture of the village of Flers. However, their small number, mechanical unreliability, and primitive tactical method meant that they were not yet a battle- or war-winning weapon. A heavier and more methodical artillery bombardment, and the strict limitation of objectives to the artillery's capacity, produced better and less-costly results than on 1 July. In a 2½-kilometre (1½-mile) advance the German front position was taken, and in follow-up operations Thiepval was finally taken on 27 September. But forward exploitation proved laborious once again as the enemy's defences were stiffened on the next ridge in front of Bapaume.

To increase the pressure on the enemy Foch and Haig chose to extend the battle to the flanks. On 4 September 11 divisions of Micheler's French Tenth Army attacked on a 10-kilometre (6-mile) front south of the Somme, between Barleux and Chilly, again breaking into the enemy's forward position. On 13 November 13 divisions of Gough's British Fifth Army launched a partially-successful advance along the valley of the river Ancre to the north of Thiepval, capturing Beaumont Hamel and Beaucourt villages. However, by September autumn rain had begun, turning the battlefield into a quagmire. Piecemeal operations continued until mid-November, when the offensive was finally halted for the winter. The Anglo-French armies had advanced some 10 kilometres (6 miles) at their point of deepest penetration, on a 40-kilometre (25-mile) front. Losses remain controversial. The British suffered nearly 420,000 casualties, their French allies just over 200,000. The German losses were at least 400,000 men, possibly as many as 650,000.

Although the German army did not collapse in 1916, in A.J.P. Taylor's phrase, at Verdun and the Somme the German army 'bled to death'. Its 1917 recruits were already in the line by the end of 1916. In spring 1917 it was obliged to withdraw its untenable front in Picardy to the prepared positions of the Hindenburg line, to liberate manpower for a renewal of the attritional struggle (see Map 32). Nor could it compete in the battle of matériel (*materialschlacht*) which the allies forced it to fight. The allied blockade was starting to impact heavily on productivity and morale on the home front (see Map 13). In December 1916 the new duumvirate at the head of the German army, Paul von Hindenburg and Erich Ludendorff, intensified mobilisation with a new Auxiliary Service Law conscripting labour on the home front into war industries. The year of attrition had cost the already tired French army and nation equally dearly. Only the British emerged from the Somme with credit. The ordinary soldiers had borne the heavy sacrifice with stoicism, and after initial failure the inexperienced army had learned to fight with skill and determination. The expectation of rapid military victory disappeared. After 1916 the war became a struggle to outlast the enemy in a brutal 'total war'. In this the allies had the upper hand.

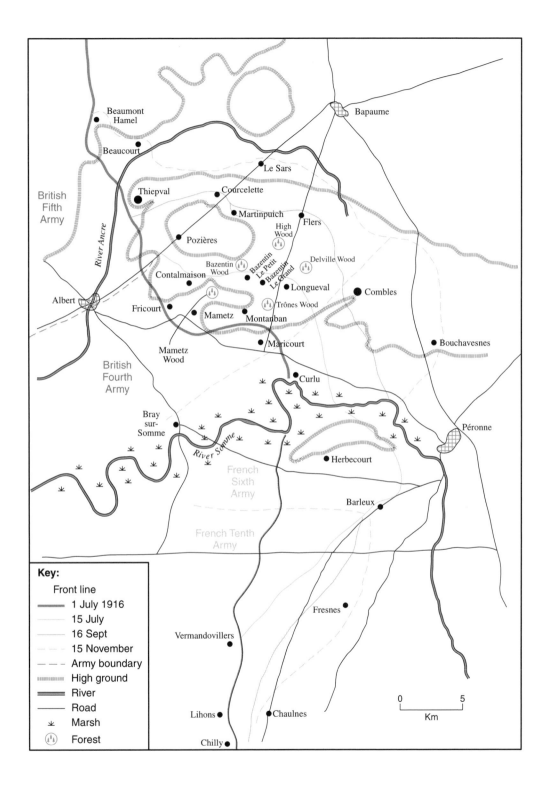

Key:

Front line
1 July 1916
15 July
16 Sept
15 November
Army boundary
High ground
River
Road
Marsh
Forest

British Fifth Army

British Fourth Army

French Sixth Army

French Tenth Army

River Ancre

River Somme

Beaumont Hamel

Beaucourt

Bapaume

Le Sars

Thiepval

Courcelette

Martinpuich

Flers

High Wood

Poziéres

Delville Wood

Bazentin Wood

Bazentin Le Petit

Bazentin Le Grand

Contalmaison

Longueval

Combles

Albert

Fricourt

Trônes Wood

Mametz

Montauban

Bouchavesnes

Mametz Wood

Maricourt

Curlu

Péronne

Bray sur-Somme

Herbecourt

Barleux

Fresnes

Vermandovillers

Lihons

Chaulnes

Chilly

0   5
Km

Map 29: The German Submarine Offensive

Although Britain and France had over twice as many submarines as the Germans in 1914, the latter had the advantage that many of their submarines (U-boats – *Unterseeboote*) had ocean-going capability. Also, rapid advances in submarine technology meant that the submarines of 1914 were very quickly obsolete, giving both sides a level start. Germany won the race to build a new ocean-going submarine fleet. On 22 September 1914, off the Dutch coast, the submarine U-9 torpedoed and sank three old British cruisers, *Aboukir*, *Hogue* and *Cressy*, a wake-up call for the British. In fact, submarines were not such a threat to fast ocean-going warships, which could outpace submarines and were protected by smaller vessels. Their danger came in the form of *Handelskrieg* – counter-blockade trade warfare against Entente and neutral merchant shipping. In retaliation against the British surface blockade of Germany (see Map 13), the Germans decided to use submarines to blockade British ports. However, this presented a practical problem: normally, intercepted merchant shipping would be turned back or have its cargo seized. But the submarine was only effective if it sank all merchant shipping it thought was bound for enemy ports – unrestricted submarine warfare. Moreover, if the submarine came to the surface to inspect cargoes and crew – restricted submarine warfare – it was at its most vulnerable. Thus, German submarines could not institute a conventional blockade. The effect of this was that for German U-boats to be effective they would need to kill civilians on enemy and neutral shipping.

On 4 February 1915, the Germans declared the waters around the British Isles a war zone, warning that any merchant vessel in this area was in danger. This declaration of unrestricted submarine warfare outraged neutral America, more especially when, on 7 May 1915, U-20 sank the passenger liner *Lusitania* off the west coast of Ireland, killing 128 US citizens (of 1198 drowned). More American lives were lost in August 1915 when the *Arabic* went down. It was a measure of American determination to stay out of the war that she remained neutral despite these outrages. Not wanting to provoke the US, the German chancellor, Bethmann Hollweg, urged the navy to be more cautious and, from late 1915, U-boat commanders, against their better instinct, moderated their war on merchant shipping, there being a mass of restrictions on what type of vessels could be sunk. Further restrictions were instituted following the sinking of the *Sussex* in the English Channel, again with loss of American life, in March 1916. The idea was that the Germans would only launch fully unrestricted warfare, which threatened to bring the US into the war, when they were sure that the end of the war was in sight and so US entry was irrelevant. Nevertheless, the Germans sank hundreds of thousands of tons of merchant shipping

in 1915, just as German shipyards were producing increasing numbers of submarines. Meanwhile the Entente struggled against the submarine threat. Despite Germany restricting the submarine war, shipping losses mounted in 1916, although Britain was still able to feed her population.

In Germany in late 1916, military and civilian advisers urged for a move to unrestricted warfare, arguing that, if sinkings could exceed 600,000 tons for six months, British imports would be reduced to an unsustainable level, thus starving the enemy into submission. If the campaign were launched in February 1917, defeat should come about before the August harvest. But the downside was that such a campaign would probably bring the US into the war as her ships would become targets. The Germans were on the horns of a dilemma. Assuming that the US military was little immediate threat as it was so small and would require a long period of mobilisation and preparation, Germany's military leaders urged that Germany move to unrestricted warfare. While unsure, Bethmann Hollweg eventually bowed to the pressure from his military advisers.

On 1 February 1917, the Germans declared that from then on they would be fighting unrestricted submarine war. The strategy came close to success. Losses between February and July 1917 averaged a little over 600,000 tons per month and Britain's stocks of food fell to dangerously low levels. What helped turn the tables was the introduction of new Royal Navy counter-measures in response to the new threat. Most importantly, from May 1917, merchant ships started to sail in protected convoys, an old naval strategy. Effective convoying of merchant shipping and better coordination, along with more aggressive means of seeking out and destroying U-boats, slowly turned the tables in the battle of the Atlantic as the Royal Navy struggled to keep open Britain's lifeline to the US. The war on submarines included attacks on their bases, such as the raid on the U-boat pens at Zeebrugge and Ostend on 22–23 April 1918. The success of convoys meant that it was extended to the Mediterranean, an important move as Italian shipping suffered badly from Austro-Hungarian and German submarines. The British also laid a blockade of mines, nets and ships across the English Channel and the Faroes gap to stop U-boats getting out into the Atlantic. The entry of the US also meant that US ships were now fully involved in hunting U-boats.

In the end, the U-boat campaign was an example of German tactical brilliance tempered by gross strategic blunders. German experts miscalculated British farmers' abilities to increase production. Moreover, by bringing the US into the war the defeat of Germany was now just a question of when, assuming that the British and French armies on the western front could hold on long enough for the arrival of large, fresh US divisions.

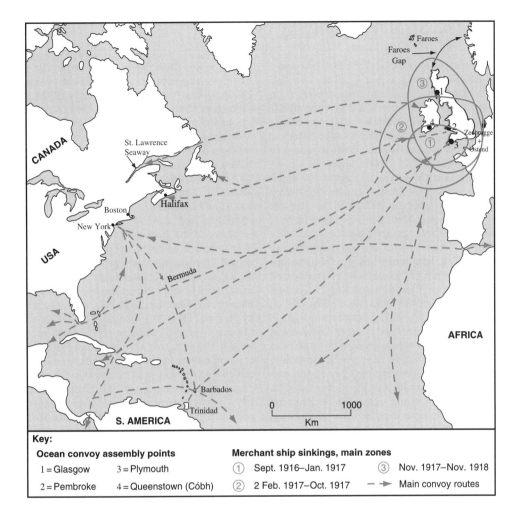

Key:

Ocean convoy assembly points

1 = Glasgow 3 = Plymouth

2 = Pembroke 4 = Queenstown (Cóbh)

Merchant ship sinkings, main zones

① Sept. 1916–Jan. 1917 ③ Nov. 1917–Nov. 1918

② 2 Feb. 1917–Oct. 1917 - → Main convoy routes

Allied and Neutral Merchant Shipping Losses, 1914–18*

1914: 100 ships (312,672 tons) sunk (248,194 British; 64,478 Allied and Neutral)

1915: 516 ships (1,307,996 tons) sunk (879,851 British; 428,145 Allied and Neutral)

1916: 1157 ships (2,348,000 tons) sunk (1,251,416 British; 1,096,584 Allied and Neutral)

Total (1914–16) = 3,968,668 tons

1917: 2676 ships (6,235,878 tons) sunk (3,751,529 British; 2,484,349 Allied and Neutral)

1918: 1209 ships (2,666,942 tons) sunk (1,699,743 British; 967,199 Allied and Neutral)

Total (1917–18) = 8,902,820 tons

*Some estimates put the total number of ships sunk at 6394 with a total tonnage of 11,900,000 tons.

U-boat Losses, 1914–1918

1914: 5

1915: 19

1916: 22

1917: 64

1918: 68

Total = 178 submarines lost

Numbers of Ships Lost, 1914–1918

	U-boats	Surface Raiders	Mines	Aircraft
1914	3	55	42	–
1915	396	23	97	–
1916	964	32	161	–
1917	2439	64	170	3
1918	1035	3	170	1

Map 30: The Strategic Bombing of Britain

The development of powered flight took war into a third dimension. As well as their significant battlefield role, aircraft would be used to strike directly at the enemy's home front. In the First World War the morale of the civilian population was considered a legitimate military target. Germany could use her air force to strike directly at the homeland of her principal enemy, Great Britain, even while she remained secure from seaborne invasion.

Germany first used her navy to strike against the British Isles. On 3 November 1914 German cruisers bombarded Great Yarmouth, although their shells failed to reach the shore. On 16 December Hartlepool, Scarborough and Whitby were shelled with greater accuracy – 133 were killed and 364 wounded. In 1915 she used single aircraft and hydrogen-filled long-range airships, the famous Zeppelins, to raid inland. The first attack came on the East Anglian ports of Great Yarmouth and King's Lynn on 19 January 1915. London was raided for the first time on 31 May. Altogether 208 successful Zeppelin raids took place. Ostensibly raids were aimed at military installations, although the inaccuracy of bombing inevitably meant that civilian targets were also hit. In July, after a particularly damaging French raid on Karlsruhe in Germany, this pretence was abandoned. Over the ensuing months London, Norwich, Harwich, Dover and other East Anglian and Kentish towns were bombed on a regular basis. More widely, Zeppelins raided as far north as Edinburgh and as far west as Liverpool. The British responded with increasingly effective counter measures, including anti-aircraft guns, barrage balloons and explosive bullets to ignite the hydrogen gas. The first Zeppelin was shot down by Lieutenant William Leefe-Robinson on 2 September 1916. Overnight he became a national hero, and was awarded the Victoria Cross for his feat. The loss of six Zeppelins between September and November 1916 forced a temporary suspension of the raids. Although casualties and damage from such small-scale raids were slight, and their impact on civilian morale was limited, they were played up by allied propagandists. German 'baby killers' had brought their atrocities from the continent to the homeland.

The raids were renewed and intensified in 1917 when Germany began using large two-engined 'Gotha' bombers based in Flanders, supplemented later by a handful of massive four-engined 'Giant' long-range heavy bombers, in massed raids on London and other towns. The first raid, by 21 Gothas against Folkestone on 25 May 1917, caught the British by surprise. Overall there were 290 civilian casualties, including 95 killed. There was uproar in Parliament at the state of Britain's air defences, and renewed panic in the streets. On 13 June Gothas raided London for the first time, killing 162 people and injuring 432 more. One bomb fell on the Upper North Street Schools in Poplar, killing 16 children and wounding 30 – a gift to British propagandists, but a tragedy for the East End of London. These early raids had caught Britain unawares, but a more effective defence was soon organised. Fighter squadrons were brought home from France and integrated with forward observers, searchlights, barrage balloons and anti-aircraft guns into the first coordinated aerial defence system, linked with a designated telephone network. Overall 16 fighter squadrons and 480 guns were assigned to the defence of London and the south east by the end of the war. If nothing else, Germany's bomber offensive tied up aeroplanes and guns which might have been better employed at the front. Over the following year Gothas, which took to raiding at night to avoid the improved British defences, became regular visitors to London and the home counties. Coastal towns and ports on the direct route from Flanders to London – Margate, Ramsgate, Sheerness, Felixstowe, Southend – were regularly targeted by passing bombers. Altogether 27 raids took place between May 1917 and May 1918, when events on the western front caused German bombing activity to be concentrated on supporting ground operations. The raids caused a lot of panic and considerable damage, although casualties were limited. Overall German air raids from 1915 to 1918 killed 1414 and wounded 3416 military personnel and civilians. Nevertheless, the psychological impact of strategic bombing on Britain's political leaders was an important influence on their decision to create their own independent strategic air force, the Royal Air Force, which came into being in March 1918.

From early on in the war the allies responded in kind. In fact the first bombs dropped from the air had been British, a naval aeroplane successfully destroying a Zeppelin in its hangar at Düsseldorf on 8 October 1914. French aircraft raided German industrial installations across the eastern frontier from 1914 onwards, and the Germans struck back at Paris. An Independent Air Force of British aeroplanes bombed industrial targets in Germany from bases in eastern France from June 1918 until the armistice. One element of the allies' plan for 1919 was large-scale bombing raids against German industrial cities by new large four-engined Handley Page bombers.

Aerial bombing had little physical or strategic impact in the First World War. The aircraft were technologically primitive and mechanically unreliable, too small and few to do more than cause minor disruption to the home front. Its main effects were psychological, although even here they were perhaps overestimated by post-war aerial strategic theorists, who liked to argue that 'the bomber will always get through'. The bomber was a weapon of terror, but it could not alone defeat an enemy without associated land and sea operations, as a second world war was to prove.

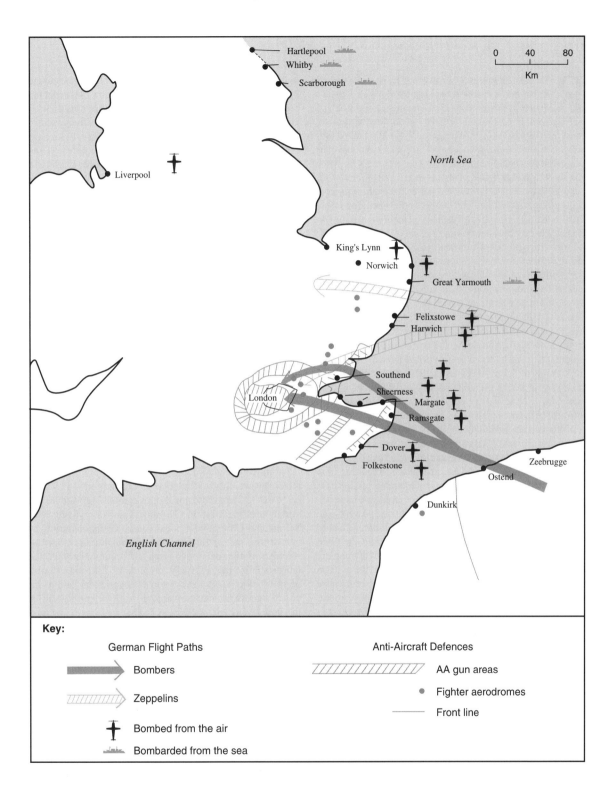

| 0 | 40 | 80 |

Km

North Sea

Hartlepool
Whitby
Scarborough

Liverpool

King's Lynn
Norwich
Great Yarmouth

Felixstowe
Harwich

Southend
Sheerness
Margate
London
Ramsgate

Dover
Folkestone
Zeebrugge
Ostend

Dunkirk

English Channel

Key:

German Flight Paths

Bombers

Zeppelins

Bombed from the air

Bombarded from the sea

Anti-Aircraft Defences

AA gun areas

Fighter aerodromes

Front line

Map 31: The Collapse of Russia, 1917

Russia's collapse in 1917 was not just a consequence of her involvement in the First World War. Russia's economy adjusted to the demands of the war and militarily she performed creditably on the battlefield, especially against Austria-Hungary. What she lacked was the cohesive civil society necessary to survive the war. The origins of the malaise stretched back to before 1914, when Russia's last two Tsars, Alexander III and Nicholas II, opposed a modern constitutional political system with concepts of citizenship, law and property that included rather than excluded ordinary Russians. Deeply reactionary, Russia's aristocratic-based ruling class refused to concede reform. This pre-1914 political problem, accelerated by the stresses of war, became a revolutionary crisis by 1917. Revolution in 1917 was revenge on a government that lacked legitimacy and that had failed to create a sense of ownership or patriotism for war. In this sense, the First World War was a gigantic test for the brittle pre-war regime.

Russian agriculture and industry performed creditably in the war. Agriculture adjusted to the demands of war, producing, for instance, a grain surplus from areas such as the Ukraine of 8.4 million tons in 1917. As for the Russian economy, while it suffered from the loss of Poland in 1915 (see Map 19), conscription of its workforce and poor internal transportation networks, it responded to demands for war production, expanding 21.6% between 1913 and 1916. The result, however, was rapid over-growth concentrated in certain key cities such as Petrograd (St Petersburg) and Moscow where, because of the difficulty of importing food from the countryside on Russia's inadequate rail system, there were food shortages by 1917. These problems, however, were identical to those faced by other warring powers. The question was whether the Russian government could respond with new initiatives that could tackle the food shortages, inflation, strikes and rural unrest threatening the country. It failed, largely because it lacked the will to reform and institute internal political change that could have mobilised Russia's population. The Russian parliament, the Duma, was prorogued in January 1915, recalled in July 1915, and then prorogued again when Tsar Nicholas II went off to the front. The absence of a representative parliament consigned government to the Tsar's wife, the German-born Alexandra, herself under the influence of a bizarre peasant holy man, Grigorii Rasputin. Voluntary and public organisations, such as the All-Russian Union of Zemstvos (rural councils) headed by Prince George Lvov (a liberal monarchist), filled the political vacuum, providing representation for ordinary people, caring for the sick and wounded, and confirming that the middle class wanted a share in the state.

The ruling regime blocked the initiatives of these patriotic self-help bodies. Its refusal to share power made industrial and agricultural reform difficult, alienated the liberal middle class and industrial working class, denied promotion to talented army officers and closed the door on land reform for the peasants. The lack of political reform also forced moderate opposition into the revolutionary camp. Moreover, the Tsar and his court dominated the army and so were intimately associated with battlefield failure. The Russian army was not as short of supplies as is often suggested; neither was its performance always poor: it captured more prisoners-of-war than the British and French armies combined and remained as a military institution until 1917. But with Germany focused on knocking Russia out of the war, Russia was hard pressed to hold her own militarily. Huge losses at the front meant that manpower became a big problem, and the Russian supreme headquarters was unable to replace the losses in men. By the autumn of 1916, there were mutinies among peasant conscripts with little stake in the war. At first, these were the result of battle fatigue and war weariness rather than revolutionary zeal, but trouble soon spread to depot troops in the major cities radicalised by contact with workers in urban areas.

On 8 March 1917 (23 February old-style Julian calendar), women textile workers in Petrograd, angry at food shortages, rioted, starting a revolution. On 11 March (26 February), the Tsar ordered troops to open fire on the rioters. They refused and mutinied. On 14 March (1 March), the Duma, sitting unofficially, declared a Provisional Government headed by Lvov (replaced by Alexander Kerensky in July). The Tsar abdicated on 15 March (2 March). The Provisional Government represented a middle-class revolution. The question was whether the Provisional Government could square up its commitment to carrying on fighting the war and instituting moderate reform with the social revolution and revolutionary parties unleashed by the February revolution. Like the Tsarist regime before it, the Provisional Government failed. Its unwillingness to end the war and institute land reform in the countryside damned it. A military offensive against Austria-Hungary in July 1917 (June 1917) collapsed, accompanied by mass desertions of Russian soldiers. With the army disintegrating and peasants seizing land across Russia, the agony of the Provisional Government dragged on as Kerensky struggled to control workers' 'soviets' and revolutionary groups such as Lenin's Bolsheviks. On 6/7 November (24/25 October), the Bolsheviks mounted a coup d'état, storming the Winter Palace in Petrograd, against a discredited regime and a demoralised army. Although a minority party with limited popular support, the Bolsheviks ruthlessly established themselves as the new ruling party in Soviet Russia and began negotiations with Germany to end the war (see Map 41).

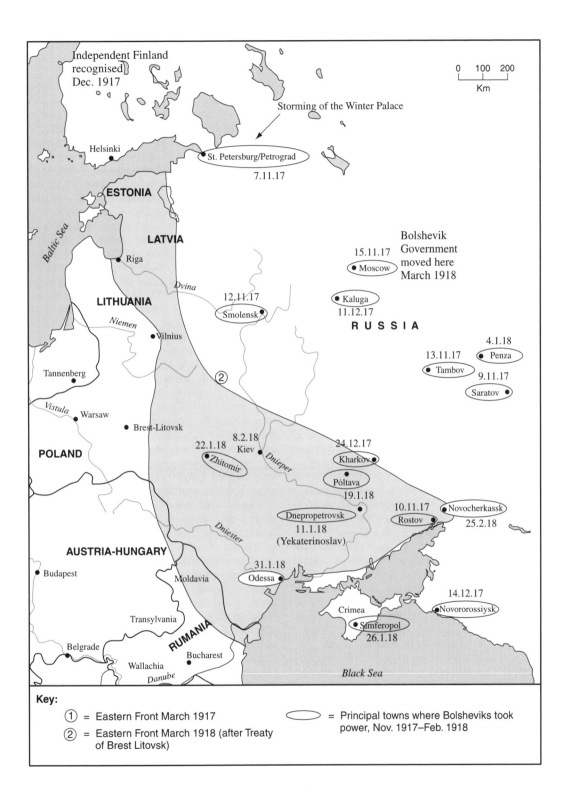

Independent Finland
recognised
Dec. 1917

Storming of the Winter Palace

Helsinki

St. Petersburg/Petrograd
7.11.17

ESTONIA

Baltic Sea

LATVIA

Riga

Dvina

Bolshevik
Government
moved here
March 1918

15.11.17
● Moscow

12.11.17
Smolensk ●

Kaluga
11.12.17

LITHUANIA

Niemen

● Vilnius

R U S S I A

4.1.18
13.11.17   ● Penza
● Tambov
9.11.17
Saratov ●

Tannenberg

②

Vistula
Warsaw

● Brest-Litovsk

POLAND

22.1.18   8.2.18
Kiev
●Zhitomir

24.12.17
Kharkov ●

Dnieper

Pòltava

19.1.18

Dnepropetrovsk

10.11.17   ● Novocherkassk
Rostov
25.2.18

11.1.18
(Yekaterinoslav)

Dniester

AUSTRIA-HUNGARY

● Budapest

Moldavia

31.1.18
Odessa

14.12.17
● Novororossiysk

Transylvania

Crimea

RUMANIA

Belgrade

Bucharest

Simferopol
26.1.18

Wallachia

Danube

Black Sea

Key:

① = Eastern Front March 1917

② = Eastern Front March 1918 (after Treaty
     of Brest Litovsk)

⬭ = Principal towns where Bolsheviks took
     power, Nov. 1917–Feb. 1918

0   100   200
Km

Map 32: The Nivelle Offensive

Efforts were to be intensified in 1917 in an attempt to force victory. In December 1916 in Britain the dynamic Welsh 'wizard', Lloyd George, supplanted Asquith as Prime Minister. In France Joffre was replaced by the rising star of the French high command, Verdun commander Robert Nivelle, who had a new plan for breaking the western front stalemate. Lloyd George, anxious to avoid further heavy casualties in a prolonged attritional struggle, and French premier Aristide Briand, anxious over his political future, both welcomed Nivelle's plan, which promised a decisive breakthrough within 48 hours. Haig's doubts were muted with his formal subordination to Nivelle's authority for the duration of the offensive, by the terms of the Calais agreement of 27 February 1917. Thus came about one of the most misguided Anglo-French strategic initiatives of the war.

Nivelle resurrected Joffre's 1915 plan of attacking both flanks of the German salient in France, but on a much greater scale. An Anglo-French holding attack, by one French and three British armies, was to take place in Artois and Picardy, between Arras and the river Oise, to draw in the enemy's strategic reserves. A breakthrough was then to be made a week later by the 53 divisions of Micheler's Reserve Army Group on the Chemin des Dames between Soissons and Berry au Bac. A third supporting attack was to be made by the French Fourth Army against the Moronvilliers massif in the Champagne. At Verdun Nivelle had made his reputation in a series of limited offensives, characterised by intensive artillery preparations, which had recaptured Forts Vaux and Douaumont (see Map 25). Such firepower-intensive methods did not translate to such a large-scale attack – instead the French were to use tanks for the first time, to compensate for weaker artillery support. Moreover Nivelle chose one of the strongest positions on the German front for his assault. Over nearly three years the German army had turned the ridge above the river Aisne into a defensive fortress, criss-crossed with trenches and barbed wire entanglements, honeycombed with dug-outs, and dotted with machine-gun nests. Even if the ridge could be stormed, fresh enemy reserves waited behind the crest, sheltered from French artillery fire on the steep reverse slope.

Things started to go wrong while the offensive was being prepared. In mid-March the Germans made a strategic withdrawal between Arras and Soissons, to the prepared defensive positions of the Hindenburg line. This both took the wind out of Nivelle's planned holding attack, and freed up more reserve divisions to meet the coming offensive. The preliminary offensive was scaled down, its centrepiece now being a British attack to capture Vimy ridge. Briand's increasingly fragile ministry fell on 17 March. Paul Painlevé, the new minister of war, had always doubted Nivelle's confident claims that he would break the German line,

and tried to scale-down the offensive. Nivelle's threats to resign and topple the new ministry dissuaded him, although by April the government no longer had confidence in its commander-in-chief. Finally, with the impending offensive the subject of intense speculation in Paris, any chance of surprise had been lost.

The British Third Army stormed Vimy ridge on 9 April 1917, demonstrating the effectiveness of the combined infantry–artillery–tank tactics which the British army had developed on the Somme. On 16 April, after a seven-day bombardment, the French assaulted on the Aisne front. Mangin's Sixth Army captured a number of their objectives on the left between Laffaux and Cerny, although in many places German counter-attacks drove the exhausted attackers back from their initial gains. On the right Mazel's Fifth Army, despite the support of 128 new Schneider heavy tanks, failed to capture Berry au Bac. The Fourth Army's supporting attack in Champagne on 17 April was also repulsed by strong enemy counter-attacks. Despite his failure to deliver the promised breakthrough in 48 hours, Nivelle decided to continue the offensive. Attacks and counter-attacks continued until 23 April, when President Raymond Poincaré intervened personally to halt the offensive. Follow-up operations in May secured a foothold on the crest of the ridge at Craonne. While the infantry had fought bravely, and penetrated between 3 to 8 kilometres (2 to 5 miles) into the enemy's deep and well-fortified defensive system, there was no decisive breakthrough. Overall the French army suffered 130,000 casualties, of which 30,000 were killed, which it could ill-afford.

Nivelle's offensive was over-ambitious. A return to manpower-intensive operations on the French front produced the same result as Joffre's 1915 attacks. Although ground was gained everywhere, it was at heavy cost since artillery support was thin. No decisive advance was made and in many places the French army was left in untenable positions, halfway up the slopes of the Chemin des Dames ridge. In this 'zone of friction' it was to suffer steady casualties throughout the summer. Above all, the failed offensive shattered the French army's weak morale, and widespread mutinies were to follow in protest against the costly offensive methods of the high command (see Map 33). The capture of Vimy ridge demonstrated what could be achieved on the battlefield if adequate material and firepower was deployed, although this first-day success was itself compromised by the follow-up attritional struggles north and south of Arras that dragged on into May. Altogether the British army suffered 158,000 casualties. Nivelle's gamble had been a costly disaster, both materially and morally. He was quickly shunted aside to a desk job, to be replaced by the more cautious Pétain, the other hero of Verdun.

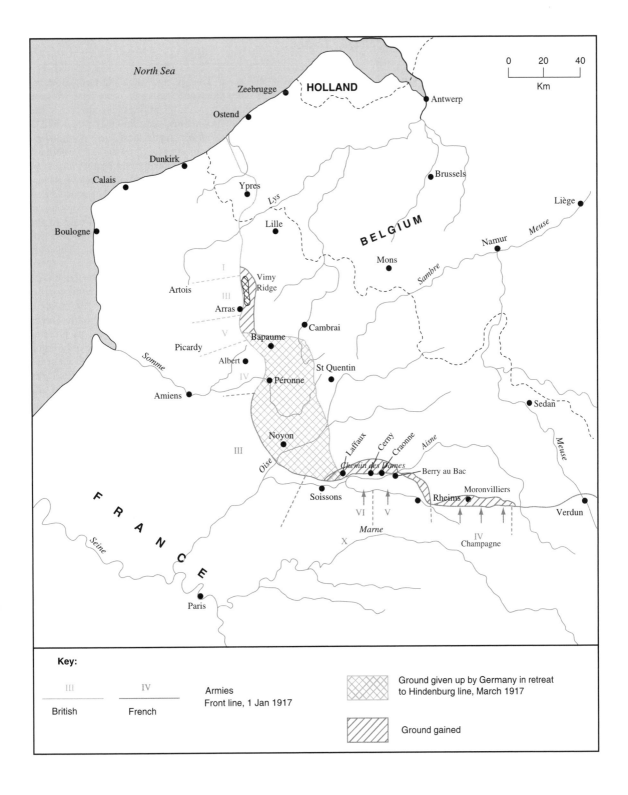

Key:

III	IV	
British	French	Armies Front line, 1 Jan 1917

Ground given up by Germany in retreat
to Hindenburg line, March 1917

Ground gained

Map 33: France Under Strain, 1917

By 1917, after three years of war, the belligerents' societies were beginning to fracture. In Russia two revolutions took the divided state out of the world war and into civil war (see Maps 31 and 49). In France, invaded and demoralised by successive failed offensives, a similar domestic crisis gripped the nation in 1917. The political consensus of the early years of the war, the so-called 'sacred union' (*union sacrée*) collapsed. Mutinies in her army, strikes in her industrial cities, a rapid turnover of ministries and calls for a negotiated peace were signs of war-weariness in the nation. Unlike backward Russia, France's modern society was able to weather the strains of 'total war' and emerge strengthened for the final fight to the finish with Germany.

Signs of political division were apparent even before Nivelle's failed spring offensive (see Map 32). Aristide Briand's government, in power since November 1915, lost the confidence of the Chamber of Deputies in March 1917 and fell. Alexandre Ribot's new government contemplated cancelling the impending offensive, which threatened a crisis in civil–military relations. When Nivelle's over-ambitious plan failed France reached her low point.

The unrest in France had military, social and political dimensions. From mid-April to early June there was widespread mutiny in the French army. Some 40,000 men in 68 divisions, mainly infantrymen who had attacked on the Aisne in April, were involved. The mutinies were primarily a soldiers' strike against conditions at the front and the way the high command was conducting military operations, rather than an anti-war protest, although there were widespread demands for a negotiated peace. In future, the ordinary soldiers insisted, their sacrifice should be in proportion to the military objectives desired. Nivelle was replaced by national hero Pétain, a soldiers' general who set about restoring order through a combination of judicious concessions, such as extra leave and a relaxation of military discipline, and selective punishment. Of over 3300 men convicted by military courts, 554 were sentenced to death, although only 49 executions were carried out. Importantly, the soldiers gained what they wanted when Pétain rethought military strategy for the western front. France was to adopt a strategic defensive while 'waiting for the Americans and the tanks' to give the allies an overwhelming material advantage. Judging it important in the interim to revive the army's morale by successful offensive action, Pétain determined on a series of limited actions to improve the army's tactical position. These offensives, at Verdun in August and on the Chemin des Dames in October (see Maps 25 and 37), were significant victories with light casualties. By the end of the year the army's fighting spirit was fully restored.

On the home front there was a wave of strikes in France's principal industrial cities. Starting in the Paris textile industry in January, and spreading throughout the spring to other cities and industries – building workers, transport workers, public employees, metalworkers and most importantly munitions workers – they threatened to undermine the war effort. Again these were not anti-war protests, but were indicative of growing war weariness and dissatisfaction at the economic and social impact of prolonged war – in particular increased prices of essential foodstuffs – which was causing hardship. Judicious concessions quelled the unrest in the short term. In Toulouse in June 1917 striking munitions workers returned to the factories once wages had been raised. However, there was simmering working-class discontent that would boil over into a general strike once the war was over.

There was no real political dimension to the strikes, although, as with the army mutinies, left-wing pacifist groups tried to take advantage of them for political purposes. This was symptomatic of a wider political crisis in France. Paul Painlevé succeeded Ribot as premier within six months, although his own ministry only lasted two months. His successor, Radical firebrand Georges Clemenceau, famously nicknamed 'the tiger', was made of stronger stuff. A long-standing critic of the way the government and high command had been conducting the war, he took a firm grip on France, in preparation for the decisive clash in 1918 – with good reason historians refer to 'Clemenceau's dictatorship'. He was not afraid to use troops against striking workers. When a further wave of strikes hit Paris in May 1918, at the height of the defensive crisis, he conscripted militant workers into the army. Left-wing defeatists were subject to 'show trials'. By these authoritarian means France was remobilised to carry on the fight, not for any imperialist agenda, but for her own freedom and security, and to justify and avenge the sacrifices of earlier years. After a crisis of confidence, government, army and citizens were prepared to see it through.

Events in France in 1917 typify the impact of total war on society. Everywhere workers were dissatisfied with prolonged economic hardship and soldiers with repeated sacrifice for no clear result. They began to question the judgement and legitimacy of traditional leaders, and the viability of the status quo. Rich industrialists were seen to be profiting from war while the workers and soldiers were making sacrifices of lifestyle and life. These developments behind the lines hastened the polarisation of society, exacerbating political and social differences and tension present before the war, and feeding into post-war radical politics. If European society was not hopelessly divided in 1914, it was by 1918. The longer the war went on the less likely it was that the old order would survive as its position was eroded by the strain.

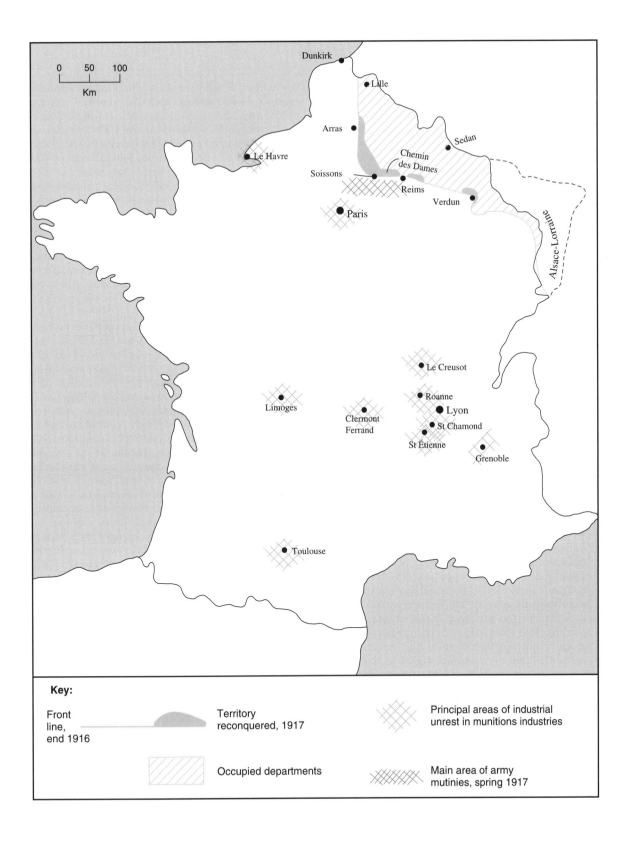

Key:

Front line, end 1916	Territory reconquered, 1917	Principal areas of industrial unrest in munitions industries
Occupied departments		Main area of army mutinies, spring 1917

Map 34: The Arab Revolt, 1916–18

During the First World War, as part of her war against the Turks, Britain attempted to build up allies among the Arab subjects of the Ottoman empire. Led by Sharif Hussain, the Hashemite Arabs of the Hedjaz region around the Muslim Holy Cities of Mecca and Medina became the most important of these allies. In 1916, they rose up in revolt against Ottoman rule. The British, and to a lesser extent the French, provided military supplies, finance and military advisers to help sustain the Arab revolt. For the British, the Hashemites were of military and imperial value: they could harry Ottoman forces in Arabia while also providing valuable allies for the British empire once the war was over and new powers replaced the old Ottoman empire. For the Hashemites, support from Britain would help them in their attempts to throw off Ottoman rule and create Hashemite-led Arab states in the Middle East. The Arab revolt began in June 1916 with a successful attack on the Ottoman garrison in Mecca. However, an assault on Ottoman troops in Medina, the terminus of the Hedjaz railway that connected the Hedjaz with Damascus to the north failed. Indeed, the garrison at Medina held out until ordered to surrender in 1919 by the Ottoman government in Istanbul.

Military operations during the Arab revolt concentrated on: firstly, hounding Ottoman forces along the Hedjaz railway; secondly, attacking Ottoman forces in the Trans-Jordan region around Amman; and, finally, supporting British-led troops of the Egyptian Expeditionary Force (EEF) based in southern Palestine in their final push at the battle of Megiddo in September–October 1918 (see Map 35).

Completed in 1906, the Hedjaz railway was ostensibly built to ferry Muslims going on the 'Hajj' pilgrimage to Mecca and Medina. It was, however, also a vital means of extending Ottoman control over the western portion of the Arabian Peninsula and became, during the First World War, a line of communication of considerable importance for the Turks. Its destruction, therefore, was a key aim for the main Hashemite army, the Northern Arab Army (NAA), led by Hussain's eldest son, Feisal. Estimates on the size of the Northern Arab Army vary from 8000 regular and 17,000 irregular troops to only 3000 rifles. Numbers of volunteers in the NAA certainly fluctuated, with periodic influxes of Arabs who had served in Ottoman forces and had been released from British prisoner-of-war (POW) camps to serve in the NAA. These former POWs helped form an officer corps for the NAA. From 1916 to 1918, NAA units attacked Ottoman blockhouses, stations and trains along the Hedjaz railway. The strategic significance of these attacks has been overestimated as Ottoman forces kept open the 1200-kilometre (750-mile) line from Damascus to Medina. However, in May 1918, an NAA force led by a British officer, Lt-Colonel Alan Dawnay, blew up a long section of the railway 80

kilometres (50 miles) south of Maan, after which the railway to Medina no longer functioned properly. The attacks on the Hedjaz railway also involved the enigmatic Colonel T.E. Lawrence ('Lawrence of Arabia'). While involved in attacks on the Hedjaz railway, Lawrence's most important task was to act as Britain's senior political liaison officer with Hussain and Feisal.

By 1918, Arab military operations had extended north to the Trans-Jordan region where, in January, a set-piece battle was fought with regular Ottoman forces at Tafilah near the shores of the Dead Sea. The battle of Tafilah was the exception to the Arab revolt, as forces of the NAA were not equipped or trained to fight Ottoman forces in open battle. Rather, the aim was to carry out a guerrilla-style campaign to worry and tie down Ottoman forces that would otherwise have been available for use against the EEF in southern Palestine.

The culmination of the Arab revolt came with the battle of Megiddo in September 1918, when the EEF launched its final assault in Palestine. In coordination with the EEF attack, the NAA attacked the Ottoman eastern desert flank before combining with EEF forces at the crucial rail junction of Deraa and pushing on to Damascus. Everything went to plan. The NAA pursued retreating Ottoman units – who were accompanied by a small German force – streaming north from Deraa. On 30 September–1 October 1918, Damascus fell.

The capture of Damascus emphasised the imperial-political element to the Arab revolt, as it was vital that the Arabs entered Damascus first to exclude French claims to the city. Therefore, the EEF tailored its operations at Damascus to give the appearance that Arab Hashemite forces entered 'first'. Once in the city, Hashemite forces took over the running of the city. The British ignored French protests that this went against the 'Sykes–Picot' Agreement of 1916. Lawrence, who rode into Damascus with Feisal's NAA, was the key liaison officer directing Arab operations and, once in Damascus, he helped establish Feisal as ruler. On 3 October 1918, the supreme commander of the EEF, Edmund Allenby, arrived in Damascus to confirm the Hashemite regime in Syria.

The Arab revolt was more significant politically than militarily. The military operations helped the main British-led force in Palestine with a guerrilla war on the Ottoman eastern flank, but the revolt was insufficiently strong to defeat the Ottoman armies in the region without the assistance of regular EEF troops. Politically, the British-sponsored Arab revolt was part of the transformation of the Middle East from one dominated by the Ottoman empire to a one ruled by local Arab rulers. Feisal's regime in Syria was eventually crushed by French forces in 1920 but Hashemite regimes in Trans-Jordan and Iraq were established and lasted until 1958 (Iraq) and to the present day in what is now Jordan.

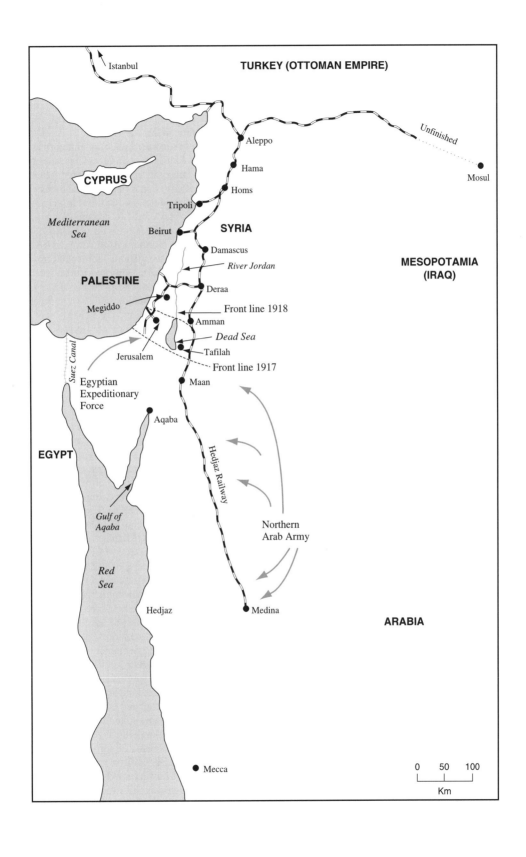

Map 35: Allenby's Offensive in Palestine

Before 1916, British-led forces in Egypt were on the defensive, keeping open the vital Suez Canal and repelling a Turkish attack across the canal at Deversoir in February 1915. In 1916, this changed as the British commander, Archibald Murray, went on the offensive, pushing forces into the Sinai Peninsula towards Palestine. His advance met with several setbacks before halting at Gaza in early 1917. In March and April 1917, Murray launched two assaults on Gaza, both of which the Turks comprehensively defeated. Murray's biggest achievement was to put in place the logistical infrastructure of railways, roads and water pipelines across the Sinai that would permit a British advance into Palestine.

After these defeats, Britain's war leader, David Lloyd George, dismissed Murray. Looking for a new, dynamic commander for the Palestine theatre of war, he chose Edmund Allenby, a western-front army commander. Allenby was unhappy at going to Palestine, seeing it as demotion, but independent command in a peripheral war theatre would make his name. In 1919, he would become a Field Marshal and a Viscount in recognition of his success in Palestine.

Allenby's arrival in Palestine in June 1917 revitalised the British-led force at Gaza, the Egyptian Expeditionary Force (EEF), whose morale had plummeted under Murray's command. Keen to push on in peripheral war theatres and to get Jerusalem as a Christmas present for the nation, Lloyd George sent Allenby the reinforcements he needed for a new offensive. Men and matériel poured into Palestine, augmenting Allenby's force to ten divisions. It was a remarkable mixture of nationalities: as well as British troops, there were Australian, Indian and New Zealand cavalry (or mounted) divisions, Arabs, Jews and contingents from the British West Indies, the French empire and Italy.

Having re-organised the EEF into two infantry corps (XX and XXI) and a cavalry corps (Desert Mounted Corps), Allenby began the Third Battle of Gaza on 31 October 1917. While he had a massive preponderance of artillery, Allenby eschewed another assault on the heavily defended Gaza town, in favour of a cavalry attack on the less well defended Beersheba at the eastern extremity of the Turkish lines. Allenby wanted to roll up the Turkish lines from the east. A dramatic Australian Light Horse cavalry charge took Beersheba on 31 October. A few days later, the infantry assaulted Gaza. Forced to retire, the Turks retreated north towards Junction station, hoping to stabilise the line south of Jerusalem. Allenby kept up the pressure, rotating his units so that fresh infantry was available for the assault on Jerusalem. After much hard fighting west of Jerusalem, the Turks withdrew from the city on 9 December 1917. Two days later, Allenby walked through the Jaffa gate into the city, read out a brief proclamation of martial law and left. For the first time since 1187, Jerusalem was back in Christian hands. The world press made much of the capture, turning Allenby into a modern-day Crusader, and it was a welcome propaganda boost for the Entente powers at a difficult time in the war.

The need to send the bulk of his infantry and some of his cavalry to France as reinforcements after Germany's March 1918 'Peace offensive' scuppered Allenby's plans to renew the offensive into north Palestine. Instead, he sent his men on two 'Trans-Jordan' raids across the river Jordan, March–May 1918, to capture Amman, break the Hedjaz railway and link up with pro-British Hashemite Arab forces in the Northern Arab Army (NAA) (see Map 34). Both raids – the official nomenclature for multi-divisional attacks – failed, lowering British prestige among Arab tribes in the region.

Allenby spent the summer of 1918 re-organising and training the raw troops – mostly Indian – sent to replace the men who had gone to France. He was not able to go back on the offensive until 19 September 1918, when his force of 11 divisions (4 cavalry, 7 infantry) attacked along the coastal plain of Palestine. The result was tremendous. After an infantry and artillery assault, the Turkish line crumbled and three cavalry divisions (one Australian and two Indian) poured through the ruptured line to exploit the victory, while 'Chaytor's' cavalry force pushed on Amman. Typically cautious, Allenby did not anticipate the extent of the Turkish collapse. Once aware of this, he ordered an advance on Damascus and beyond. Damascus fell on 1 October to Indian and Australian mounted troops. The cavalry – suffering badly from endemic malaria – then pushed on to Aleppo and Cilicia. The infantry, meanwhile, advanced up the coast, taking Beirut on 8 October. Helping the British from the desert flank, Arab troops of the NAA joined British forces at Deraa for the push on Syria. The attacking force had passed by the ancient mound of Megiddo in northern Palestine, the site of many battles, and this lent its name to Allenby's final battle. The victory at the Battle of Megiddo should be set against the poor state of the Turks in Palestine in September 1918. The Turkish high command denuded Palestine of troops and the Turks in Palestine in September 1918 were in no state to offer a protracted defence.

Allenby's victories in 1917 and 1918 were a welcome alternative to the mud and misery of France. His cavalcade through the holy land captured the imagination of the British public, and gave Britain a commanding position when it came to negotiating the political settlement in the Middle East after the war as British troops were in control of the whole region. While cavalry was used after 1918 in the Russian Civil War (even in the Second World War) the Palestine campaign was the swansong of cavalry; the last time that it acted as a decisive weapon of war.

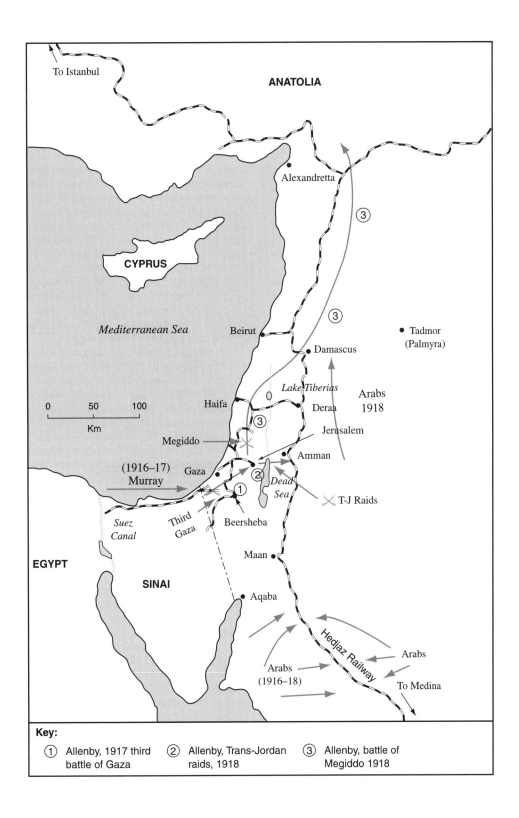

To Istanbul

ANATOLIA

Alexandretta

③

CYPRUS

Mediterranean Sea

③

Beirut

Damascus

• Tadmor
(Palmyra)

Lake Tiberias

Arabs
1918

Haifa

Deraa

③

Megiddo

Jerusalem

(1916–17)
Murray

Amman

Gaza

② *Dead
Sea*

T-J Raids

①

Third
Gaza

Beersheba

*Suez
Canal*

Maan

EGYPT

SINAI

Aqaba

Hedjaz Railway

Arabs

Arabs
(1916–18)

To Medina

0   50   100
Km

Key:

① Allenby, 1917 third
    battle of Gaza

② Allenby, Trans-Jordan
    raids, 1918

③ Allenby, battle of
    Megiddo 1918

Map 36: The Third Battle of Ypres (Passchendaele)

Since October 1914, when Germany had established naval bases on the Belgian coast, at Ostend and Zeebrugge, British strategists had advocated a military offensive in Flanders to nullify this threat to British maritime communications. By the summer of 1917 the strategic situation dictated an attack from the Ypres salient to capture those ports. Germany's unrestricted submarine offensive from February 1917 (see Map 29) obliged the army to do something before the war was lost at sea. The French army's temporary incapacity following the May 1917 mutinies meant that the British army also had to do something to take pressure off its ally. Freed from his obligation to conform to French strategy, Haig would be able to mount an independent British offensive for the first time.

Haig's plan had four stages. Firstly, a preliminary 'bite and hold' offensive to capture the commanding Messines–Wytschaete ridge to the south of the Ypres salient. This attack was executed with considerable skill by Herbert Plumer's Second Army on 7 June 1917. Assisted by 19 huge underground mines, 12 British divisions stormed the ridge, advancing up to 3 kilometres (2 miles) and taking 7500 prisoners. Stage two was to take the high ground east of Ypres, between the villages of Gheluvelt and Passchendaele. The third stage was an assault from this ridge against the railway junctions of Roulers and Thourout, to interrupt German communications in the coastal sector. Finally British divisions would break out along the coast from Nieuport, to support an amphibious landing between Middelkerke and Ostend. Attacking in Flanders had advantages and disadvantages. The low-lying water-logged ground would be difficult to negotiate in wet weather – 'a duck's march' as Foch pithily described it. However, with vital railways and ports to protect, the German army would be obliged to stand and fight. Although Haig recognised that the advance would be slow and systematic, as on the Somme, he believed that by forcing the enemy to battle further attrition might finally break their will to resist. Although after the Somme Haig's political masters in London had deep misgivings about such a method, they felt unable to overrule their military advisers who were unanimously in favour of the offensive.

The offensive – officially the Third Battle of Ypres – opened on 31 July 1917, a week later than planned after poor weather delayed artillery preparation. The initial assault was entrusted to Hubert Gough's Fifth Army. Unlike the more methodical Plumer, Gough hoped to take advantage of the preliminary bombardment to push on as far as possible on the first day, and to establish his army firmly on the main ridge at Gheluvelt. This was over-ambitious. Although the French First Army and XIV Corps on the left secured their objectives, the XVIII and XIX Corps in the centre failed to reach their final objective before being heavily counter-attacked. On the right the II Corps, charged with capturing the key Gheluvelt plateau, lost touch with its creeping barrage and was halted by enemy strongpoints and artillery. The next day the weather broke. Gough's divisions found themselves engaged in a succession of small-scale actions as they attempted to push on up the forward slopes of the ridge. Better progress was made when the weather improved in September. Plumer's Second Army was entrusted with the southern sector of the front, and in three carefully planned assaults using massive artillery support – the battles of the Menin Road Ridge (20 September), Polygon Wood (26 September) and Broodseinde (4 October) – it pushed slowly towards the crest. In mid-October the weather deteriorated again. On 26 October Gough's army made its final major push, the Canadian Corps securing the shattered village of Passchendaele on the northern end of the crest on 6 November. Thereafter the battle wound down into desultory trench fighting as the winter set in.

The German defence-in-depth, based around five lines of machine-gun nests and fortified strong-points rather than linear trench positions, was tenacious. For the first time a new and deadly poison, mustard gas, was employed to break up allied assaults. Although the German army held on against relentless pressure, the material and human costs were high: nearly 300,000 casualties and the realisation that the German army could not endure such spirit-sapping attrition indefinitely. Conditions were appalling for both sides: 'Lice, rats, wire entanglements, corpses, blood, schnapps, gas, guns and rubbish,' recorded German artist Otto Dix. 'This is the true nature of war.'

In three months the British army had advanced 8 kilometres (5 miles), at the cost of 280,000 casualties. Such losses were difficult to sustain; over the winter of 1917–18 British divisions had to be reduced from 12 to 9 fighting infantry battalions. Moreover, the enthusiastic volunteers of 1916 were now the tired 'old sweats' of 1917. British army morale reached a low point over the ensuing winter.

The allies' 1917 offensives had finally wrested control of the western front's strategic high ground from the enemy. With the allies poised to attack again in 1918 the German high command was forced to make a final gamble on a spring offensive to win the war (see Map 42).

The Passchendaele campaign remains controversial. Whether it should have taken place, or should have been continued given the heavy casualties and slow progress, is open to debate. The terrible weather – the wettest in Flanders for many years – certainly contributed to the fact that Haig's full intentions could not be realised. Yet Plumer's successful set-piece battles indicate that the British army did have the method and means to mount such an extensive operation, indicative of the progress made since the Somme.

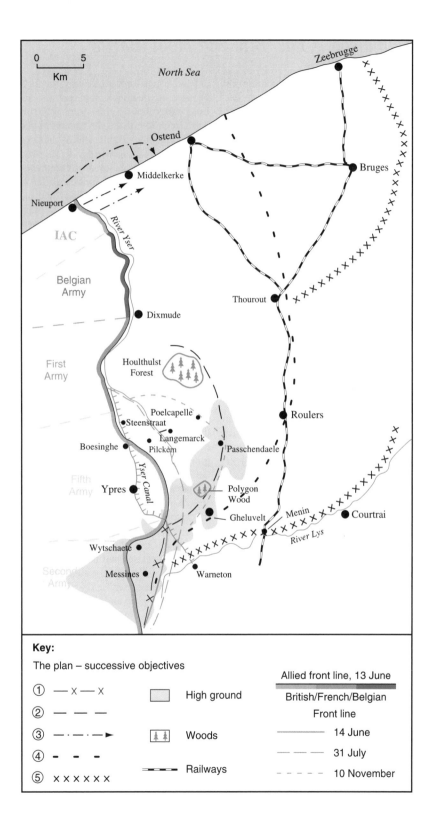

Key:

The plan – successive objectives

① — x — x

② — — —

③ —·—·—►

④ — — —

⑤ x x x x x x

| High ground |
| Woods |
| Railways |

Allied front line, 13 June

British/French/Belgian
Front line

——— 14 June

— — — 31 July

— - — - 10 November

Map 37: Malmaison – The 'Bite and Hold' Battle

The historian Cyril Falls dubbed the French army's autumn 1917 offensive to capture the Chemin des Dames ridge – the Battle of Malmaison – 'the perfect offensive'. In a meticulously planned and well-provisioned assault the French army threw the enemy off the commanding heights of the ridge in a matter of days. It was a striking contrast to its failure to take the position in Nivelle's spring offensive.

This success arose from the adoption of new methods by the French army after the mutinies of spring 1917. Nivelle's successor as commander-in-chief, Philippe Pétain, was an artillerist who as a corps and army commander had demonstrated consistent success with his methodical style of attack. His catchphrase, 'the artillery conquers, the infantry occupies', implied the use of massed artillery to facilitate the advance of the infantry with minimal casualties. It represented a sharp contrast to the manpower-intensive French offensives of the past. Over the summer of 1917, as the French army recovered from the mutinies, Pétain trained the whole French army in his offensive methods. Although strategically he felt that the allies should adopt a generally defensive posture until they were fully equipped for artillery-intensive warfare, and reinforced by American manpower, Pétain felt that to restore his army's morale after the mutinies it was necessary for it to mount successful limited offensive operations. These might not win the war, but were designed to improve the French army's tactical position for a later strategic offensive. Three such attacks were mounted by the French army in the summer and autumn of 1917: by the First Army in support of the British offensive at Ypres; by the Second Army at Verdun in August; and by the Sixth Army at Malmaison in October.

Nivelle's offensive had left a 'zone of friction' between the French army and the Germans along the southern slopes of the Chemin des Dames ridge. Repeated attacks and counter-attacks over the summer of 1917 were causing steady losses to the French, at a rate equivalent to that of Verdun in 1916, and they were determined to capture the crest of the ridge to end this wastage and gain observation over the German rear areas. General Maistre, commanding the Sixth Army, planned to assault the western end of the ridge, which formed a wide plateau, between Laffaux and Filain. The German defensive position, constructed over three years, was formidable: three lines of forward trenches backed by a support line of strongly fortified villages and farms – Allemant–Vaudesson–Malmaison Farm–Malmaison fort–Pargny–Filain – with intermediate pill-boxes, machine-gun nests and fortified quarries. To conquer the position Maistre prepared an intricate four-part artillery fire plan which demonstrates the sophistication of artillery techniques by this stage in the war. Heavy guns and trench mortars were to be precisely targeted on the enemy's

defensive positions to destroy them. Gas shells were to be used to neutralise the enemy's supporting artillery. Long-range heavy guns were to be used to isolate the battlefield, to prevent the enemy bringing up supplies and reinforcements. Lighter field guns were to be used to provide a creeping barrage to support the infantry as it advanced. Over 2000 artillery pieces were employed altogether, and over 3 million shells were stockpiled for the offensive. The reorganised and meticulously-trained infantry were to assault using new small-unit 'combined-arms' tactics, and were to be closely supported by tanks.

After a six-day bombardment the French attacked by stealth, with no change in the intensity of the bombardment to warn the enemy, on 23 October. Going 'over-the-top' before dawn and shrouded by thick fog, eight divisions advanced on a 12-kilometre (7½-mile) front. The artillery had done its job. One advancing French infantryman noted in his diary: 'What a terrain! It's frightful – everything is devastated, we stumble into huge craters, German corpses everywhere blown to pieces. Others overcome by gas dying. It's dreadful, but superb.' This overwhelming bombardment greatly facilitated the infantry advance; most of the shell-shocked German infantry who survived surrendered immediately the attackers fell upon them, and those who did not were unable to put up much resistance. It hampered the advance of the tanks however. Two-thirds of the 68 tanks deployed broke down or bogged down in the churned-up ground before they got beyond the German forward defences. Those that did get through proved valuable in the advance across the open plain on top of the plateau. Where resistance was met it was quickly overcome, either by close-range tank fire, or tactically sophisticated infantry assaults with hand grenades, machine guns, light trench mortars and flamethrowers. By the afternoon all the Sixth Army's objectives had been captured. On 27 October the Sixth Army followed up with an advance to the river Ailette. German losses were heavy: 38,000 killed and wounded, 12,000 prisoners, and 200 guns and 720 machine guns captured. The French had suffered fewer than 14,000 casualties. They were able to follow up their success in early November, when the Tenth Army to the east evicted the Germans from their now-untenable positions on the eastern extension of the ridge.

The battle of Malmaison is the definitive example of the 'bite and hold' tactics which the allied armies developed in 1917. This combination of massed artillery, well-armed and well-trained infantry, and close tank support, enabled them to conquer sections of the German defensive system at will. Yet while they could 'break in' to the enemy's deep defences, however strong, they had not yet developed techniques to 'break out' and restore mobile warfare to the battlefield.

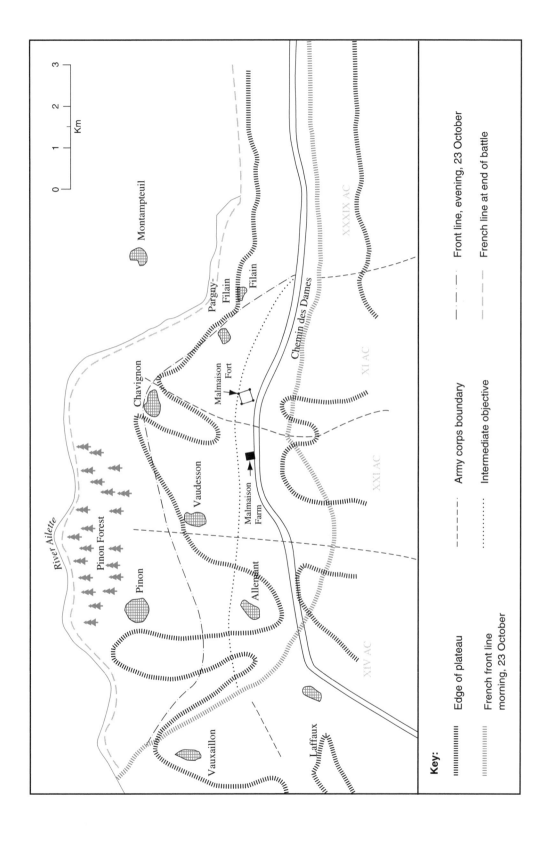

Key:

⊪⊪⊪⊪⊪ Edge of plateau	– · – · – Front line, evening, 23 October
▓▓▓▓▓ French front line morning, 23 October	– – – – French line at end of battle
– – – – Army corps boundary	
· · · · · · · Intermediate objective	

Montampteuil

Parguy-Filain

Filain

Chavignon

Malmaison Fort

River Ailette

Pinon Forest

Pinon

Vaudesson

Vauxaillon

Allemant

Malmaison Farm

Laffaux

Chemin des Dames

XXXIX AC

XI AC

XXI AC

XIV AC

Km
0 1 2 3

Map 38: The Battle of Caporetto – The Collapse of the Italian Army

The Battle of Caporetto, or the Twelfth Battle of the Isonzo, in October 1917 was a spectacularly successful Austro-Hungarian/German offensive against Italian forces on the upper reaches of the river Isonzo. It led to the collapse and retreat of Italian forces across the whole of north-eastern Italy. The origin of the Battle of Caporetto lay in the eleven Italian offensives led by Luigi Cadorna along the Isonzo river from May 1915 to September 1917, that threatened to break Austro-Hungarian resistance (see Map 20). Had Austro-Hungarian units broken, as seemed possible in August 1917, Italy could have captured the port of Trieste. Austria-Hungary appealed to Germany for help. In response, Germany sent six divisions, grouped with nine Austro-Hungarian divisions into the Fourteenth Army commanded by the German general, Otto von Below, and planning began for an assault against the Italians.

The Austro-Hungarian salient of Trentino (Alto Adige or South Tyrol) in the Italians' rear threatened their troops in the province of Venezia and along the Isonzo and was a possible launching point for an attack. However, the plan eventually agreed on was to deploy the Fourteenth Army opposite the town of Caporetto (Kobarid or Karfreit) in the southern part of the Julian Alps, relegating the Trentino salient to a subsidiary role. Central alliance forces would mass along a 25-kilometre (16-mile) stretch of front by Caporetto, utilising a small bridgehead held by Austria-Hungary on the west bank of the Isonzo river at the town of Tolmino (Tolmin or Tolmein) as a launching-off point for the assault. The initial attack plan was limited in scope: while the German-led Fourteenth Army attacked along the upper reaches of the Isonzo at Caporetto, two Austro-Hungarian armies would advance along the coast to the south. The objective was to push the Italians back from Trieste.

The terrain in the area chosen for the assault was very rough. While the mountains of the Caporetto sector did not reach the heights of the Carnic (Carnia) Alps, they still represented a formidable obstacle to any attacking force, especially with the presence of numerous fast-flowing rivers and steep rocky outcrops that would tangle up any advance. The Germans' response to this challenge was to employ new infiltration and shock tactics, first used at Riga on the Eastern Front in September 1917, to achieve maximum offensive punch. The new tactics dictated that fast-moving, highly trained storm-troops would attack after an intense gas and artillery bombardment. To keep up the momentum of the attack, once through the enemy front line they would bypass enemy strong points.

The Italians had an overall numerical advantage along the whole of the front but their troops suffered from poor command and low morale, the latter not helped by the casualties suffered in the earlier Isonzo battles. Along the Caporetto section of the front, the Italian Second Army, commanded by Luigi Capello, had just two battalions per mile of front, as opposed to the usual seven per mile. Although warned by Austro-Hungarian deserters of the impending attack, Capello, who was in ill-health in October 1917, did little to improve his weak defences. Greatly helped by morning mist, when the attack came on 24 October 1917, Italian battalions crumbled and German and Austro-Hungarian shock troops poured through the central part of the Italian line at Caporetto. Commanding an *Abteilung* – an ad hoc unit of several companies of mountain infantry of the *Alpenkorps* – was Erwin Rommel, later famous as the 'Desert Fox' of the Second World War, who won the *Pour le mérite* medal for his part in capturing the 1643-metre (5400-feet) Monte Mataiur (Matajur), one of only 687 Germans awarded the medal in the war. By 30 October, the breakthrough at Caporetto threatened Italian forces to the north and north-west (the Fourth Army and Carnic Force) and to the south (the Third Army), and soon a withdrawal along the whole front from the Gulf of Trieste to the Trentino was underway. The rout at Caporetto meant that the Italians surrendered territory along the Isonzo, on the Bainsizza plateau and the town of Gorizia (Görz or Gorica), all won at great cost in the earlier Isonzo battles. The trauma of Italy's mass withdrawal is vividly described in Ernest Hemingway's novel *A Farewell to Arms* (1929). 300,000 Italians surrendered, 350,000 deserted or simply went missing. The Second Army was destroyed as a fighting force. In addition, the Italians lost 10,000 men killed and 30,000 wounded. While logistical problems held up the advance, German and Austro-Hungarian units were across the river Tagliamento by 2–3 November. Italian forces then retired to the river Piave. Meanwhile, an Austro-Hungarian thrust down from the Trentino salient on 12 November threatened to turn the Piave defences. This attack was held, largely due to better-prepared Italian defensive positions. By 10 November, the last Italian units crossed the river Piave, just 30 kilometres (19 miles) from Venice, and set up a new defence line.

The defeat at Caporetto prompted the formation of the inter-allied Supreme War Council (9 November) to coordinate Entente strategy, whose first job was to rush to Italy an expeditionary force of six French and five British divisions to stiffen the Italian line along the Piave and at Asiago. The Italians, led by Armando Diaz, who replaced Cadorna as Italian commander on 8–9 November, held the line of the Piave against further Austro-Hungarian attacks in June 1918, before counter-attacking at the battle of Vittorio Veneto (23 October–3 November 1918), forcing back the Austro-Hungarian army, taking 300,000 prisoners and revenging the humiliation of Caporetto.

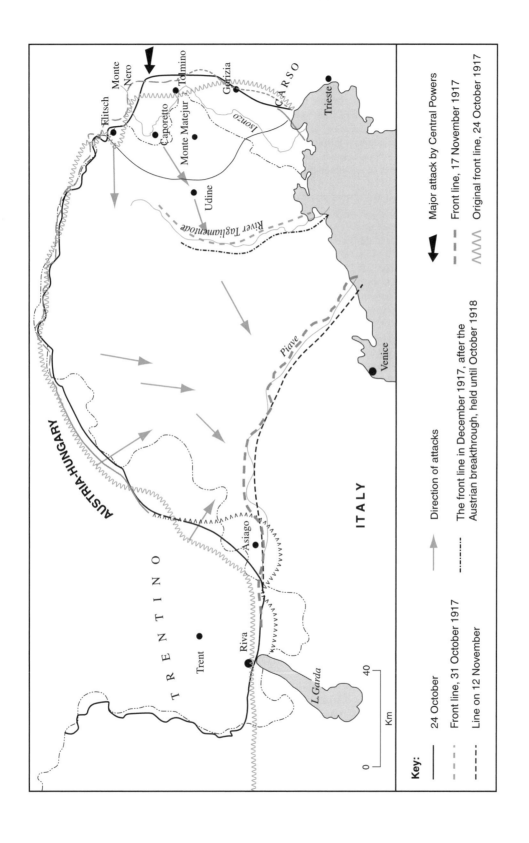

Key:

⎯⎯⎯⎯	24 October
– – – –	Front line, 31 October 1917
– · – · –	Line on 12 November
⬛	Major attack by Central Powers
– – – –	Front line, 17 November 1917
∧∧∧∧	Original front line, 24 October 1917
→	Direction of attacks
· · · · · ·	The front line in December 1917, after the Austrian breakthrough, held until October 1918

Labels on map: Monte Nero, Tolmino, Gorizia, CARSO, Trieste, Flitsch, Caporetto, Monte Matejur, Isonzo, Udine, River Tagliamento, AUSTRIA-HUNGARY, TRENTINO, Trent, Riva, L. Garda, Asiago, Piave, Venice, ITALY, Km, 0, 40

Map 39: The Battle of Cambrai – The Use of the Tank

The battle of Cambrai is generally remembered for the employment of tanks *en masse* for the first time. In reality it was not a tank battle, but the first example of a new style of mechanised 'combined-arms' warfare in which all the elements of the army – artillery, infantry, cavalry and tanks – would be synchronised in a new type of attack, foreshadowing the main features of twentieth-century land combat.

Unlike the set-piece battles of 1917, with their lengthy preliminary bombardment, Cambrai was conceived as a surprise. The British Third Army's objective was to break into Germany's Hindenburg line defensive system on a hitherto quiet sector of the British front, and to isolate and capture the communications centre of Cambrai, turning the flank of the German forces to the north. In this plan each fighting arm had a clearly defined role. The artillery was to neutralise the enemy's defences with an intensive surprise 'hurricane' bombardment before the infantry advanced, closely supported by the tanks. Once the infantry–tank assault had broken the Germans' second defensive position cavalry were to be pushed through to capture Cambrai.

The front of attack lay between two canals – the St Quentin canal to the south, and the dry Canal du Nord to the north. The attacking tanks and infantry would have to capture two ridges: Flesquières ridge topped by the village of the same name, and Bourlon ridge, crowned by Bourlon Wood. Capturing the second would give observation over the German communications in this sector and support the cavalry advance on Cambrai itself.

In Third Army's meticulous preparations priority was given to maintaining surprise. The presence of Havrincourt Wood behind the British line allowed tanks to be brought up in secret and concealed. The artillery was pre-registered silently by novel map-plotting and sound-ranging techniques, rather than observed ranging fire. The chosen point of attack was a strong sector of the Hindenburg line, with an outpost line backed by two deep and heavily wired fortified positions (Siegfried I and Siegfried II). However, being a 'quiet' sector, the line was thinly held by two German divisions with weak artillery provision and no close reserves.

The British attacked at 6.20am on 20 November. Six infantry divisions went over the top supported by 378 fighting and 98 support tanks, covered by morning mist and a smoke screen. The sudden bombardment by 1000 guns effectively neutralised and demoralised the defenders, allowing a rapid 'break-in' to the enemy defences. The Siegfried I position was overrun by midday and 4000 prisoners and 100 guns were taken. Advance guards established themselves across the St Quentin canal and the leading cavalry units pushed into the German rear areas. However, since they could only advance slowly across the open battlefield, not enough cavalry could be got across the canal to push on to Cambrai. The enemy had blown most of the bridges – one left intact at Marcoing was unfortunately demolished by a British tank. Altogether a penetration of 5–8 kilometres (3–5 miles) was achieved on the first day, about the same as the French had achieved at Malmaison the previous month (see Map 37). Yet all the first day's objectives had not been captured. The fortified village of Flesquières held up the centre of the attack, and Bourlon ridge remained in enemy hands.

The attack at Cambrai was initially perceived as a great success. For the first time church bells were rung in England to celebrate a victory. As with earlier battles, however, once initial momentum was lost and enemy reserves were encountered progress stalled. On 21 November it was decided to capture Bourlon ridge, rather than to push on towards Cambrai. However, tank support was much reduced owing to mechanical breakdown and the exhaustion of the crews, and a grim infantry slogging match ensued. Bourlon village was never captured. On 30 November the German defenders counter-attacked on the southern flank of the British penetration, using new 'storm-troop' tactics to break into the British defences. Only the recapture of Gouzeaucourt by the Guards Division prevented a disaster. However, in the face of continuous enemy pressure the British position was now untenable and they were forced to withdraw to a more defensible line.

Overall the battle of Cambrai must be judged a draw. Both armies demonstrated new and effective offensive methods, a forerunner of those to be employed in the more mobile operations of 1918. The tanks, while effective on the first morning, were as yet only a one-shot weapon, effective for 'break-in', but not 'break-out'. A combination of mechanical breakdowns, crew exhaustion and vulnerability to well-aimed artillery fire put 179 tanks out of action by the evening of 21 November. By the end of the battle fewer than a dozen tanks were still operational. More significant was the effective integration of tanks into an infantry–artillery–cavalry battle plan, and the positive results from careful preparation and thorough training before the attack. Despite its technical and tactical limitations, the tank's value in combined-arms warfare was confirmed at Cambrai, and it became an integral component of later allied offensives. By the end of the war the British had produced nearly 5000 tanks, and the French almost 4000. In 1918 new fast light tanks, the British Medium Mark A 'Whippet' and the French Renault FT-17, also appeared on the battlefield, to take on the mobile exploitation and pursuit roles previously assigned to the vulnerable cavalry. The German army, however, at Cambrai and in 1918, was able to demonstrate equally successful offensive tactical results with few or no tanks.

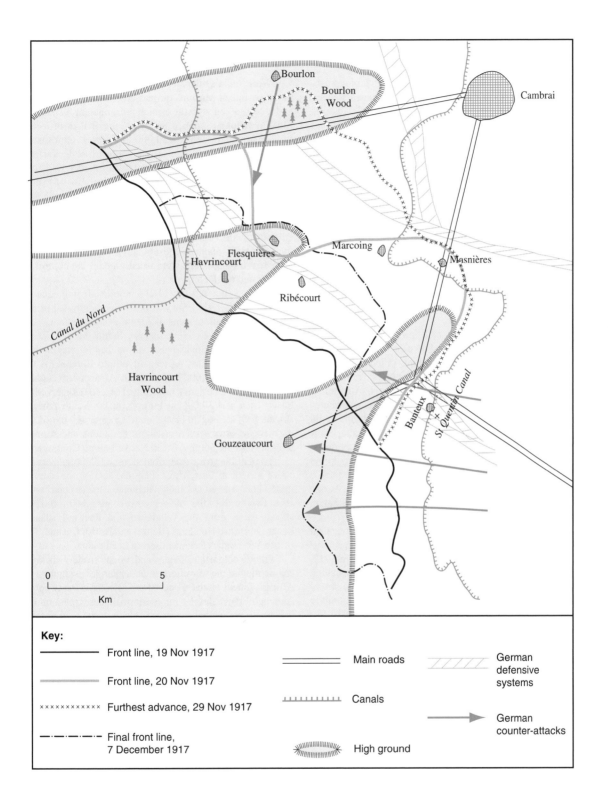

Bourlon

Bourlon
Wood

Cambrai

Canal du Nord

Flesquières
Havrincourt

Marcoing

Masnières

Ribécourt

Havrincourt
Wood

Banteux

St Quentin Canal

Gouzeaucourt

0   5

Km

Key:

———	Front line, 19 Nov 1917
———	Front line, 20 Nov 1917
××××××××××	Furthest advance, 29 Nov 1917
—·—·—·—·—	Final front line, 7 December 1917

═════	Main roads
⊥⊥⊥⊥⊥⊥	Canals
𝍢𝍢𝍢𝍢	High ground

▨▨▨	German defensive systems
➝	German counter-attacks

Map 40: Empires at War

When war broke out in 1914, the protagonists' empires automatically joined. Britain's imperial contribution varied between the 'white' (Australia, Canada, Newfoundland, New Zealand and South Africa), 'brown' (India) and 'black' (Africa/West Indies) dominions/colonies. While 'white', 'brown' and 'black' dominions all provided combat troops, black African soldiers (some 56,000) were usually deployed outside Europe. Britain, however, employed black Africans in labour units in Europe. Excepting India, in 1914 Britain's imperial territories had tiny armies supported by part-time militias. Once war started, the white dominions had to create expeditionary forces from scratch. Meanwhile, France recruited indigenous soldiers from her empire in Africa and Indo-China for the war fronts and for labour duties behind the lines. Belgium and Portugal also tapped the resources of their empires, as did Russia, whose land-based empire stretched into the Caucasus, Central Asia and Siberia.

Australia (13.4% white male population mobilised) formed an Australian Imperial Force for service overseas and in late 1914 the first troopships sailed for Europe. With only 5 million inhabitants, Australia, like most of the empire, gave heavily for the war. Although Australians never voted for conscription, they nevertheless contributed five volunteer infantry divisions, mounted troops (light horsemen), sailors and airmen. Unlike Australia, New Zealand (19.3% mobilised) introduced conscription in 1916. While Maoris were exempt, over 2000 joined up. As a proportion of her 1.1 million population, New Zealand's contribution to the war effort was extraordinary. She raised a New Zealand Division that fought with Australian forces (as ANZACS).

In Canada (13.4% mobilised), the only dissent against the war came from the minority French-speaking separatist Quebecois community. Conscription, introduced in 1917, met with little opposition from the English-speaking majority. While the Canadian army was only 3100 strong in 1914, Canada organised a Canadian Expeditionary Force, the first recruits reaching Britain in late 1914. By early 1915, the 1st Canadian Division entered the line. By late 1915, there was a second Canadian division (in a Canadian corps), augmented by two more divisions in 1916 and a fifth in 1917 (later disbanded). The Canadian-born Arthur Currie took command of the corps in June 1917. Considered something of a shock force, the Canadians stormed Vimy Ridge in April 1917 (see Map 32) and performed well against the Germans in late 1918. Newfoundland, separate from Canada until 1949, contributed 6500 men of the Newfoundland Regiment; others served with Canadian forces, the Royal Navy (through the Newfoundland Naval Service) and in a forestry battalion. The Canadian navy, formed in 1910, was a tiny force.

While India's rulers feared revolt from the large Muslim minority, Indian Muslims did not upset Britain's war effort and many served with the British in campaigns against the Muslim Ottoman empire. In 1914, the British-officered Indian army of some 150,000 men was unprepared materially and psychologically for modern-style warfare. Nevertheless, an Indian corps of two infantry divisions and a cavalry brigade served in France in 1914–15 where it suffered badly, some 'native' battalions suffering 100% casualties before being pulled out in late 1915. Thereafter, Britain used Indian troops for peripheral operations in Palestine, Gallipoli, Mesopotamia and East Africa. Except for campaigns such as Mesopotamia (before 1916) (see Map 16), Indian troops were usually under the control of London and not Delhi.

While South Africa (11.1% mobilised) immediately offered help in 1914, this was not welcomed by all of her Afrikaner population, some of whom revolted in September 1914 (see Map 12). Nevertheless, South African forces invaded German South-West Africa before contributing troops to fight in East Africa, Egypt and Europe. Of the approximately 145,000 white South Africans (excluding 5716 white Rhodesians) who joined up, 40,000 served in East Africa and 30,000 in Europe (in the South African Brigade). Of the 86,000 black South Africans who joined up, the vast majority served in labour battalions and support units such as the South African Native Labour Contingent.

The Caribbean area contributed some 15,000 soldiers for active service in East Africa, Palestine and on the western front. Others served in labour battalions. Jamaica contributed about two-thirds of the soldiers; other contingents, 100–1000 strong, came from the Windward and Leeward islands, Bahamas, British Honduras (Belize) and British Guyana. The British West Indies Regiment served in Palestine.

French colonial resources and troops made a massive contribution to the war effort. In particular, large numbers of Africans fought on the western front in colonial army corps. Although France did not impose formal conscription on the indigenous population (excepting Algeria), she used a series of coercive measures to encourage recruitment in Algeria, Madagascar, Morocco, Senegal and Tunisia. Colonial *Tirailleur* (rifle) units served (mainly) on the western front. The French recruited the *Tirailleurs Sénégalais* predominantly from French West Africa. French Equatorial Africa was not considered 'martial' enough for recruitment purposes until 1917 when manpower shortages became acute. The French also deployed 42,883 men of the Foreign Legion. Amid the mud and misery of the western front, France's African troops generally performed well, sharing with the French *poilu* a sense of common suffering, notwithstanding the fact that they were kept in special camps when resting to avoid contact (especially sexual) with French civilians.

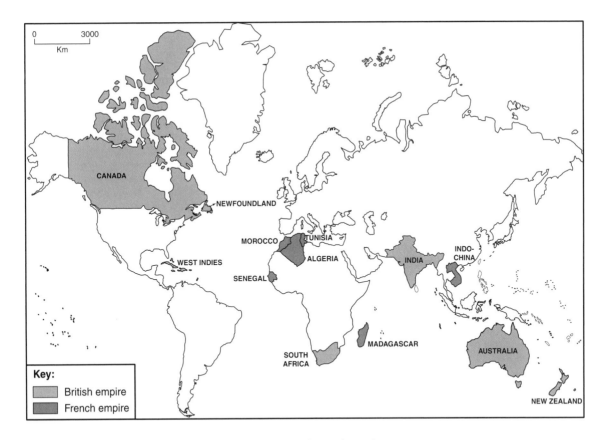

Estimated mobilisation and expenditure of the British and French empires

	Troop mobilisation	Approximate cost of the war (US$ 1981 equivalent)	Casualties
British empire			
Australia	412,953 (*c*.381,1000)	$1.4 billion	208,690 (*c*.60,000)
Canada	628,964 (*c*.442,400)	$1.7 billion	208,700 (58,990)**
India	1,440,437* (1,096,000)	$601 million	128,750 (62,060)
Newfoundland	11,922		(1–2000)
New Zealand	128,525 (*c*.98,900)	$378 million	58,030 (16,710)
South Africa	145,000 (white) (136,000)	$300 million	19,150 (7000)***
	86,000 (black) (77,000)		Unknown
West Indies	(12–15,000)		Unknown
*French empire****			
Algeria	(150,000)		(36,000)
Indo-China	(43,000)		(2000)
Malagasy/Madagascar	(34,000)		(4000)
Morocco	(14,000)		(Unknown)
Sénégalais*****	(150,000)		(29,000)
Tunisia	(39,000)		(10,000)

Number in brackets equals those who served abroad and those killed.

*Some put this figure at 1,680,000.

**Including Newfoundland.

***Whites only. Some authors give a much lower figure of 76,000 for numbers of South Africans who served abroad.

****These figures are for European service and include white settlers. A further 150,000 indigenous troops served in Africa and Indo-China.

*****The term Sénégalais was used for all sub-Saharan French African regiments with the exception of Malgache troops from Madagascar/Malagasy.

Map 41: The Treaty of Brest-Litovsk, March 1918

The November 1917 revolution (all dates Gregorian calendar) brought to power a Bolshevik regime willing to agree a separate peace. Not only did the Bolsheviks feel that Russia could stand no more war, they were sure that peace would presage wider workers' revolutions across Europe. For the Central Powers, peace with Russia meant that they could tap into Russia's grain supplies to feed Austria-Hungary's starving cities, and it would release German troops for offensive operations in France.

In November 1917, Leon Trotsky approached the Central Powers about an armistice and a Bolshevik delegation set off for Brest-Litovsk, in German-occupied Russia, to join diplomatic delegations from Austria-Hungary, Bulgaria, Germany, Turkey and the Ukraine. Notwithstanding these delegations, the real arbiter of power at Brest-Litovsk was the German military. Led by Adolf Yoffe, Lev Kamenev and Lev Karakhan, the Bolshevik team included workers, sailors, soldiers and women, all symbols of the new regime and its revolutionary democracy. But what of the peasants? They had been forgotten and so as he sped through Petrograd (St Petersburg) on the way to the station Yoffe picked up off the street an old peasant man, Roman Stashkov. Expecting to be taken to Petrograd's Nikolaevsky station, from whence he could get to his village, Stashkov instead set off in the opposite direction to Brest-Litovsk from Petrograd's Warsaw station with Yoffe and he duly entered diplomatic history at Brest-Litovsk as the 'plenipotentiary representative of the Russian peasantry'. While his crude table manners raised eyebrows at the lavish banquets held at Brest-Litovsk, Stashkov did get a smile from one stony-faced German waiter when he, in response to the question at supper of whether he wanted red or white wine, asked 'which one is the strongest?'

In early December, the Bolsheviks accepted a temporary one-month armistice, thereafter dragging out the talks while simultaneously agitating for revolution among the German workers and soldiers present, and distributing revolutionary anti-war literature behind enemy lines. In late December/ early January, Trotsky arrived to replace Yoffe, planning to use his negotiating skills to stall the talks for as long as possible. Meanwhile, the German Third Supreme Command of Erich Ludendorff and Paul von Hindenburg, tiring of Bolshevik methods, looked to get tough by once again driving east (*Drang nach Osten*), fulfilling a long-held German aim of imperial expansion into Russia.

The Germans also hoped to sign a separate peace with Ukranian nationalists, thus splitting the Russians and turning the rich lands of the Ukraine into vassal territory. At the end of December, the Germans demanded Poland and large parts of Latvia (Courland), Lithuania and Estonia from the Bolsheviks. Trotsky wanted to walk out of the talks, declare the war over but refuse to sign a peace. Instead, he stalled,

spinning out the talks into January 1918. On 9 February, the Germans presented him with a final ultimatum: if a peace were not signed, the Central Powers would attack. Having signed a separate peace with the Ukraine on 9 February – after which the Ukraine sent 300 truckloads of grain per day as a tribute to Austria-Hungary and Germany – the Germans had a strong hand, although Trotsky still refused to sign, declaring the slogan of 'no peace no war', and walking out of the talks on 10 February. Perplexed by this approach to diplomacy, the Germans attacked on 17/18 February (Operation *Faustschlag*), German and Austro-Hungarian troops advancing the huge distance of 240 kilometres (150 miles) in five days against almost no resistance.

It was now that the Bolshevik leader Lenin intervened. On 18 February, Lenin sent a telegram to Berlin accepting enemy terms. It was now Germany's turn to play for time, believing that she might be able to capture Petrograd. In a panic, Lenin now called for resistance and planned to evacuate Petrograd. Finally, on 23 February, the Germans accepted Lenin's offer. The Germans now asked for more, demanding all the land that their troops had occupied in the war, including the territory taken in the recent fighting (18–25 February). This meant the loss of Poland, Ukraine, White Russia (Belorussia), most of the Baltic states and parts of Russia proper. On 24 February 1918, Russia accepted Germany's terms.

The treaty was finally signed on 3 March. As no one wanted to put their names to such a shameful peace, a second-rate Bolshevik delegation went to Brest-Litovsk for the signing. Russia paid 6 billion gold marks in reparations and lost Poland, White Russia, Finland, Latvia, Estonia and Lithuania. She also lost swathes of territory in Transcaucasia to Turkey. All in all, she lost 34% of her population (55 million people), 32% of her agricultural land, 54% of her industrial base and 89% of her coal mines. This was a ruthless peace that showed what a German 'peace' for Europe would have looked like if she had won the war.

Brest-Litovsk facilitated the movement of German troops to France for the 'Peace offensive' (see Map 42). However, this was not straightforward as some 1.5 million German soldiers had to remain in Russia to keep order and enforce the treaty. Indeed, a breakdown of the German divisions used in the Ludendorff offensives shows that many of them had never come from the eastern front. However, psychologically Russia's defeat confirmed the strategy of Ludendorff and Hindenburg that the moment had come to launch their final offensive in the west. Brest-Litovsk also caused friction within the Central bloc with Bulgaria and Austria-Hungary resentful at the emphasis given to German interests. The armistice of 11 November 1918 voided the Treaty of Brest-Litovsk.

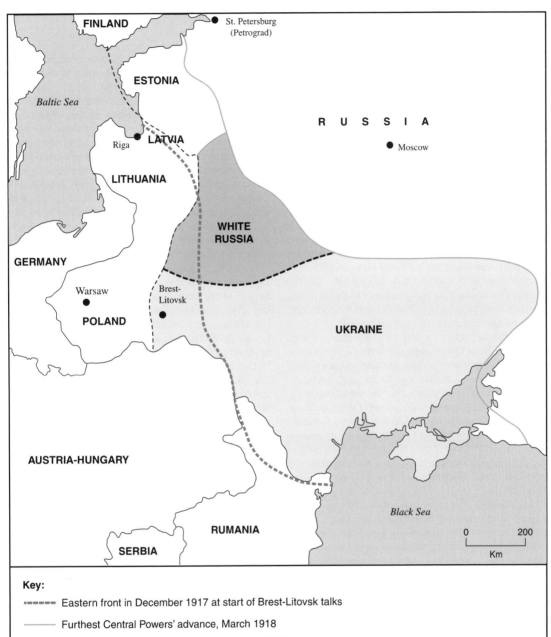

FINLAND

St. Petersburg
(Petrograd)

ESTONIA

Baltic Sea

R U S S I A

Riga · LATVIA

Moscow

LITHUANIA

WHITE
RUSSIA

GERMANY

Warsaw

Brest-
Litovsk

POLAND

UKRAINE

AUSTRIA-HUNGARY

Black Sea

0   200

Km

RUMANIA

SERBIA

Key:

━━━ Eastern front in December 1917 at start of Brest-Litovsk talks

──── Furthest Central Powers' advance, March 1918

- - - - Russia relinquishes rights to area to west of this line
after Brest-Litovsk

━ ━ ━ Northern and western boundary of independent Ukraine agreed with
Central Powers, Jan. 1918

Independent Ukraine 1917–1920

White Russia (Independent 1919–21)

Map 42: The German Spring 1918 Offensive

By the end of 1917 the allies had gained tactical ascendancy on the western front, although the Bolshevik revolution and Lenin's immediate call for a peace in the east handed the strategic initiative back to Germany. In the war of attrition, Anglo-French forces were feeling the effects. Both allied armies had to reduce the fighting strength of their divisions over the winter, and to disband some divisions entirely to fill up others. Additional weaponry and battalion reorganisation made up for this reduction in manpower with greater tactical flexibility and firepower, making the smaller divisions of 1918 more effective than their larger predecessors in the new 'combined-arms' warfare. Nevertheless, until the expanding American army could make its weight of numbers count, the allies chose to follow Pétain's defensive strategy in the west. The British army was obliged to take over more of the French defensive line, stretching its line dangerously thin. In order not to hand the initiative completely to the Germans, plans were made to create an allied General Reserve under Foch to counter-attack any German offensive.

In contrast, victory in the east freed-up German resources which could be re-deployed to the west. However, problems of transportation, food supply and policing obliged Germany to keep 1.5 million men in the east. As battle-hardened veterans were shipped to the west, moreover, many deserted as their troop trains crossed Germany. It was symptomatic of the crisis of morale that gripped Germany by this point. Hindenburg and Ludendorff were determined to launch a final 'Victory Offensive' to try to force a military decision before the German home front, starving after four winters of allied blockade and crippled by industrial strikes, collapsed.

The German offensive, codenamed 'Michael', was designed to split the British and French armies in front of Amiens. A short but immensely powerful hurricane bombardment to neutralise the enemy's defences was to be followed by an assault by elite 'storm-troop' divisions, tasked with bypassing points of resistance and infiltrating the enemy's deep defensive system. Second-class 'mopping-up' divisions would then subdue any resistance. Although tactically sophisticated, the German offensive had no strategic rationale other than to break the allied front and restore mobile warfare, in an attempt to defeat the allied armies in the field.

On 21 March 1918, 76 German divisions, supported by over 10,000 guns, 1070 aeroplanes, and 160 tanks (mostly captured from the allies) attacked the Anglo-French front between Arras and La Fère, in the biggest attack seen on the western front since 1914. Covered by fog, the storm-troopers penetrated the British Fifth Army's thinly held front. Nevertheless, fierce resistance by rear-area troops in hastily organised defensive positions took a heavy toll of the advancing German divisions. It took three days for the attackers to pass through the Fifth Army's 'battle zone', during which they suffered heavy losses. The British Third Army to the north, and the French Sixth Army to the south of the gap, held the enemy in their 'battle zone'. Although a genuine breakthrough had been achieved on the western front for the first time, the impetus of the German advance had been absorbed, and allied resistance had not been destroyed. Hungry and well-beyond their own supply lines, those German troops who did push through fell to looting the well-stocked allied supply dumps which they found behind the front. Although the Germans had inflicted 248,000 casualties and taken 90,000 prisoners, they suffered 239,000 casualties themselves, exhausting their 90 best assault divisions in the process.

Although Anglo-French arrangements for mutual support at the junction of the two armies rapidly collapsed in face of the strength and speed of the German assault, the allies improvised effectively to contain the German breakthrough. At Doullens on 26 March, Foch was appointed to coordinate the operations of the allied forces in front of Amiens. On 3 April at Beauvais he was given powers to coordinate all allied operations on the western front. For the first time the allies had a unified military command. French reserves were hurried north to maintain contact with the retiring British right wing, and fresh American divisions were pushed into the breach. A defensive line was re-established before the Germans reached the vital rail-junction at Amiens.

Germany followed up with a series of smaller offensives in the following months. On 9–10 April 55 divisions attacked the British First and Second Armies around Armentières, south of the Ypres salient, in operation 'Georgette'. Although obliged to give up the ground won in the Third Battle of Ypres the previous autumn, the British, reinforced by fresh French divisions, contained the attempt to break through to the Channel ports. On 27 May, in operation 'Blücher', 43 divisions attacked the French on the Aisne front. The heaviest German artillery bombardment of the war smashed in the thinly-held allied front, and within five days the Germans had captured Soissons and once again reached the river Marne at Château-Thierry. Hastily improvised American resistance held them before they could break through and threaten Paris. A final assault, 'Marneschüte-Reims', by 52 under-strength divisions on either side of Reims on 15 July, was contained, and counter-attacked successfully on 18 July (see Map 44).

In their 1918 offensive Hindenburg and Ludendorff achieved notable tactical successes, but strategic purpose was lacking, and victory eluded them. Their army could ill-afford the casualties, or to weaken their own defensive positions. Their last push for military victory – always a gamble – had failed.

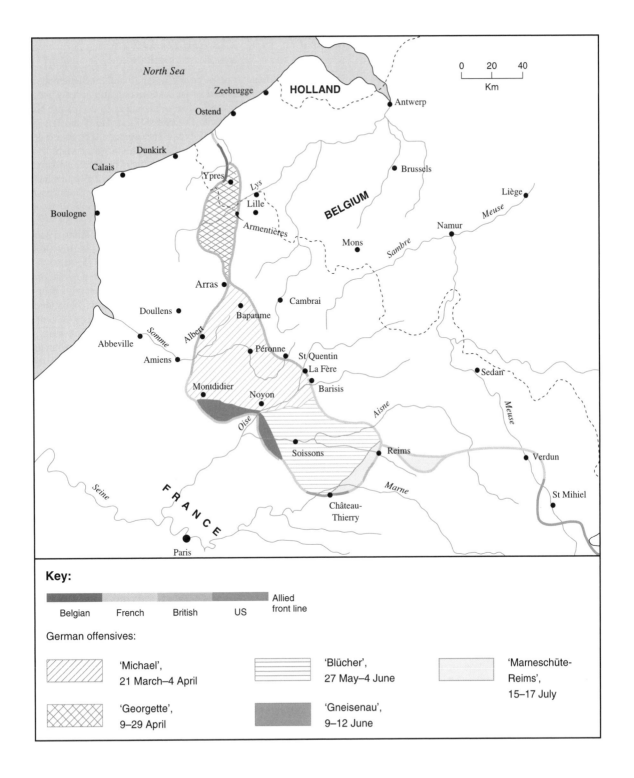

Key:

Allied front line

Belgian   French   British   US

German offensives:

'Michael', 21 March–4 April

'Georgette', 9–29 April

'Blücher', 27 May–4 June

'Gneisenau', 9–12 June

'Marneschüte-Reims', 15–17 July

North Sea

HOLLAND

Zeebrugge

Ostend

Antwerp

Dunkirk

Calais

Ypres

Lys

Brussels

Liège

Boulogne

Lille

Armentières

BELGIUM

Meuse

Namur

Mons

Sambre

Arras

Cambrai

Doullens

Bapaume

Albert

Abbeville

Somme

Péronne

St Quentin

La Fère

Sedan

Amiens

Montdidier

Noyon

Barisis

Aisne

Meuse

Oise

Soissons

Reims

Verdun

Seine

F R A N C E

Marne

St Mihiel

Château-Thierry

Paris

0   20   40

Km

Map 43: Foch's Advance to Victory – The 'Hundred Days'

Throughout the months of defence against Germany's spring offensive, Foch, the new allied generalissimo, had looked for the opportunity to counter-attack and regain the initiative. The opportunity came in July, when four French armies (including British and American divisions) supported by 750 tanks, 2100 guns and over 1000 aircraft, attacked the flanks of the German salient on the river Marne. The Second Battle of the Marne was a decisive success, the German army being driven back 35 kilometres (21 miles) to the rivers Aisne and Vesle. It was the first of a concerted series of successful allied offensives, the 'hundred days', which broke the fighting power of the German army and forced Germany to sue for an armistice.

Foch's counter-offensive strategy, the 'General Battle' (*bataille generale*), represented the outcome of four years of experience and reflection upon the new style of matériel-intensive warfare. Foch recognised that the enemy's line could not be decisively broken – enemy reserves could always plug any gap in the line before the allies could push through. Nevertheless he concluded that by concerted and unrelenting pressure the enemy's whole line could be destabilised. A successful 'break-in' offensive on one section of the front would allow for exploitation laterally rather than forwards. A series of 'waves' would wash the enemy out of France. At the same time constant fighting would complete the attrition of the enemy's divisions, allowing them no time for rest or reinforcement. By the summer of 1918 Foch had the manpower and matériel, and the necessary authority over the various allied armies, to put this strategy into practice.

On 8 August the British Fourth Army, attacking with over 400 tanks alongside the French First Army, launched a surprise offensive to disengage Amiens. In one day the allies advanced 7 kilometres (4 miles), and by the end of the battle four days later they had captured almost 30,000 prisoners and over 650 guns. The 8 August, Ludendorff later recorded in his memoirs, was the 'black day' of the German army. From now on Germany would be fighting for survival. The German retreat from Amiens was followed up by British and French attacks on either side of the Amiens front, against Bapaume and Lassigny. By mid-September the British army had broken the Drocourt–Queant 'switch line', the forward position of the Hindenburg line, and French and American forces had re-crossed the river Aisne. The Germans had been driven from all the ground they had gained in the spring, and were back in their main defensive system, the Hindenburg line.

Foch was faced with a crucial decision. Should he continue to attack and hope to win the war in 1918, or wait until 1919 when American manpower and allied munitions and weapons production would give the allies an overwhelming superiority? After consulting his army commanders, Foch chose to press on. Between 26 and 29 September a general offensive was launched along the allied fronts, armies coming successively into action to destabilise the whole German front. The British First, Third and Fourth Armies attacked and broke the western section of the Hindenburg line, enveloping Cambrai (see Map 45). Simultaneously the French First Army broke the Alberich defensive position, the eastern extension of the Hindenburg line, while a Franco-Anglo-Belgian army group broke through in Flanders, and a Franco-American army group advanced in the Meuse-Argonne sector.

As the army's resistance collapsed at the front, a constitutional revolution took place in Germany (see Map 46). The new liberal-socialist government asked the allies for an Armistice on 4 October. While armistice negotiations went on the allied armies followed up the retreating enemy. By the cessation of hostilities, at 11am on 11 November 1918, the allied armies had reached the line Ghent–Maubeuge–Mezières–Sedan. Symbolically the British army ended the war at Mons, the scene of its first encounter with the enemy. Foch's next planned offensive, on the hitherto quiescent Lorraine front on 14 November, which would have taken the allied armies into German territory, did not take place. Foch knew that the German army was beaten. Over the course of the 'advance to victory' the allied armies between them had captured 385,000 prisoners and 6600 guns. Germany's already weakened divisions had been fought to standstill, suffering 420,000 casualties on top of those of the spring. Attrition had worked. Only twelve battle-ready divisions could be found on the western front by November. Knowing that the war was lost, soldiers' morale had collapsed, with hundreds of thousands deserting or refusing to fight. Yet the allies' failure to take the battle onto German soil convinced many on the home front that the German army had not been beaten in the field, inspiring the 'stab in the back' myth, a potent factor in the rise of militant nationalism in Germany after the war's end.

In their final advance the allied armies suffered heavy casualties too, at a rate only exceeded in the mobile fighting of 1914. Yet allied fighting methods had advanced significantly from the manpower-intensive frontal assaults of 1914. The matériel-intensive 'combined-arms' warfare of 1918 had more in common with that of 1940 than 1914. Artillery was the dominant fighting arm, supporting assaults by tanks and well-armed infantry squads. Low-flying ground-attack aircraft added a new dimension to the battlefield – war now took place in three dimensions. Experience and clear doctrine allowed sophisticated, large-scale attacks to be executed successfully at short notice, while logistics and industrial production allowed them to be supplied on a hitherto unknown scale. Victory in 'total war' required total effort and total commitment, which the allies had mastered by 1918.

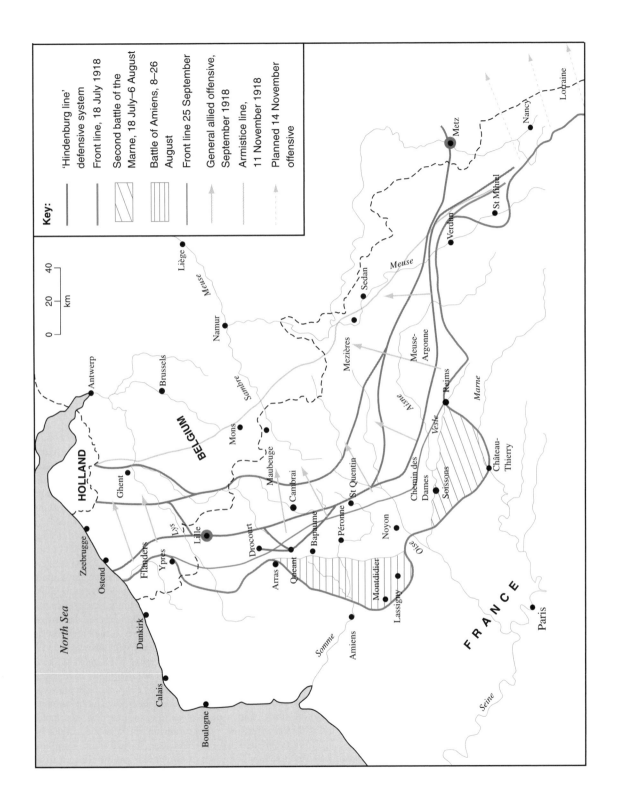

Key:

	'Hindenburg line' defensive system
	Front line, 18 July 1918
	Second battle of the Marne, 18 July–6 August
	Battle of Amiens, 8–26 August
	Front line 25 September
	General allied offensive, September 1918
	Armistice line, 11 November 1918
	Planned 14 November offensive

North Sea

HOLLAND

BELGIUM

F R A N C E

Calais
Boulogne
Dunkirk
Ostend
Zeebrugge
Flanders
Ypres
Lys
Arras
Quéant
Drocourt
Lille
Ghent
Antwerp
Brussels
Mons
Maubeuge
Cambrai
Bapaume
Péronne
St Quentin
Noyon
Montdidier
Lassigny
Amiens
Somme
Oise
Sambre
Namur
Liège
Meuse
Mézières
Sedan
Meuse
Verdun
St Mihiel
Metz
Nancy
Lorraine
Meuse-Argonne
Chemin des Dames
Aisne
Vesle
Soissons
Reims
Marne
Château-Thierry
Seine
Paris

0 20 40
km

Map 44: American Operations on the Western Front

America entered the war in April 1917 with a small professional army of 100,000 men. To intervene decisively in the conflict she would have to draft an army on a continental scale, and deploy it to the western front before her allies were defeated. It was expected, by both allies and enemies, to be the decisive factor in the war of attrition. America's allies saw an unlimited pool of manpower. Fresh US recruits, they hoped, would be shipped over to fill up the ranks of depleted British and French divisions. This went against US policy. Only by committing her forces as a separate national army could she intervene decisively to bring about a just peace. She was, however, willing to accept British and French training and equipment to speed the deployment and combat-readiness of her army. For Germany, it was a race against time. Could she defeat the Entente at sea or on land before American manpower tipped the military balance decisively against her?

There was no expectation that American manpower would make a significant difference before late-1918, or even 1919. The American 1st Division reached France on 26 June 1917, and went into the line in October. Further divisions followed slowly but steadily. By spring 1918 there were six American divisions in France, four of which had spent time at the front. The American army was assigned a sector on the eastern end of the western front, in Lorraine. John Pershing, commander of the American Expeditionary Force (AEF), hoped to be ready to launch his first major attack, to pinch out the St Mihiel salient, in the summer of 1918. In 1919 he envisaged a large-scale American offensive to capture Metz and the important coal and iron-ore fields of the Saar and Longwy-Briey behind. The development of events following Germany's March 1918 offensive obliged Pershing to compromise his policy of strict national independence. At the 3 April Beauvais conference he agreed that the AEF should come under the general control of the newly appointed allied Generalissimo, Foch. American divisions were put into the line piecemeal as they reached the front, either to hold quiet sectors and free British and French divisions for the main battle, or to shore up the crumbling allied line. The AEF made its first major independence offensive on 28 May, when the 28th Regiment of 1st Division captured the village of Cantigny. It was a small but significant step in the AEF's acclimatisation to the battlefield. Their contribution to the defensive battle was also important – at Château-Thierry on 31 May the US 3rd Division repulsed German efforts to cross the river Marne.

As the defensive battle continued, the despatch of American reinforcements to France was accelerated. Twenty-five divisions had arrived by July, and the AEF was to play an increasingly important part as the allied counter-attack developed. Eight divisions were integrated into French armies for Foch's Second Battle of the Marne counterstroke in late July (see Map 43). While a significant boost to the manpower of the attack, they were as yet raw and ill-trained, and suffered disproportionate casualties as a result. Two more divisions, the 27th and 30th, supported the British army in its advance across the Hindenburg line (see Map 45). In August the American First Army was officially formed. On 12 September over 500,000 American troops, equipped with French tanks and artillery and supported by the French Colonial Corps, carried out Pershing's long-desired offensive to pinch-out the St Mihiel salient. The 23,000 defenders, forewarned of the attack, withdrew from their untenable position in the face of overwhelming odds. To Pershing's displeasure, Foch's overall plan obliged the AEF to switch their next attack westwards from the Lorraine front. The Meuse-Argonne offensive, mounted in conjunction with the French Second Army across the wooded hills west of Verdun, was the largest operation carried out by the AEF. Progress was slow until German resistance crumbled in late October as the front-line soldiers realised that the war was lost. Between 26 September and the armistice the Americans advanced 65 kilometres (40 miles), reaching the line of the river Meuse opposite Sedan.

American soldiers made a significant military contribution in 1918, fighting as national formations in close coordination with their allies. In the 'hundred days' the AEF captured 43,000 prisoners and 1400 guns. Nevertheless, its battlefield performance was often indifferent. Although there was no doubting the zeal and bravery of the men, the AEF's inexperienced commanders frequently repeated the sort of tactical blunders which the Anglo-French armies had made earlier in the war, attacking en masse with inadequate artillery support. In its repeated assaults on Belleau Wood between 6 and 25 June 1918, often made without artillery support, the 4th Marine Brigade lost over 5000 men to well-positioned enemy machine guns. American divisions were large – at over 28,000 men more than twice the size of other allied divisions – and so such manpower-intensive attacks could still be successful. However, with less naive self-confidence, and more willingness to draw on the experience of their allies, the AEF may have saved many of its 260,000 casualties. Yet the impact on the morale of ally and enemy alike, as inexhaustible numbers of fresh, highly-motivated troops arrived in the main theatre after four years of attritional stalemate, cannot be overestimated. Overall America drafted some 4 million men, almost 2 million of whom reached the western front before the armistice. America won a psychological victory, even if her battlefield contribution was more limited than Pershing implied in his post-war memoirs.

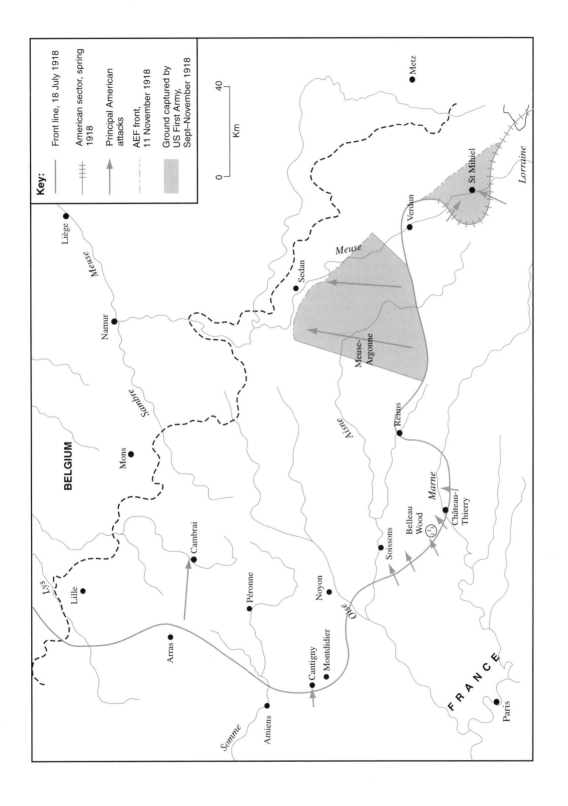

0   40

Km

Metz

Liège

Meuse

Sedan

Meuse

Verdun

St Mihiel

Lorraine

Namur

Sambre

Rêms

Aisne

Meuse-
Argonne

BELGIUM

Mons

Lys

Lille

Cambrai

Péronne

Noyon

Oise

Soissons

Belleau
Wood

Château-
Thierry

Marne

Arras

Cantigny
Montdidier

Amiens

Somme

Paris

F R A N C E

Map 45: Breaking the Hindenburg Line, September 1918

By the middle of September 1918 the allies had forced the German army back to the defensive line which it had occupied at the start of the year, before their spring offensive. Although the German army's attempt to win a decisive military victory on the western front had failed, both armies had fought themselves to a standstill, suffering the heaviest rate of casualties since 1914. The German defensive position, the carefully cited and heavily fortified *Siegfriedstellung* and its supporting systems (known to the allies as the 'Hindenburg line'), represented a formidable obstacle. The allies debated whether to attack the German position immediately, to try to force victory in 1918, or to wait until 1919 when allied productive capacity and the further increase of American manpower would give them overwhelming military superiority in the west. It was Foch's intention to follow up the victories of the summer to deny the German army any breathing space in which to recover from their earlier defeats. To do so meant an immediate assault on the Hindenburg line, which was mounted by three British and one French armies at the end of September.

The attack was to be spearheaded by the British Fourth Army, which faced the main section of the Hindenburg line between Vendhuille and Le Tronquoy. The German defences had been constructed behind the natural obstacle of the St Quentin Canal. It consisted of two main positions, some six lines of defences, well provided with concrete dugouts and machine-gun posts, altogether some 5 kilometres (3 miles) in depth. However, there were clear weaknesses in the defensive system which an attacker could exploit. For 6 kilometres (4 miles) between Le Catelet and Bellicourt the canal entered a tunnel, which would allow an attack with tanks across a flat plain. To protect the main line behind the canal from allied artillery observation a forward 'outpost line' had been established on the ridge between Epéhy and St Quentin to the west of the canal. Moreover, the heavy losses of the previous six months had weakened the German army to such an extent that many of its divisions were greatly under-strength and manned by second-class soldiers combed out from the rear areas. In trying to hold both the outpost and main lines the defending divisions were overstretched.

By 18 September the Fourth Army had established itself on the ridge, ready to assault the main defensive line behind the canal, although strongpoints in the northern sector of the outpost line in front of Bony remained in enemy hands, and would have to be assaulted again on the day of the main attack. That attack, launched on 29 September following a 56-hour bombardment, demonstrated the sophistication of combined-arms offensive methods employed by the end of the war. Two large American divisions, the 27th and 30th, supported by the 3rd and 5th Australian Divisions, were to attack across the tunnel. Since the tunnel sector was not considered wide enough for the assault, the 46th (North Midland) Division was also to assault across the canal itself between Bellicourt and Le Tronquoy. A heavy and carefully targeted artillery bombardment was the key to success. As strong as the bombardment which the Fourth Army had fired on the Somme on 1 July 1916, its method and objectives were very different. Destructive fire was precisely directed against wire entanglements and known strongpoints: a map of the enemy's main defences had luckily been captured some months before, and the ridge gave good observation over the enemy's positions. Much fire – including mustard gas shells for the first time – was to be used to neutralise enemy infantry and artillery. An intensive 'creeping' barrage would then carry the attackers on to their objectives before the enemy had time to react. In all over 1600 guns were employed and nearly 1 million shells were fired on 28 and 29 September.

On the northern sector of the attack, where the artillery barrage concentrated on the main defensive line rather than the remaining defences of the outpost line, the 27th American and 3rd Australian Divisions failed to reach the tunnel. In the centre the 30th American and 5th Australian Divisions forced their way across the tunnel and broke into the German second position around Nauroy. To the south the 46th Division, supported by the 32nd and 1st Divisions, and under cover of the heaviest barrage ever fired to support a single division's attack, crossed the canal by means of rafts and lifebelts. Their crossing obscured by thick fog, they took the enemy, who had not expected an attack on such a strong sector, completely by surprise, breaching the German front position at Bellenglise, and pushing on into the second position at Magny la Fosse. Simultaneously to the north the British First Army attacked across the Canal du Nord north of Cambrai, while the British Third Army pushed across the St Quentin canal south of Cambrai. South of St Quentin the French First Army stormed the 'Alberich' position, the southern extension of the Hindenburg line. In the week that followed the allied armies pushed the Germans back from the reserve position of the Hindenburg line to makeshift defences along the river Suippe. The German high command acknowledged that the war was lost, and asked the government in Berlin to open negotiations for an armistice.

In breaking the Hindenburg line the British army demonstrated a mastery of new military techniques, excellent staff work and a dynamic offensive spirit. Not only the supposedly elite imperial formations, but also ordinary British divisions such as the 46th, had turned three years of hard and often bloody experience to good account, to produce the most efficient and militarily effective army Britain had ever put into the field.

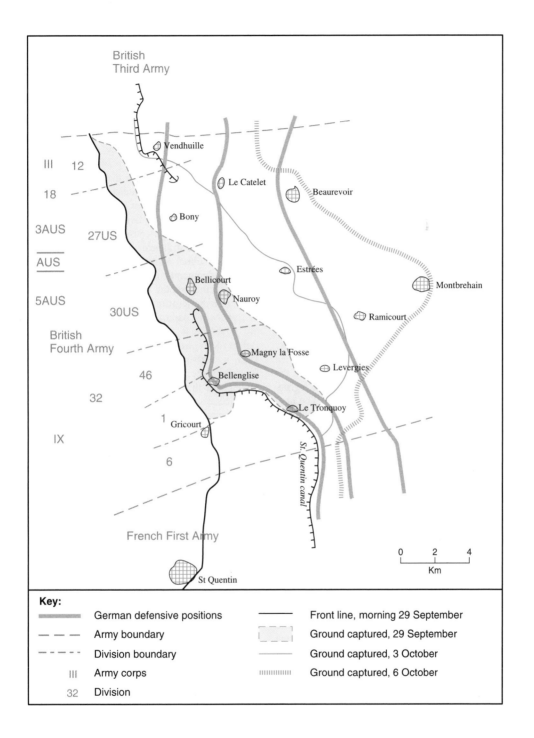

British
Third Army

Vendhuille

III 12

18

3AUS

27US

AUS

5AUS

30US

British
Fourth Army

46

32

1

Gricourt

IX

6

Le Catelet

Bony

Beaurevoir

Estrées

Bellicourt

Nauroy

Magny la Fosse

Bellenglise

Levergies

Le Tronquoy

Ramicourt

Montbrehain

St. Quentin canal

French First Army

St Quentin

Key:

German defensive positions

Army boundary

Division boundary

III   Army corps

32   Division

Front line, morning 29 September

Ground captured, 29 September

Ground captured, 3 October

Ground captured, 6 October

0   2   4
Km

Map 46: The Collapse of Germany

There is no truth in the 'stab in the back' myth, so prominent in nationalist politics after the war, that revolution on the German home front caused the army to sue for an armistice without having been defeated. Realising that the war was lost, the Kaiser and his ministers and generals attempted to carry out a constitutional 'revolution from above', an ill-fated attempt to share responsibility for the defeat with the political centre and left. In doing so they precipitated a wider political crisis which toppled the Kaiser and plunged Germany into domestic chaos. Against a background of defeat, demobilisation, ongoing peace negotiations, hunger caused by continued allied blockade, and international Bolshevik agitation, Germany's new leaders struggled to construct a new Germany. The result, the ill-fated Weimar republic, was built on political compromise and weak social foundations, perpetuating domestic divisions which would destroy it in the difficult economic circumstances of the 1920s and 1930s.

At the end of September 1918 a new Chancellor, Prince Max of Baden, who had the confidence of all democratic parties including the Social Democrats (SPD), assumed power in Germany. Constitutional reforms transferred the powers to appoint and dismiss ministers and initiate legislation from the crown to parliament (*Reichstag*). The new government sought an armistice on 4 October. The sudden announcement that the war was lost came as a great surprise to a German nation fed for four years on nationalistic propaganda tales of military victory and territorial conquest. Tensions were exacerbated by an order, at the end of October, for the High Seas Fleet to put to sea for a final 'clash of honour' with the Royal Navy. The sailors at Kiel and Wilhelmshaven mutinied. Local workers rallied to the strike, and a popular uprising – a 'revolution from below' – spread rapidly through Germany. The workers, sailors and soldiers set up political councils on the model of the Bolshevik soviets, and called for an end to the Imperial regime and for wide-reaching social reforms.

The Kaiser was forced to abdicate, and fled to Holland. Prince Max resigned, formally handing over authority to Friedrich Ebert, head of the SPD. A republic was declared on 9 November, Ebert soliciting approval for his assumption of office from representatives of the Berlin workers' and soldiers' councils. A situation of 'dual control', akin to that in Russia in 1917, now existed in Germany.

Ebert's Provisional Government had more success than Kerensky's Russian equivalent in establishing its authority against the threat from the revolutionary left, embodied in the council movement. The legitimacy of the new republic was quickly established on the basis of a 'corporate partnership' between Germany's democratic political parties, private capitalists and moderate trade unionists, and the remnants of the 'old order'. On 10 November Ludendorff's successor, Wilhelm Groener, placed the army at the disposal of the new government, on condition that it support the officer corps against the soldiers' councils. On 15 November Hugo Stinnes, representing Germany's private employers, agreed to major workplace concessions, including the long-sought-after eight-hour day, to defuse worker unrest in the factories. To maintain public order and oversee the demobilisation required by the terms of the armistice, existing civil servants and judiciary were confirmed in their posts. The first elections for a new constitutional assembly, which met in the small provincial town of Weimar because the capital Berlin was considered too politically volatile, hurriedly called in January 1919, confirmed the success of the new 'Weimar coalition', whose centre and moderate left-wing democratic parties won 76% of the vote.

Nevertheless, the radical left and right continued to challenge the legitimacy of the republic. With the help of right-wing paramilitary formations, the 'Freikorps', the government put down a left-wing uprising by the Bolshevik-inspired 'Spartacus League' in Berlin in January 1919, a short-lived 'Soviet republic' which sprung up in Bavaria in the spring, and other workers' movements in Baden and the Ruhr industrial region. This successful 'defence against Bolshevism' helped to reinforce the new government's position. During the course of 1919 the council movement was suppressed by force where it did not melt away of its own accord.

While order had been restored by the end of 1919, politics, which had been highly militarised by war and defeat, remained polarised and volatile. Elements in the army backed the right-wing Kapp putsch in Berlin in March 1920, which was only defeated with the aid of a general strike by Berlin workers. It was followed by left-wing uprisings in the Ruhr and Saxony. The French occupation of the Ruhr in 1923 provoked a further wave of left-wing agitation in the Ruhr, Saxony and Thuringia. A new anti-republican political movement, Adolf Hitler's National Socialists, signalled their intentions with the failed 'beer hall putsch' in Munich in November 1923.

In the difficult circumstances of 1918–19 Germany's moderate democratic leaders did their best. Essentially they consolidated the political revolution which removed the old imperial system, but resisted any move towards genuine social revolution which might have given the republic a more solid foundation in German society. They had achieved what they wanted, a share of power in a constitutional system. But the compromises which they made with elements of the old order – army, bureaucracy, judiciary, employers – and their failure to deal effectively with the social demands of the revolutionary left, or the nationalist demands of the radical right, meant that the new republic was living on borrowed time.

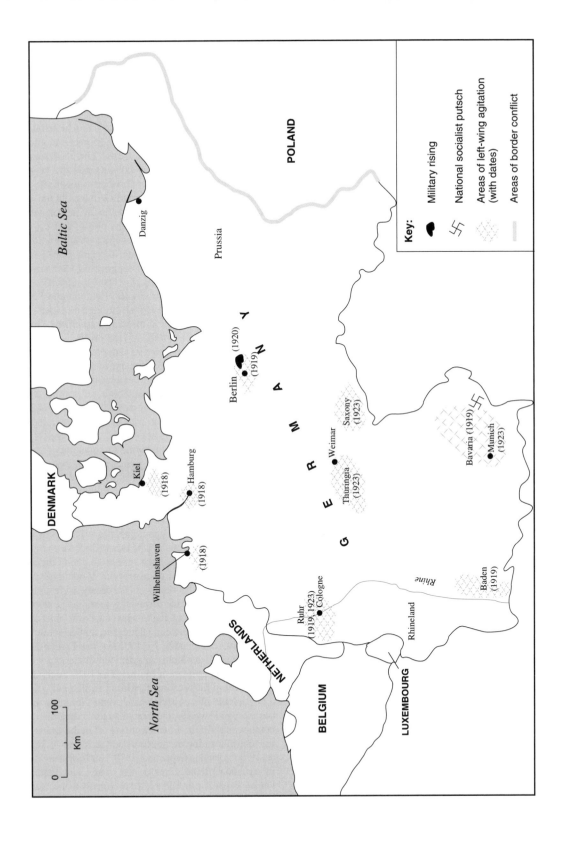

Map 47: Peace in the West – The Versailles Settlement

Although an armistice was signed on 11 November 1918, a final peace with Germany, the Treaty of Versailles, would not be signed until 28 June 1919. In the interim a peace conference met in Paris to decide the fate of the defeated Central Powers, and to divide the spoils amongst the victors. Germany was not invited to attend the conference. She would only be allowed to comment in writing, before accepting or rejecting the terms drawn up by the allies. The allies' differences over war aims (see Map 24), suppressed while the fighting continued, became manifest as negotiations went on. In particular, Woodrow Wilson's internationalist agenda clashed with France's punitive approach to dealing with Germany. Great Britain found herself acting as intermediary between her two principal allies, while trying to secure her own global security and imperial power.

It was Clemenceau's intention to impose a victors' peace on Germany, to ensure France's long-term security against renewed German aggression. Four principles underpinned French peace diplomacy: that Germany should pay reparations to compensate for the financial costs of the war, and material damage in France and Belgium; that the German economy should be permanently weakened, possibly by splitting off her principal industrial regions, the Ruhr and Saar; that Germany's war-making capacity should be severely reduced, by limiting her armaments; that the security of France's eastern frontier should be assured by splitting off or demilitarising the Rhineland. Wilson, who travelled to Paris to chair the peace conference, had a more liberal agenda. He was especially concerned with ensuring the rights of national minorities in Germany, particularly the Poles. However he did not want to cripple Germany unduly, seeing her as the economic power-house of continental Europe and the newly democratised bastion against the westward spread of Bolshevism. Britain was more willing than France to treat Germany leniently, fearing the rise of a strong France in Germany's place. Her security concerns were mainly outside Europe – the future of Germany's African and Asian colonies, and above all the fate of Germany's High Seas Fleet, interned at Scapa Flow since the armistice, were central to her peace agenda.

The actual peace terms were thrashed out by the victors over several months in a series of complex, detailed negotiations, in which none got exactly what they wanted. The principle that Germany should pay reparations was accepted, although a sum could not be agreed; the issue was referred to a reparations commission that would meet after the peace conference. To justify imposing reparations, the allies assigned responsibility for causing the war to Germany. Clause 231 of the Treaty of Versailles, the infamous 'war guilt clause', was an international humiliation which did much to fuel radical right-wing nationalism in Germany in the inter-war period. The territorial settlement returned the 'lost provinces' of Alsace and Lorraine to France. Belgium received the cantons of Eupen and Malmédy. The Rhineland remained part of Germany, although it was to be demilitarised and occupied by an allied army for 15 years, to guarantee Germany's fulfilment of the treaty. The Saar was to be controlled by the League of Nations, its industrial production going to France, for 15 years, when a plebiscite would decide whether it remained part of Germany. In the east the new state of Poland was to gain much German territory, including access to the sea via the port of Danzig. Upper Silesia, Allenstein and Marienwerder were to hold plebiscites to decide whether to join the new Polish state or remain part of Germany. Schleswig was to vote on whether to become part of Denmark. Germany's African colonies were mandated to Britain, France, Belgium and Portugal; her Asian colonies to the British empire and Japan.

By the terms of the armaments settlement, Germany was to retain only a long-service professional army of 100,000 men (the *Reichswehr*) and a small coastal-defence fleet. She was not allowed weapons of aggressive warfare – tanks, heavy artillery, aircraft and submarines.

The German government objected strongly to the proposed peace terms, which they termed a *diktat* (dictated peace). The first Weimar ministry resigned rather than accept the proposed peace terms, before the National Assembly, held to ransom by the continuation of the allied economic blockade while peace negotiations went on, reluctantly accepted the proffered terms. Rejecting them would have led to the renewal of fighting and the likely dismemberment of a defenceless Germany.

The Paris Peace Conference produced a fudged settlement that satisfied no one completely. Therefore neither the victors, and certainly not the vanquished, were committed to upholding its terms. Foch refused to attend the signing ceremony in the Hall of Mirrors at Versailles since he considered that the terms on the treaty were not harsh enough – 'an armistice for twenty years' as he dubbed it. The treaty's shadow hung over inter-war international relations. France's forceful attempts to implement the peace settlement, culminating in 1923 in the Franco-Belgian occupation of the Ruhr, undermined attempts to restore international harmony in Europe. The 1925 Locarno Pact, guaranteeing the western territorial settlement, signified a new phase of cooperation between Germany and her conquerors. However, the treaty had left a diplomatic time-bomb which Adolf Hitler was to set off in the 1930s. From the remilitarisation of the Rhineland in March 1936, to the attack on Poland in September 1939, Nazi Germany's forceful revision of the terms of the treaty, and Britain and France's appeasing response, led inexorably to the renewal of hostilities which Foch had predicted.

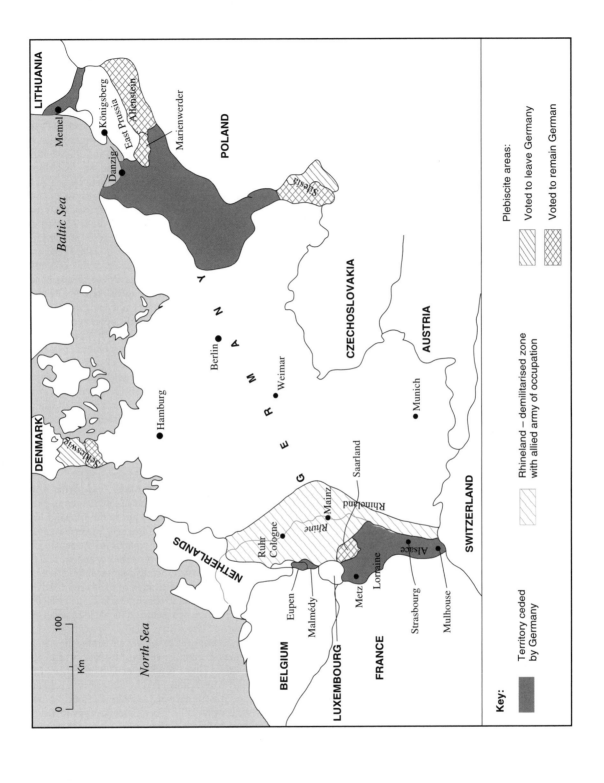

Map 48: The Eastern Peace Settlements

In Austria-Hungary from late 1917, there were food riots and strikes, accompanied by mutinies in the Austro-Hungarian navy in February 1918. Notwithstanding the fact that Austria-Hungary felt short-changed by the treaties of Brest-Litovsk (3 March 1918) (see Map 41) and Bucharest (7 May 1918), her deteriorating internal situation meant that, in May 1918, she accepted German economic and military control of her affairs. After the defeat of her last major offensive against Italy in June 1918, Austria-Hungary's army decayed. On 27 October 1918, Italian forces along the Piave attacked (Battle of Vittorio Veneto) and the Austro-Hungarian army collapsed. With revolution threatening on the home front, Austria-Hungary began talks for an armistice on 1 November and agreed an armistice for 3/4 November. The result was the treaties of Saint-Germain-en-Laye with Austria (10 September 1919) and Trianon with Hungary (4 June 1920). From the ruins of Austria-Hungary, there emerged an expanded Rumania and the new states of Austria, Czechoslovakia, Hungary, Poland and Yugoslavia. After Saint-Germain-en-Laye, Austria became little more than a rump state with a population of 8 million, 14% of its pre-war territory, a questionable economic future and forbidden to enter a political union (*Anschluss*) with neighbouring Germany. The Béla Kun communist revolution in Hungary in March 1919 and a Rumanian invasion of Hungary delayed the final settlement with Hungary until Trianon in June 1920. Like Austria, this was a harsh settlement: Hungary lost 68% of her territory and 33% of her Hungarian (or Magyar) population. As it left so many Hungarian minorities living beyond her borders, Hungary was bitterly opposed to the peace settlement and was very keen after 1920 to revise the treaty to bring these minorities back into a greater Hungary.

A starving Bulgaria, angry (like Austria-Hungary) at the fact that she was sidelined by the treaties of Brest-Litovsk and Bucharest, started to collapse from within in late 1918. Food shortages on the Bulgarian home front were matched by war weariness within the Bulgarian army stationed along the Salonika front (see Map 22). On 15 September 1918, the Entente armies at Salonika launched a final offensive. By 21 September the Bulgarian defence had collapsed. On 27 September 1918, a Bulgarian delegation arrived in Salonika to sue for peace, and an armistice was signed on 29 September. The last state to join the Central Powers was the first to leave. The peace treaty with Bulgaria was signed on 27 November 1919 at Neuilly-sur-Seine. Bulgaria was required to relinquish all the territory occupied by her in the recent war, as well as some areas on her western border with (what would become) Yugoslavia. She also lost Thrace and the port of Dedéagatch (Alexandroúpolis) and direct access to the Aegean Sea, although article 48 of the treaty offered a guarantee of economic access to the Aegean. In all, she lost 5500 square miles of territory along with 90,000 Bulgarians. These were added to the almost 1 million Bulgarians already living outside Bulgaria, fanning the fires of nationalist resentment in the inter-war years. The Bulgarian army was limited to a 20,000-strong volunteer army. She also paid reparations: Yugoslavia, Rumania and Greece were to receive deliveries of coal, livestock, railway equipment and other items, while a massive 2.25 billion gold francs would be paid in reparations to the Entente powers within 37 years. The last was an impossible burden and it was reduced in March 1923: 550 million was to be paid over 60 years and the remainder in a further 30 years. Between 1925 and 1929, 41 million gold francs was paid, a sum equivalent to the budget deficits of those years. The reparations were finally abandoned at the Lausanne economic conference in 1932.

The most immediately disastrous peace settlement was with the Ottoman empire (Turkey). As with Austria-Hungary and Bulgaria, a war-weary Turkey was under considerable internal stress when, in September 1918, she was attacked in Palestine (see Map 35) and from Salonika. The break-out of the Salonika force was especially dangerous as a direct advance along the Thracian coast threatened the capital, Istanbul (Constantinople). Having agreed an armistice on the island of Mudros on 31 October 1918, the Ottoman empire signed the Treaty of Sèvres on 10 August 1920. The terms of Sèvres were harsh: while the Sultan remained as a titular figurehead, the Ottoman empire ceased to exist and it lost all its territory in the Arab Middle East. What would become Turkey was reduced to an Anatolian rump, plus a small strip of European Turkey up to the Chatalja lines 32 kilometres (20 miles) west of Istanbul. Sèvres added parts of eastern Anatolia to a new republic of Armenia, gave substantial parts of Thrace to Greece and raised the possibility of an autonomous Kurdistan. In addition, the settlement gave the administration of the town of Smyrna (Izmir) and its hinterland to Greece, Turkey's long-standing rival, with the promise of a plebiscite for the local population after five years of Greek rule. Finally, Sèvres allowed for international control of Istanbul and the surrounding Straits zone. This was a punitive settlement made worse by a British-sponsored Greek invasion of Turkey in May 1919 that threatened to destroy Turkey altogether. The Turks rallied under Mustafa Kemal (Atatürk) and fought a bitter war with the Greeks (1919–22), ejecting them from Turkey and Smyrna, before negotiating a new more realistic peace at Lausanne in 1923. This marked not only the birth of the modern republic of Turkey but also proved to be one of the most durable peace settlements of the twentieth century.

PEACE SETTLEMENT WITH AUSTRIA-HUNGARY

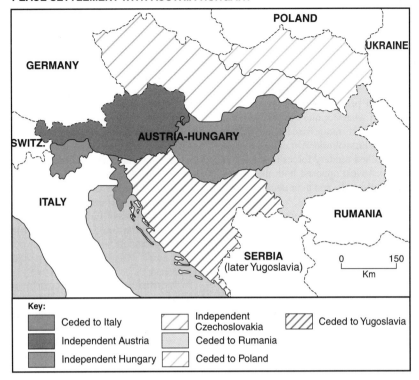

Key:

	Ceded to Italy		Independent Czechoslovakia		Ceded to Yugoslavia
	Independent Austria		Ceded to Rumania		
	Independent Hungary		Ceded to Poland		

PEACE SETTLEMENT WITH BULGARIA

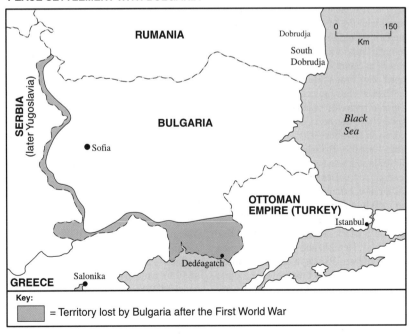

Key:

= Territory lost by Bulgaria after the First World War

Map 49: Allied Intervention in the Russian Civil War

The Russian revolution (see Map 31) was not followed by a global workers' revolution. Instead, the Bolsheviks consolidated their power base inside Soviet Russia (the Soviet Union in 1922). 'White' anticommunist armies led by former Tsarist generals, and 'Green' autonomous local peasant militias, opposed the Bolsheviks (or 'Reds') in what became the Russian civil war (1917–1921/22), in which more Russians (including civilians) died than in the First World War. The battle for Russia's future drew in allied military forces in support of the Whites. The capitalist west opposed both the revolutionary ideology of the Bolsheviks and their decision to sue for peace at Brest-Litovsk (see Map 41), a decision that would allow Germany to move troops from Russia to the western front. Direct allied intervention in the Russian civil war came in six theatres of operation.

(1) In Russia's far-east Maritime Province, Japanese and American troops landed at Vladivostok. Japanese forces landed first, on 30 December 1917, ostensibly to maintain order, but with the objective of annexing parts of Russia. Fearful of Japanese expansion in Siberia, in August 1918 American troops landed at Vladivostok. The Americans were there partly to help evacuate the 35,000-strong Czech Legion of Czech nationalists (including former Austro-Hungarian POWs of Czech origin) who had been fighting for Russia and who were now trying to escape east down the Trans-Siberian railway; but they were also there to check the Japanese. The American force of two regiments came close to clashing with the Japanese. The US also had differences with the British and French, who assumed that it would join them in supporting Admiral Alexander Kolchak's White forces in central Russia/Siberia. American troops helped guard the Trans-Siberian railway from Vladivostok to Lake Baikal (thus protecting Kolchak's rear) until the Czech Legion arrived for evacuation by sea from Vladivostok. In April 1920, the last US troops withdrew. The Japanese withdrew in October 1922.

(2) Allied forces – notably British and French – were involved in the civil war in southern Russia and the Crimea in support of White generals Anton Denikin and Peter Wrangel. In December 1918, France established a base at Odessa from which to support White counter-revolutionary forces in the Ukraine, while Britain concentrated its attention on the eastern littoral of the Black Sea. In 1919 and 1920, with local Cossack support, Denikin and Wrangel fought a series of actions across southern Russia, assisted by British and French naval forces. This support, however, failed to avert a defeat, with the last remnants of White forces evacuated from the Crimea by British ships in November 1920. During the intervention in southern Russia, French Black Sea sailors mutinied in protest against French support for the Whites.

(3) British, French and American troops landed at Murmansk (June 1918) and Arkhangelsk (August 1918) (Canadian, Italian and Serbian troops were also involved). The avowed purpose of these expeditions was to retrieve allied war-time military stockpiles, but the allies also had the objective of striking south to link up with the Czech Legion. This would it was hoped lead to a resurgence of the Whites and Russia's re-entry into the war. For more than a year, the allied troops skirmished with Bolshevik forces along the Severnaya Dvina river, using poison gas in these clashes. The Americans withdrew their Arctic force in August 1919; the British and French by October 1919.

(4) British naval units supported White forces operating in the Baltic states of Latvia, Lithuania and Estonia. These counter-revolutionary forces were also being helped by German forces left behind in the region after the treaty of Brest-Litovsk (Germany also supported Finland against Red forces).

(5) Britain sent two specialist missions into Trans-Caucasia and Trans-Caspia. The largest of these, 'Dunsterforce', led by Lionel Dunsterville left Mesopotamia in January 1918 for the Persian shore of the Caspian Sea. It sailed with its own small navy to Baku in Trans-Caucasia where it fought the Turks in September 1918. In Turkestan (Trans-Caspia), Britain sent (June 1918) another force under Wilfred Malleson to block German and Turkish penetration into Russian central Asia.

(6) The French provided military help (including a young officer, Charles de Gaulle) for the Polish army for its invasion of Russia and subsequent war with the Bolsheviks (1919–20).

The desire to keep Russia in the war prompted the interventions in Russia. After November 1918, intervention and support for the Whites (and Poland) was a means of fighting the Bolsheviks and communism. Allied intervention came in the form of supplies of matériel and specialist military support rather than the large-scale deployment of troops. This help was substantial: in 1919, Kolchak, for instance, received 1 million rifles, 15,000 machine guns, 700 guns, 800 million rounds of ammunition, and clothing for half a million men. This was equivalent to all Soviet Russian munitions production for 1919. However, numerically 'White' armies were small and fragmented – total strength in the field against the Bolsheviks never exceeding 250,000 men at any one time. In contrast the Red army reached a peak strength of over 5 million men by the end of 1920. Much of their equipment was captured from the defeated Whites – allied stockpiles were turned against their former owners. With home fronts and soldiers sick of war (and at times revolutionary), the allied interventions in the Russian civil war were half-hearted, and ill-coordinated. It prolonged the conflict but was insufficient to prove decisive.

Key:

— Boundary of Russian empire, 1914

---- Area controlled by Bolsheviks, Aug. 1918

NORWAY

SWEDEN

Entente fleet

Murmansk

British
French
Canadians
Italians
Serbs

Canadians
Americans

FINLAND

Finns

White Sea

Arkhangelsk

British
French

White
Sea

Severnaya
Dvina

0   500

Km

Petrograd
(Leningrad)

Yudenich

ESTONIA

British/French
naval assistance

LATVIA

Baltic
Germans

Kolchak 1918–19

Czech Legion
(escapes to Vladivostok)

LITHUANIA

Moscow

Czechs

East Prussia

POLAND

CZECH.

Poles

UKRAINE

Denikin
1919

Don Cossacks
1917–19

Ural Cossack Army
1918–20

ROMANIA

Wrangel 1920

BULGARIA

French

Crimea

British

Georgians 1919–20

Caspian Sea

Mensheviks

Dunsterforce

Transcaspia

Entente fleet

Black Sea

Baku

Istanbul

Transcaucasus

Malleson
Mission

TURKEY

Territory lost by Russia
to Turkey after the war

British
1918–19

Map 50: The Costs of the War, 1914–19

The human and material cost of the Great War was immense. Known military deaths and missing totalled some 10 million. The map opposite shows the breakdown of military deaths country-by-country, with the caveat that many of these figures are estimates and many vary depending on the source. This is especially the case with countries such as Rumania, Russia, Serbia and Turkey that suffered turmoil and occupation during and after the war, and where government records on war losses were lost, destroyed or not properly kept. The same is true for deaths among local inhabitants and soldiers in peripheral campaigns such as in Africa.

These statistics, however, do not take into account civilian deaths, the wounded and those killed in an influenza epidemic (possibly as many as 21 million) that swept across war-ravaged Europe in 1918 and 1919. In terms of civilian deaths, for instance, 2 million Russians, 650,000 Serbians, and 500,000 Rumanians died, most as a direct result of the damage and dislocation caused by the war. In 1915, a genocidal campaign by the Ottoman government led to the deaths of some 1 million Armenians in eastern Asia Minor. In addition, invading armies raped local women, notably (but not exclusively) in the campaigns in the Balkans and eastern Europe/Russia. In Belgium, recent studies argue that outrages by the Germans in that country were real and not simply propaganda stories. As for the wounded, every country had its sad quota of limbless, scarred, gassed, blinded and psychologically traumatised veterans: long-term reminders of the cost of the Great War (in 1977, Britain still had 3000 limbless veterans). In Germany, over 4 million men were wounded; in Austria-Hungary, 3.6 million; in Britain, the figure exceeded 2 million; even the US, which arrived late in the war, suffered over 200,000 wounded. France's c.3 million war wounded – the *mutilés de guerre* – included the *gueules cassées* ('smashed faces'), for whom, in an era before effective plastic surgery, facial masks had to be made to hide their disfigurements. At the same time, the mental trauma of the war led to the birth of 'shell shock': soldiers mentally unbalanced by the shock of service in the trenches.

The cost of the war also extended to the empires of the protagonists. For instance, some 3 million men enlisted from the British empire (excluding Ireland), of whom approximately 200,000 died: Africans, ANZACS, Canadians, Indians, South Africans and West Indians, all of whom had responded to the call for war in 1914. Likewise, France mobilised 475,000 men from her empire, and over 60,000 French African and Indochinese troops died, mostly on the western front. Large numbers of men were also taken prisoner, many of whom never found their way home, an example of the social dislocation wrought by the war. In terms of social change, the involvement of women in the war accelerated their move towards equality with, for instance, women (over the age of 30) voting for the first time in Britain in the December 1918 general election – a positive 'cost' of the war.

Alongside the loss of life, the war caused massive material physical damage: German troops devastated north-west France; churches, libraries and monuments were destroyed across Europe; cities were wrecked and railways ripped up by retreating armies. Moreover, the war bankrupted Europe's treasuries. For instance, Britain, a 'victor' in the conflict, incurred debts equivalent to 136% of her gross national product, a fifth of which she owed to foreign powers, mainly America. In this sense, the war began a process whereby Europe was financially bankrupted by war, increasingly dependent on the emerging financial and economic power of the US.

The war also threatened Europe's global dominance. Servicemen from Africa and Asia who had served in Europe took back to their home countries new ideologies and ideas such as communism, nationalism, and socialism that would help to upset traditional notions of colonial authority, something already dented by the experience that Africans and Asians had had of seeing Europeans kill each other on the western front. New forms of nationalism also upset the balance of power in Europe. The war destroyed four great European empires: Austria-Hungary, Germany, the Ottoman empire and Russia. In their place, new nations emerged: Austria, the Baltic states, Czechoslovakia, Finland, Weimar Germany, Hungary, Poland, the Soviet Union, Turkey and Yugoslavia. These new states – many of which were small, economically weak and politically immature – transformed Europe, making it, in the long run, a less stable place than it had been before 1914.

In all sorts of ways, the First World War upset the normal balance of life and overturned the pre-1914 sense of cultural certainty. In the arts, the war accelerated the emergence of a new spirit of modernism, scepticism and irony, expressed in, *inter alia*, T.S. Eliot's poem 'The Wasteland' (1922), James Joyce's book *Ulysses* (1922), Bertolt Brecht's and Kurt Weill's play 'The Threepenny Opera' (1928), and absurd valueless art movements of the 1920s such as Dada.

Meanwhile, war veterans unfit for normal, civilian life, looked to new, extreme anti-liberal and anti-democratic ideologies. Communism was one such movement; the other was fascism. Many fascist leaders who challenged the status quo in the new Europe of the 1920s and 1930s – such as Hitler and Mussolini – had served in the trenches during the war. They found support from other disgruntled war veterans willing to act as foot soldiers for the Second World War. Europe in the inter-war years was the 'dark continent', struggling to re-assert the liberal values destroyed by the First World War. The Europe of 1914 had vanished forever.

Estimated Military War Dead and Missing, 1914–1918

Germany: 2,000,000 (out of 13,250,000 mobilised)
Russia: 1,700,000 (out of 13,000,000 mobilised)
France (excluding empire): 1,300,000
    (out of 8,500,000 mobilised)
Austria-Hungary: 1,200,000
    (out of 9,000,000 mobilised)
Great Britain (excluding empire): 750,000
    (out of 6,200,000 mobilised)
Italy: 460,000 (out of 5,900,000 mobilised)
Ottoman empire (Turkey): 400,000
    (out of 2,850,000 mobilised)
Serbia: 322,000 (out of 1,000,000 mobilised)
Rumania: 158,000 (out of 1,000,000 mobilised)
USA: 116,000 (out of 3,800,000 mobilised)
Bulgaria: 49,000 (out of 950,000 mobilised)
Belgium: 41,000 (out of 380,000 mobilised)
Portugal: 7222 (out of 100,000 mobilised)
Greece: 5000 (out of 200,000 mobilised)
Montenegro: 3000 (out of 50,000 mobilised)
Japan: 2000 (out of 800,000 mobilised)

Cost of War (US $ billion, current)

Germany	37.7
GB	35.3
USA	22.6
France	24.2
Russia	22.6
Austria-Hungary	20.6
Italy	12.4
Canada	1.66
Rumania	1.6
Ottoman empire	1.43
Australia	1.42
Belgium	1.1
Bulgaria	0.8
India	0.6
Serbia	0.4
New Zealand	0.37
South Africa	0.3
Greece	0.27
Japan	0.04
	$186 billion total*

* Other sources give a total of $208.5 billion for war expenditure

Bibliography

Historical writing on the First World War is extensive and often of questionable quality. In this bibliography the authors have included standard works on the war, recent up-to-date introductory texts, and influential scholarly studies which treat military, political and social aspects of the conflict in greater depth. While not exhaustive, it provides both a wide-ranging introduction to further reading, and an indication of the many aspects of the First World War which are currently being studied. In addition there are many studies of the individual battles and campaigns, and biographies of the principal political and military figures, which are not listed here. There is also an extensive literature on the origins and consequences of the war which cannot be included here.

Ashworth, Tony, *Trench Warfare, 1914–18: The Live and Let Live System* (London: Macmillan, 1980)

Asprey, Robert, *The German High Command at War: Hindenburg, Ludendorff and the First World War* (London: Little Brown & Co, 1991)

Bailey, Jonathan, 'The First World War and the Birth of Modern Warfare', in Macgregor Knox & Williamson Murray (eds), *The Dynamics of Military Revolution, 1300–2050* (Cambridge: Cambridge UP, 2001)

Banks, Arthur, *A Military Atlas of the First World War* (London: Heinemann, 1975)

Becker, Annette & Audoin-Rouzeau, Stéphane, *1914–1918: Understanding the Great War* (London: Profile Books, 2002)

Becker, Annette, Smith, Len & Audoin-Rouzeau, Stéphane, *France and the Great War, 1914–1918* (Cambridge: Cambridge UP, 2003)

Beckett, Ian, *The Great War, 1914–1918* (Basingstoke: Macmillan, 2001)

Bourne, John, *Britain and the Great War 1914–1918* (London: Arnold, 1989)

Bourne, John, Liddle, Peter & Whitehead, Ian, *The Great World War: 1914–45: Vol. 1: Lightning Strikes Twice* and *Vol. II: Who Won? Who Lost?* (London: Harper Collins, 2000 & 2001)

Braddon, Russell, *The Siege* (London: Cape, 1969)

Brown, Ian, *British Logistics on the Western Front* (Westport, CT: Praeger, 1998)

Bruce, Anthony, *The Last Crusade: The Palestine Campaign in the First World War* (London: John Murray, 2002)

Cecil, Hugh & Liddle, Peter, *Facing Armageddon: The First World War Experienced* (London: Leo Cooper, 1996)

Chickering, Roger, *Imperial Germany and the Great War, 1914–18* (Cambridge: Cambridge UP, 1998)

Chickering, Roger & Förster, Stig, *Great War, Total War: Combat and Mobilization on the Western Front, 1914–1918* (Cambridge: Cambridge UP, 2000)

Clayton, Anthony, *Paths of Glory: The French Army, 1914–1918* (London: Cassell, 2003)

Cruttwell, Charles, *A History of the Great War* (Oxford: Clarendon, 1936)

Dutton, David, *The Politics of Diplomacy: Britain and France in the Balkans in the First World War* (London: IB Tauris, 1998)

Ellis, John & Cox, Mike, *The World War One Databook* (London: Arum, 1993)

Erickson, Edward, *Ordered to Die: A History of the Ottoman Army in the First World War* (Westport, CT: Greenwood, 2001)

Falls, Cyril, *Caporetto 1917* (London: Weidenfeld & Nicolson, 1966)

Feldman, Gerald, *Army, Industry and Labor in Germany 1914–1918* (Princeton, NJ: Princeton UP, 1966)

Ferguson, Niall, *The Pity of War* (London: Allen Lane, 1998)

Figes, Orlando, *A People's Tragedy: The Russian Revolution, 1891–1924* (London: Cape, 1996)

Gilbert, Martin, *First World War Atlas* (London: Weidenfeld & Nicolson, 1970)

Gilbert, Martin, *The First World War* (London: Weidenfeld & Nicolson, 1994)

Griffith, Paddy, *Battle Tactics of the Western Front: The British Army's Art of Attack, 1916–18* (New Haven, CT: Yale UP, 1994)

de Groot, Gerard, *The First World War* (New York: Palgrave, 2001)

Halpern, Paul, *A Naval History of World War 1* (London: UCL Press, 1994)

Herrmann, David, *The Arming of Europe and the Making of the First World War* (Princeton, NJ: Princeton UP, 1996)

Howard, Michael, *The First World War* (Oxford: Oxford UP, 2002)

Liddell Hart, Basil, *The Real War, 1914–1918* (London: Faber, 1930)

Herwig, Holger, *The First World War: Germany and Austria-Hungary, 1914–1918* (London: Arnold, 1997)

Hughes, Matthew, *Allenby and British Strategy in the Middle East, 1917–1919* (London: Frank Cass, 1999)

Joll, James, *The Origins of the First World War* (2nd edn, London: Longman, 1992)

Keegan, John, *The First World War* (London: Hutchinson, 1998)

Kennedy, Paul, *The War Plans of the Great Powers, 1880–1914* (London: Allen & Unwin, 1979)

Macmillan, Margaret, *Peacemakers: The Paris Conference of 1919 and its Attempt to End War* (London: J. Murray, 2001)

Millet, Allan & Murray, Williamson, (eds) *Military Effectiveness, Vol. 1: The First World War* (London: Allen & Unwin, 1988)

Nicolson, Colin, *The Longman Companion to the First World War, Europe 1914–1918* (Harlow: Pearson, 2001)

Ousby, Ian, *The Road to Verdun* (London: Jonathan Cape, 2002)

Palmer, Alan, *The Gardeners of Salonika* (London: Deutsch, 1965)

Philpott, William, *Anglo-French Relations and Strategy on the Western Front, 1914–1918* (Basingstoke: Macmillan, 1996)

Pope, Stephen & Wheal, Elizabeth-Anne, *The Macmillan Dictionary of the First World War* (London: Macmillan, 1995)

Prior, Robin & Wilson, Trevor, *Command on the Western Front: The Military Career of Sir Henry Rawlinson* (Oxford: Blackwell, 1992)

Samuels, Martin, *Command or Control? Command, Training and Tactics in the British and German Armies, 1888–1918* (London: Frank Cass, 1988)

Schindler, John, *Isonzo: The Forgotten Sacrifice of the Great War* (Westport, CT: Praeger, 2001)

Sharp, Alan, *The Versailles Settlement: Peacemaking in Paris, 1919* (London: Macmillan, 1991)

Sheffield, Gary, *Forgotten Victory: The First World War, Myths and Realities* (London: Review, 2001)

Showalter, Dennis, *Tannenberg: Clash of Empires* (Hamden, CT: Archon, 1991)

Steel, Nigel & Hart, Peter, *Defeat at Gallipoli* (London: Macmillan, 1994)

Stevenson, David, *The First World War and International Politics* (Oxford: Oxford UP, 1988)

Stevenson, David, *Armaments and the Coming of War: Europe, 1904–14* (Oxford: Clarendon Press, 1996)

Stone, Norman, *The Eastern Front 1914–1917* (London: Hodder & Stoughton, 1975)

Strachan, Hew, *The Oxford Illustrated History of the First World War* (Oxford: Oxford UP, 1998)

Strachan, Hew, *The First World War. Volume I. To Arms* (Oxford: Oxford UP, 2001)

Strachan, Hew, *The First World War* (London: Simon & Schuster, 2003)

Terraine, John, *White Heat: The New Way in Warfare* (London: Sidgwick & Jackson, 1982)

Terraine, John, *Business in Great Waters: The U-Boat Wars, 1916–1945* (London: Leo Cooper, 1989)

Trask, David, *The AEF and Coalition Warmaking, 1917–18* (Lawrence, KA: UP of Kansas, 1993)

Travers, Tim, *The Killing Ground: The British Army, the Western Front and the Emergence of Modern Warfare, 1900–1918* (London: Allen & Unwin, 1987)

Travers, Tim, *How the War was Won: Command and Technology in the British Army on the Western Front* (London: Routledge, 1992)

Williams, John, *The Home Fronts: Britain, France and Germany, 1914–1918* (London: Constable, 1972)

Wilson, Keith, (ed.) *Decisions for War, 1914* (London: University College London Press, 1995)

Wilson, Trevor, *The Myriad Faces of War* (Oxford: Blackwell, 1986)

Wrigley, Chris, (ed.) *Challenges of Labour: Central and Western Europe, 1917–1920* (London: Routledge, 1993)

Index

Numbers refer to individual maps. The names of ships are given in italic script.

Abercorn, 12
Aboukir, 9, 29
Africa, 1, 6, 47, 50
   recruitment in, 12, 40
   war in, 12, 40
Aisne, battle of the, 1914, 4
Al ʿAmārah, 16
Albania, 14, 21, 22
Albert I, King of the Belgians, 10
Alexander III, Tsar, 31
Alexandra, Tsarina, 31
Allenby, Edmund, 34
   commander-in-chief in Palestine, 35
Alps, the, 20, 38
'Alliance system', the, 1
Al Kūt (Kūt al Imārah)
   siege of, 1916, 16
   battle of, 1917, 16
Alsace, 3, 24, 47
America
   American Expeditionary Force
      (AEF), 44
   army, 42, 43, 44
   casualties, 44, 50
   entry into war, 24, 29
   intervention in Russian civil war, 49
   neutrality, 8, 13, 29
   war aims, 24, 47
Amiens, 3, 42
   battle of, 1918, 43
Amman, 34, 35
Ancre, battle of the, 1916, 28
An Nāsirīyah, 16
Antwerp, 3, 6
   siege of, 1914, 4, 7
ANZACs, 17
Anzac Cove, landing at, 1915, 17
Arabic, sinking of, 1915, 29
Arab revolt, the, 34
Archangelsk, 49
Ardennes, 3
Armenia, 23, 48
   genocide in, 16, 50
Armentières, 7, 42
Armistice, the, 1918, 6, 43, 46, 47
arms races, 2
Arras, 7, 42
   battle of, 1917, 32
Artois, 32
   battles in, 1915, 15

Asia, 1, 47
   war in, 12
Asiago plateau, 20, 38
Asquith, Herbert, 15, 30
Atlantic, battle of, 1917, 29
attrition, 15, 25, 27, 28, 36, 42, 43, 44
Aubers ridge, 10, 15
Australia, 12, 40
   recruitment in, 40
Austria, 48, 50
Austria-Hungary, 1, 14, 41
   army, 8
      on eastern front, 19
      on Italian front, 20, 38, 48
   casualties, 8, 50
   defeat of, 48
   navy, 2
   peace with, 24, 48
   and Serbia, 1, 2, 21
Auxiliary Service Law, 1916, 28
Baden, 46
Baghdad, 16
Bainsizza plateau, 20
Baku, 16, 49
Balfour Declaration, 1917, 23
Balkans, the 14
   war in, 1912–13, 1, 2
Baltic Sea, 6
Bapaume, 27, 28, 43
Barisis, 10
Barleux, 28
Basra, 16
Bavaria, 46
Beatty, David, 9, 26
Beaucourt, 28
Beaumont Hamel, 28
Beirut, capture of, 1918, 35
Béla Kun, 46
Belgium, 6, 24, 47
   army, 3, 4, 7, 10
   atrocities in, 50
   empire, 40
   violation of, 2
Belgrade, 21, 22
Belleau Wood, 44
Bellenglise, 45
Bellicourt, 45
Below, Otto von, 38
Belfort, 3
Benedict XV, Pope, 24

Berlin, 46
Berlin–Baghdad railway, 1
Berry au Bac, 32
Bethmann-Hollweg, Theobald von,
   6, 29
Béthune, 7
Bismarck, Otto von, 1
Black Sea, 2, 49
blockade, 13, 28, 29, 47
Blücher, 9
'Blücher', operation, 1918, 42
Bolsheviks/Bolshevism, 14, 24, 31,
   41, 46, 47, 49
bombing, 30
Bony, 45
Bosnia, crisis over, 1908, 1
Bourlon ridge, 39
   Wood, 39
Bouvet, 17
Breslau, 9
Brest-Litovsk, 19
   treaty of, 1918, 6, 41, 48, 49
Briand, Aristide, 32, 33
British Expeditionary Force (BEF),
   2, 3, 4, 7
Brusilov, Alexei, 8
   offensive, 1916, 8, 21, 28
Bucharest, treaty of, 1918, 21, 48
Bukovina, 21
Bulair, 17
Bulgaria, 1, 41
   defeat of, 22, 48
   enters war, 21, 22
Bülow, Bernhard von, 14
Bülow, Karl von, 4
Cadorna, Luigi, 14, 20, 38
Calais agreement, 1917, 32
Cambrai, 45
   battle of, 1917, 39
Cameroons, 12
Canada, 40
   in battle of Ypres, 1915, 18
   recruitment in, 40
Cantigny, battle of, 1918, 44
Cape Helles, landings at, 1915, 17
Capello, Luigi, 38
Caporetto, battle of, 1917, 20, 38
Caribbean, recruitment in, 40
Carpathian mountains, 2, 8, 19, 21
Carso plateau, 20

casualties, 50
Caucasus, campaign in the, 16
Cerny, 32
Champagne
    battles in, 1915, 15
    battles in, 1917, 32
Chanak, 17
Chantilly Plan, 1916, 20, 27
Charleroi, 3
Château-Thierry, 4, 42, 44
Chemin des Dames, 10, 32, 33, 37
Chilly, 28
China, war in, 12
Christmas truce, 1914, 10, 18
Churchill, Winston, 7, 17
Clemenceau, Georges, 33, 47
Combles, 27, 28
Communism, 50
'Concert of Europe', the, 1
Conrad von Hötzendorff,
        Franz, 8
Constantine I, King of Greece, 22
Contalmaison, 28
convoys, 29
Corfu Island, 21, 22
Coronel, battle of, 1914, 9
Cracow, 19
Craonne, 32
Cressy, 9, 29
Crimea, the, 49
Ctesiphon, battle of, 1915, 16
Currie, Arthur, 40
Czech Legion, 49
Czechoslovakia, 48, 50
Czernowitz, 19
Damascus, 23, 34
    capture of, 1918, 34, 35
D'Annunzio, Gabriele, 14
Danzig, 47
Dardanelles Campaign, 1915, 17
Dawnay, Alan, 34
De Bunsen, Maurice, 23
Dedéagatch, 48
Delville Wood, 28
Denikin, Anton, 49
Denmark, 47
Derfflinger, 26
De Robeck, John, 17
Diaz, Armando, 38
Dix, Otto, 36
Dixmude, 10
Dobrudja, the, 21
Dodecanese Islands, 14
Dogger Bank, battle of the,
    1915, 9

Douai, 15
Douaumont, fort, 25, 32
Doullens agreement, 1918, 42
Dover, 30
    patrol, 13
Dresden, 9
Dual Alliance, 1879, 1
Dunsterville, Lionel, 49
Durazzo, 21
Düsseldorf, 30
eastern front, 5, 8, 19, 21,
    22, 31, 41
East Prussia, 2, 5, 19
Ebert, Freidrich, 46
Edinburgh, 30
Egypt, 35
Egyptian Expeditionary Force
    (EEF), 34, 35
Einem, Karl von, 18
Emden, 9
Entente, the
    Anglo-French, 1904, 1
    Anglo-Russian, 1907, 1
    General Reserve, 1918, 42
    intervention in Russian civil war, 49
    Mediterranean strategy, 14
    naval strategy, 9
    unified command, 1918, 42
    war aims, 24, 47, 48
Enver Pasha, 16
Epéhey, 45
Erzurum, 16
Es Sinn, battle of, 1915, 16
Estonia, 41, 49
Eupen, 47
Evert, Alexei, 8
Falkenhayn, Erich von, 4, 7, 19,
    21, 25
Falkland Islands, battle of the,
    1914, 9
Fascism, 50
Fatherland Party, 6
Felixstowe, 30
Filain, 37
Finland, 41, 49, 50
Fiume, 14
Flanders, 7, 30, 36, 43
Flers, 28
Flesquières ridge, 39
Foch, Ferdinand, 3, 4, 7, 27,
    28, 36, 42
    strategy, 43, 44, 45, 47
Folkestone, 30
Fort Ruppel, Greece, 22
'Fourteen Points', 1918, 6, 24

France, 1, 6, 24
    army, 2, 4, 15, 25, 27, 32, 37, 43, 45
        mutinies, 25, 33, 36
    casualties, 7, 15, 28, 32, 37, 50
    empire, 1, 40, 50
    home front, 33
    strategy, 2, 15
    war aims, 23, 24, 47, 48
Franchet d'Esperey, Louis, 22
Franco-Russian alliance, 1892, 1
Franz Ferdinand, Archduke
    assassination of, 1914, 1, 2
'Freikorps', 46
French, John, 18
Fricourt, 27
Frontiers, battle of the, 1914, 3
Galicia, 8, 19
Gallipoli, 17, 22
gas, 15, 18, 36
Gauloise, 17
Gaza, battle of, 1917, 35
'Georgette', operation, 1918, 42
German East Africa, 12
German South West Africa, 12
Germany, 1, 24, 47
    army, 2, 3, 4, 5, 18, 19, 25, 28, 37,
        38, 39, 42, 43, 45, 46
    bombing of, 30
    casualties, 7, 15, 28, 36, 37, 42,
        43, 50
    home front, 42, 43, 46
    impact of blockade on, 13
    intervention in Russian civil war, 49
    naval strategy, 2, 9, 13, 26
    1918 offensive, 6, 35, 36,
        41, 42
    peace diplomacy, 6, 41
    strategy, 2, 19, 29, 30, 42
        on eastern front, 19, 41
    tactics, 38, 39, 42
    war aims, 6
Gheluvelt, 7, 36
Ghent, 43
'giant' bombers, 30
Gneisenau, 9
Gnila Lipa, battle of, 1914, 8
Goeben, 9
Gommecourt, 27
Good Hope, 9
Gorizia, 20, 38
Gorlice–Tarnów, battle of, 1915,
    8, 19
'Gotha' bombers, 30
Gough, Hubert, 28, 36
Gouzeaucourt, 39

Great Britain, 1, 6, 24, 25, 30
　　army, 4, 7, 15, 16, 17, 18, 27, 28,
　　　　32, 35, 36, 39, 42, 43, 45
　　casualties, 7, 15, 28, 30, 32, 36, 50
　　empire, 40, 50
　　strategy, 2, 34
　　　　in Mediterranean, 17
　　　　war aims, 23, 24, 47, 48
Great Yarmouth, 30
Greece, 1, 14, 22, 48
Grey, Edward, 1
Grodno, 19
Groener, Wilhelm, 46
Guillaumat, Marie, 22
Guise, battle of, 1914, 3
Gumbinnen, battle of, 1914, 5
Hague Convention, 1899, 18
Haig, Douglas, 15, 27, 28, 32, 36
Hamilton, Ian, 17
Hartlepool, 30
Harwich, 30
Havrincourt Wood, 39
Hedjaz, the, 23
　　railway, 34, 35
Heligoland Bight, battle of the,
　　1914, 9
Hentsch, Colonel, 4
High Seas Fleet, Germany's, 26,
　　46, 47
High Wood, 28
Hindenburg, Paul von, 5, 19, 28,
　　41, 42
Hindenburg Line, 10, 28, 32, 39, 43,
　　44, 45
Hipper, Franz von, 9, 26
Hitler, Adolf, 18, 46, 47, 50
Hoffmann, Max, 5
Hogue, 9, 29
Holland (the Netherlands), 6,
　　13, 46
'hundred days' offensive, 1918,
　　43, 44
Hussain, Prince Feisal, 23, 34
Hussain, Sharif, 34
India
　　in Mesopotamia, 16
　　on western front, 40
　　recruitment in, 40
Indo-China, 40
Indefatigable, 26
Independent Air Force, 30
Inflexible, 9, 17
Influenza epidemic, 1918, 50
Inter-Allied Economic Conference,
　　1916, 24

Invincible, 9, 26
Iraq, 23, 34
Iron Duke, 26
Irresistible, 17
Isonzo, battles of the, 1915–17, 14,
　　20, 30
Istanbul (Constantinople), 17, 21,
　　23, 48
Italy, 1
　　army, 20, 38
　　casualties, 20
　　navy, 2
　　war aims, 14, 23, 24
Japan, 2, 47
　　intervention in Russian civil war, 49
　　in China, 12
Jaurès, Jean, 2
Jellicoe, John, 26
Jerusalem, capture of, 1917, 35
Joffre, Joseph, 3, 7, 15, 25, 27, 32
Jünger, Ernst, 25
Jutland, battle of, 1916, 9, 26
'Kapp' putsch, 46
Karlsruhe, 30
Kavala, 22
Kemal, Mustafa, 17, 48
Kerensky, Alexander, 31, 46
'Kerensky' offensive, 1917, 8, 31
Kiel, 46
King's Lynn, 30
Kitchener, Herbert, 4, 15
Kluck, Alexander von, 4
Kolchak, Alexander, 49
Köln, 9
Komaróvw, battle of, 1914, 8
Königsberg, 5
Königsberg, 9, 12
Kovon, 19
Kraków, 8
Krithia, 17
Kum Kale, 17
La Fère, 42
Laffaux, 32, 37
Langemarck, 7
Lanrezac, Charles, 3
Lassigny, 43
Latvia (Courland), 19, 41, 49
Lausanne, treaty of, 1923, 48
Lawrence, Colonel T.E., 34
League of Nations, 47
Lebanon, 23
Le Cateau, battle of, 1914, 3
Leefe-Robinson, William, 30
Leipzig, 9
Lemberg, 8, 19

Lemnos, 17
Lenin, 24, 31, 41, 42
Le Tronquoy, 44
Lettow-Vorbeck, Paul von, 12
Liège, 3
Lille, 7, 15
Liman von Sanders, Otto, 17
Lion, 9, 26
Lithuania, 41, 49
Liverpool, 30
Lloyd George, David, 15, 32, 35
Locarno Pact, 1925, 47
London
　　air raids on, 30
　　Declaration of, 1909, 13
　　Pact of, 1914, 24
　　treaty of, 1915, 14
Longueval, 28
Longwy-Briey coalfield, 6, 44
Loos, battle of, 1915, 15
Lorraine, 3, 24, 43, 44, 47
Ludendorff, Erich, 5, 19, 28, 41, 42,
　　43, 46
Lusitania, sinking of, 1915, 8, 29
Luxembourg, 6, 24
Lvov, Prince George, 31
Macedonia, 21
Mackenson, August von, 19, 21
Mainz, 9
Maistre, General, 37
Malleson, Wilfred, 49
Malmaison, battle of, 1917, 37, 39
Malmédy, 24, 47
Mametz, 27
Mangin, Charles, 32
Manoury, Michel-Joseph, 3, 4
Mărăşeşti, battle of, 1917, 21
Marcoing, 39
Margate, 30
Marinetti, Filippo, 14
Maritz Revolt (South Africa), 1914,
　　12, 40
Marne
　　battle of the, 1914, 4
　　battle of the, 1918, 43, 44
'Marneschute-Reims', operation,
　　1918, 42
Marshall, William, 16
Martinpuich, 27
Masurian lakes
　　battle of, 1914, 5
　　battle of, 1915, 19
Maubeuge, 4, 43
Maude, Stanley, 16
Max of Baden, Prince, 46

Mazel, General, 32
Mecca, 34
Medina, 34
Megiddo, battle of, 1918, 34, 35
Mesopotamia, 16, 23, 49
  campaign in, 40
Messines ridge, 10
  battle of, 1917, 36
Metz, 44
Meuse-Argonne offensive, 1918,
  43, 44
Mézières, 15, 43
'Michael', operation, 1918, 42
Micheler, Joseph, 28, 32
Micronesia, 12
Middelkerke, 36
Middle East,
  peace settlement, 35, 48
Minsk, 19
Mittelafrika, 6
Mitteleuropa, 6
Moldavia, 21
Moltke, Helmuth von, 2, 3, 4, 5
Monastir, 22
Monmouth, 9
Monro, Charles, 17
Mons, 3, 43
Montauban, 27
Montenegro, 21
Morhange, 3
Morocco, 1
Mort Homme, 10, 25
Moscow, 31
Mosul, 16, 23
Mousquet, 9
Mozambique, 12
Mulhouse, 3
Munich, 46
Murmansk, 49
Murray, Archibald, 35
Mussolini, Benito, 14, 20, 50
Namur, 3
Nancy, 3
Nauroy, 45
Netherlands, the (see Holland)
Neuilly-sur-Seine, treaty of, 1919, 48
Neutrality, 13
Neuve Chapelle, battle of, 1915, 15
New Armies, 27
Newfoundland, 40
New Zealand, 12, 40
  recruitment in, 40
Nicholas II, Tsar, 31
Nieuport, 7, 10, 36
Nish, 21

Nivelle, Robert, 25, 32, 33
Nivelle Offensive, 1917, 32,
  33, 37
Nixon, John, 16
Northern Arab Army (NAA), 34, 35
Norwich, 30
Notre-Dame-de-Lorette, 15
Nürnburg, 9
Nyasaland, 12
Ocean, 17
Odessa, 49
Ostend, 6, 36
  raid on, 1918, 29
Ottoman Empire (Turkey), 1, 6, 14,
  41, 50
  defeat of, 48
  enters war, 21
  navy, 2
  peace settlement, 23, 48
  war with, 16, 17, 34, 35
  war with Greece, 1919–22, 48
Padua, 20
Painlevé, Paul, 32, 33
Palestine, campaign in, 23, 34, 35,
  40, 48
Papua New Guinea, 12
Paris, 2, 3, 4, 24, 30, 32, 33, 42
  Declaration of, 1856, 13
  peace conference in, 1919, 24,
    47, 48
Passchendaele, 10, 36
'Peace Resolution', 1917, 6
Penang, 9
Péronne, 27
Pershing, John, 44
Persia, 16
Pétain, Philippe, 3, 25, 32, 33, 37, 42
Picardy, 10, 28, 32
Pirot, 21
Plan XVII, 2
Plebiscites, 47
Plumer, Herbert, 36
Poelcapelle, 10, 18
Poincaré, Raymond, 32
Poland, 5, 6, 8, 41, 47, 48, 49, 50
  occupation by Central Powers,
    19, 31
Portugal, 47
  empire, 40
Potiorek, Oskar, 21
Pozières, 28
Princip, Gavrilo, 1
Prittwitz, Max von, 5
Provisional Government, in Russia,
  1917, 31

Prussia, 1
Przemyśl, 19
  siege of, 1914, 8
Putnik, Radomir, 21
Queen Mary, 26
'race to the sea', 1914, 7
Ramsgate, 30
Rasputin, Grigorii, 31
Rawlinson, Henry, 15, 27
Red Army, 49
Reims, 42
Rennenkampf, Pavel, 5
Reparations, 47, 48
Rhineland, 47
Ribot, Alexandre, 33
Riga, 19
River Clyde, 17
Robertson, William, 22
Rommel, Erwin, 38
'Room 40', 26
Roulers, 36
Royal Air Force (RAF), 30
Ruffey, General, 3
Ruhr, 24, 46, 47
Rumania, 22, 48, 50
  defeat of, 21
  enters war, 21
Russia, 1, 6, 24, 40
  army, 2, 31
  casualties, 8, 50
  navy, 2
  revolutions, 1917, 16, 21,
    24, 31, 33, 41, 42
  strategy, 2, 5, 8, 16
  war aims, 23
Russian civil war, 1918–21, 35, 49
Saar/Saarland, 24, 44, 47
Sainte Adresse, Declaration of,
  1916, 24
Saint-Germain-en-Laye, treaty of,
  1919, 48
St Gond marshes, 4
Saint-Jean-de-Maurienne, treaty of,
  1917, 23
St Mihiel salient, 10
  capture of, 1918, 44
St Petersburg (Petrograd), 31, 41
St Quentin, 45
Salandra, Antonio, 14
Salonika, campaign, 21, 22, 48
Samoa, 12
Samsonov, A., 5
Sarajevo, 1
Sarrail, Maurice, 3, 22
Sarrebourg, 3

Saxony, 46
Scandinavia, 6, 13
Scapa Flow, 26, 47
Scarborough, 30
Scharnhorst, 9
Scheer, Reinhardt, 26
Schleswig, 47
Schlieffen, Alfred von, 2
Sedan, 43, 44
'September Programme' (see
    Germany, war aims)
Serbia, 1, 2, 14, 50
    army, 22
    defeat of, 21
Serres, 22
Sèvres, treaty of, 1920, 48
Seydlitz, 9
Sheerness, 30
'shells scandal', 1915, 15
Silesia, 47
Sistove, 21
Skopje, 22
Smith-Dorrien, Horace, 18
Smyrna, 48
Socialist International, 6
Soissons, 7, 10, 32, 42
Somme, battle of the, 1916, 15, 25,
    27, 28, 32, 36, 45
Sonnino, Sydney, 14
South Africa, 40
    recruitment in, 40
Southend, 30
southern front, 20, 38
South Tyrol, 14
Soviet Union, 49, 50
'Spartacus League', 46
Spee, Maximillian Graf von, 9
Steenstraat, 18
Stinnes, Hugo, 46
'Strafexpedition', 1916, 20
Straits, the, 17, 23, 48
submarine warfare, 9, 14, 29, 36
    declaration of unlimited, 29
Suez Canal, 35
Supreme War Council, 38

Sussex, 29
Suvla Bay, landing at, 1915, 17
Sydney, 9
'Sykes–Picot' agreement, 1916,
    23, 34
Syria, 23, 34, 35
tactics, 10, 27, 28, 36, 37, 38, 39, 42,
    43, 44
Tafilah, battle of, 1918, 34
Tanga, battle of, 1914, 12
tanks, 28, 32, 37, 38, 39
Tannenberg, battle of, 1914, 5, 19
Thiepval, 10, 27, 28
Thourout, 36
Thrace, 48
Three Emperors' League
    (Dreikaiserbund), 1881, 1
Thuringia, 46
Togoland, 12
Toulouse, 33
Townshend, Charles, 16
Trabazon, 16
Transcaucasia, 41, 49
Trans-Jordan, 23, 34, 35
Transylvania, 21
trench warfare, 10
Trentino, 14, 20, 38
Trento, 20
Trianon, treaty of, 1920, 48
Trieste, 14, 20, 38
Triple Alliance, 1882, 1, 14
Trônes Wood, 28
Trotsky, Leon, 41
Tsingtao, siege of, 1914, 12
Turkestan, 49
Turkey (see Ottoman Empire)
U-boats, 8, 29
United States (see America)
Ukraine, 6, 8, 41, 49
'Union Sacrée', 25, 33
Valona, 14, 21
Vaux, fort, 25, 32
Vendhuille, 45
Venice, 38
Venizelos, Eleutherios, 22

Verdun, 3, 4, 7, 14, 8, 32, 44
    battle of, 1916, 15, 25, 27, 37
    battle of, 1917, 25, 33, 37
Vermandovilliers, 28
Versailles, treaty of, 1919, 6, 47
Victor Emmanuel III, King of Italy,
    14
'Victory Offensive', 1918 (see
    Germany, 1918 offensive)
Vienna, 20
Vilnius, 19
Vimy ridge, 10, 15, 32, 40
Vittorio Veneto, battle of, 1918,
    38, 48
Vladivostok, 49
'Voie Sacrée', 25
Von der Tann, 26
war debts, 50
Warsaw, 19
Weimar Republic, 46, 47
western front, 3, 4, 7, 10, 15, 18, 25,
    27, 28, 32, 36, 37, 39, 42, 43,
    44, 45
Whitby, 30
White Russia, 41
Wilhelmshaven, 46
William II, Kaiser of Germany,
    1, 46
Wilson, Woodrow, 6, 24, 47
women at war, 50
Wrangel, Peter, 49
Yoffe, Adolf, 41
Ypres, 27
    battle of, 1914, 7
    battle of, 1915, 18
    battle of, 1917, 36, 37, 42
    salient, 10, 42
Yugoslavia, 48, 50
Zeebrugge, 6, 36
    raid on, 1918, 29
Zemstvos, 31
zeppelins, 30
Zhemchug, 9
Zionism, 23
Zlóta Lipa, battle of, 1914, 8

DATE DUE
